# The Grand Illusion

*and 20 Habits of Spiritual Transformation*

Christopher Speer

**BALBOA.**
PRESS
A DIVISION OF HAY HOUSE

Balboa Press books may be ordered through booksellers or by contacting:

Balboa Press
A Division of Hay House
1663 Liberty Drive
Bloomington, IN 47403
www.balboapress.com
1-(877) 407-4847

Printed in the United States of America.

ISBN: 978-1-4525-7192-8 (sc)
ISBN: 978-1-4525-7194-2 (hc)
ISBN: 978-1-4525-7193-5 (e)

Library of Congress Control Number: 2013909009

Balboa Press rev. date: 12/3/2013

# Contents

Introduction                                              vii

Dedications and Acknowledgments                           xv

**BOOK 1** The Events and Realizations of a Spiritual
              Awakening                                   1

1. Death and a New Beginning                              3
2. Another Lesson                                         11
3. All Change                                             17
4. Separation From Ego                                    28
5. Tribalism—The Collective Ego Consciousness            44
6. Here and Now                                           61
7. A Further Freedom                                      82
8. I Have Seen Such Beauty                                92
9. The Grand Illusion                                     96
10. An Introduction To Your Chakras                       103

**BOOK 2** The 20 Habits of Spiritual Transformation—
              Awakening From the Grand Illusion           117

Prologue                                                  119

1st Habit of Transformation: Staying Conscious of
     Your Spiritual Nature                                122

2nd Habit of Transformation: Staying Focused on the
     Present Moment                                       130

3rd Habit of Transformation: Remaining Separate
     From Ego                                             134

4th Habit of Transformation: Accepting Reality 147

5th Habit of Transformation: Practicing Forgiveness 164

6th Habit of Transformation: Practicing Gratitude 188

7th Habit of Transformation: Non-Judgment, Tolerance, and Love 198

8th Habit of Transformation: Integrity—The Hero's Journey 208

9th Habit of Transformation: Practicing Positive Communication 234

10th Habit of Transformation: Helping Others 252

11th Habit of Transformation: Empowering Ourselves—Not Blaming Others 255

12th Habit of Transformation: Daily Meditation 273

13th Habit: Opening Your Heart Chakra 288

14th Habit of Transformation: Prayer and Accepting Guidance 305

15th Habit of Transformation: Cultivate Humor and Joy 323

16th Habit of Transformation: Bringing Your Life Into Balance 331

17th Habit of Transformation: Changing Negative to Positive 338

18th Habit of Transformation: Controlling Your Internal World 358

19th Habit: Letting Go of Attachments 374

20th Habit of Transformation: Becoming Centered 381

Summary—The Spiritual Laws 399

Recommendations: Other Books, CDs and DVDs 431

Bibliography 443

Index 457

# Introduction

Spirituality Is An Experience Not Just A Concept—We Are All Governed By Universal Spiritual Laws—To Change Our Lives We Have To First Change Our Ideas

*We're so engaged in doing things to achieve purposes of outer value that we forget that the inner value, the rapture that is associated with being alive, is what it's all about. ~ Joseph Campbell, The Power of Myth*

*Doubt everything, find your own light.~ Buddha*

This book is the account of one person's journey from a crisis of devastating emotional pain to an experience of profound joy and peace. It is about the discovery of those workable principles that, *when applied*, always permit a return to an experience of inner peace, love, and the pure joy of existence, despite the ups and downs of "real life."

At first, I thought I should write this book without reference to my own experiences. It seemed too self-absorbed to talk about my life, and uncomfortably revealing. But as I reviewed what I had written without including the process that led to my realizations, it seemed that something important was missing.

It occurred to me that perhaps my own difficulties, and

the solutions that had worked for me, might actually be the most useful thing I could write about. It seemed clear that they must be universal experiences that other people could relate to as well. Maybe describing what had gotten me out of my hole would help others out of theirs.

The book's title—*The Grand Illusion*—is the phrase that occurred to me as I was trying to describe the mass of negative emotions, thoughts, and false beliefs that keep us from experiencing our natural state of love, compassion, kindness, joy, and connectedness to life.

Negative emotions such as anger, anxiety, grief, jealousy, and resentment can darken our lives and sap our energy. Beliefs about all that is wrong with ourselves, others, and the world around us can enmesh us in a web of conflicts and turmoil, and can turn our lives into a soap opera of drama and tragedy. We can be living our lives still stuck in painful incidents that happened decades ago, and needlessly still be carrying around toxic resentments.

This book is about the path away from this "Grand Illusion" of suffering, and into the light of joy and contentment.

The path is organized to be accessible and understandable as 20 habits which when practiced in daily life will bring about spiritual transformation and take us out of suffering. The only requirement on the part of you, the reader, is a desire to experience positive change in your life, the openness of mind to consider new ideas without immediately dismissing them because they are new, and the persistence to actually apply them and see if they work in your own life.

For most people however this is all too much effort, they just want to be comfortable and entertained or reassured or medicated into oblivion. Or they don't believe real change is possible to achieve. Or they are still convinced by the falsehood that the physical universe can provide all they need. And so nothing much changes as they make their way through their life. And then one day they die.

This book is not aimed at those people. This book is written for those people who are motivated by a strong internal desire to find something beyond everyday life: beyond a job to pay the bills, a beer, some laughs, the TV and a comfortable place to sleep. The fact is that life will give you what you ask for—mundane or extraordinary.

I am not a member of any organized religion or philosophy, so I have no agenda to forward. I am open to wisdom wherever I find it.

I have collected and included quotes from spiritual teachers and others with insight throughout the book to show the universality of the truths I discuss—that they show up in many places and come from many religions, traditions, and just people of perception. In fact, the more I looked, the more amazed I became that people from completely diverse walks of life and totally different cultures were saying the same things over and over, proving how similar the human experience of the divine really is. We are far more similar than we are different.

But most of these teachings were *not* the source of my own insights. I gathered most of them *after* the fact, to give my writing context and to illustrate that these truths indeed are universal. Many of the religious quotes only made sense to me *after* my own experiences.

I mention this for those who mistakenly believe that spirituality can be achieved by intellectual pursuit alone. It cannot. It is beyond intellect, it is an *experience,* and must be found through the *application* of spiritual truths. This is a very important distinction.

Once I had some very transformative experiences, I then understood some religious teachings for the first time; suddenly I was able to comprehend what had often been a foreign language. And then I started to collect them.

They showed me that others had experienced the same things before me, and that they can be experienced by everyone who reaches for them. But you cannot *logic* or *think* your way to changes in spiritual consciousness; the wisest concepts are only sign-posts to what lies beyond the territory of the mind.

And this is why no one can say what is the right path of experience for another. Each of us is somewhere our own journey to awakening, whether we realize it or not. And this is why tolerance is so important.

This book isn't about adopting new ideas; its concepts are not mine, or even new. It is about the truths that always surround us and of which we are a part, which we can recognize within our own innate wisdom. They are always waiting and accessible if we take the time to look for them.

This is because spiritual truths are universal to *all* people, and apply to those of *all* races, religions, and cultural backgrounds. We all carry this wisdom within us, even though it may be covered up.

This book is an introduction to the Spiritual Laws of the Universe, which exist just as gravity and the speed of light do in the physical universe, without regard to our opinions or judgments.

I invite you to test the workability of the principles in this book in your own life.

One way is by using the type of "bracketing" approach that anthropologists often do in studying other cultures, wherein one's own personal belief system is suspended while learning about another system of thought in a non-judgmental way.

So you are not required to accept new ideas until you first know what they are, and have had a chance to see if they work in your life when you apply them. If you simply reject new concepts as you encounter them, just because they are different to that with which you are already familiar, you are closing the door to the possibility of change or advancement.

The beginning of wisdom, as Socrates pointed out, is for us to realize we don't know anything.

To declare: "I am dissatisfied with my life, and I want it to change for the better, but without considering the possibility of changing any of my ideas"—is describing a strategy that I guarantee is simply not going to work!

**Changing your life in a positive way requires first changing your ideas in a positive way**.

If you are skeptical about spirituality, or if the very word makes you cringe, you may be interested in knowing upfront that this is the story of the gradual transformation of someone who had pretty much rejected spiritual matters and religions. I was so embittered by what I felt was my earlier betrayal in following what I mistakenly took to be a valid spiritual path, that for thirteen years I focused only on material achievements, my career, family, and friends. But then I was presented with an experience of tangible spirituality so undeniable and profound that it forced me again to include spirituality in my worldview.

This book describes personal work we need to do in order to bring about change. *Then* we can experience the results. It is not just about absorbing concepts. Otherwise it is like reading a book on weightlifting without lifting any weights and then saying, "Well, that didn't work!"

I believe in pragmatism—that which can be experienced to be true because of its workability in the real world. Reading an idea is just the first step. Then the reader needs to practice the principles in his or her daily life to experience the results—just as they can experience the workability of gravity.

Don't ever accept anything just because it is found in books. There is a great deal of nonsense written in books.

It will help to let the concepts seep into you, and to become aware of your own internal responses to them. What is important here is not my words but your own awareness at a level beyond words. These are truths that you already know at some deep level, but you need to let your recognition of them surface.

As Thomas Dewar famously noted, *Minds are like parachutes; they work best when open.* In order to change one's situation, one has to be willing to consider and be open to new ideas. One has to first be willing to learn, in order to learn anything. If you are dissatisfied with your life in some way and would like it to improve, but are convinced you already know everything and are dismissive of considering new ideas, you aren't likely to get anywhere.

Knowing that you don't know is the first step to knowledge.

You may initially feel cynical or even antagonistic as you read this book. One's own pain can rise up like an angry dog that has been awakened and finds itself still tied to a chain. If you give in to negative emotion, you will stay trapped by it. There is a way out—but it requires patience, self-examination, and work. It is just a matter of priorities and deciding what is important to you.

For some people, the concepts will already be familiar

friends, or to others may be life-changing revelations—depending on how open they are to their own internal wisdom.

I have tried to be careful about my use of words—words like *God* or *spiritual* can be very emotionally loaded to some individuals, either positively or negatively, according to their life experiences. So if you encounter words you find off-putting, I ask you to be patient until you understand the concept being described. Please don't assume if you see a word that is emotionally charged to you, that it is being used in the same way as you previously encountered it.

If the concepts in this book are within the scope of your consciousness, you may feel recognition of them reverberating deep within you. It has often happened that once I became aware of something, I saw examples of it everywhere. But before that awareness, it was invisible. The day you drive your new car home from the dealer, you see the same model everywhere.

You may recognize some concepts are being repeated in the book—all the spiritual laws in the book interlock and work with each other, and so they are repeated in different contexts when necessary.

Those who are seeking truth are like people walking into the darkness with a flashlight. We cannot see what is beyond the beam of our light, but sometimes, we come across a signpost that tells us we are on the right road. Eventually, our own internal compass will steer us in the right direction.

Picture yourself in a box. The box is in the middle of a beautiful garden full of flowers and trees, streams and lakes. But you believe in the reality of the box, and so it contains you and you cannot reach the garden outside it. You are not even aware of its existence. But the moment you cease to believe in the box, it vanishes, and you are free to walk in the garden. The condition of most Homo sapiens is the same, unaware of our natural spiritual state and of the possibilities and freedoms that lay just beyond our grasp, beyond the prison of our false beliefs and trapped attention—our box—beyond the Grand Illusion.

This book is like offering a man locked in a cell the keys to his freedom. It is your choice whether to pick up the keys and try them in the lock.

I have written this book in the sincere hope you may find it useful. I wish I had been able to read it myself when I was young. It could have saved me a great deal of trouble!

With love,
Christopher Speer,
Santa Fe, N.M.
2012

# Dedications and Acknowledgments

I wish to dedicate this book and acknowledge my help and support to the following people: To my beautiful and talented wife of thirty-five years, Vicky, who has always supported and encouraged me, has inspired and taught me with her wisdom, intuition, intelligence, love, kindness, creativity and her ability to manifest, and to raise the emotions of those she encounters—she is truly a force of nature.

To my beautiful, loving and wonderful daughters: Sara, Erin, Suzy, and Devin.

To my marvelous sons in law, Darren and Lance. To my wonderful grandchildren, Joya, Rumi, Liam and Jack.

To my parents Betty and Stan, who gave me life and love and a foundation from which to make my way in the world. To my parents in law, Louise and Patrick for all their support and kindness.

To my extended family, for all the love and kindness they have given me.

To my dear friends, Tom Morgan, Paul Humphrey, Clive Henderson and Pam Hurwitz, who became part of my own tribe since a young age, who supported me and gave me an emotional family, and listened to me throughout the years, who have taught me by their examples.

To my friends in England who gave me support, friendship, help, and welcomed me into their homes during dark days: Tom & Lindy Morgan, Paul & Jane Humphrey,

Ron & Liz Hopkins, Pam & Jay Hurwitz, Allan & Wendy Mason—my thanks and love to you all. To the children of all these friends and their families, whose friendship and wisdom gives me optimism for the future.

To my friend and mentor Douglas Buchanan, who edited the initial version of this book with skill and wisdom and for his contributions and encyclopedic knowledge, until his passing. Douglas started my spiritual education at a young age and reappeared in my life many years later to help me with this book. Sadly, he passed on before the book was completed, but his guidance remains.

To my friend Allen Buchanan for his friendship and his parting gift which jump started my spiritual journey.

To Quinn Gleeson, Devin and Lance Kelly, Marty Gerber, and Vicky Speer, for their additional assistance in editing this book.

To Eckhart Tolle, whose writings and lectures, applied during a time of personal crisis, re-opened the door to my own spiritual awakening.

To Dr. Darren Weissman for his friendship and Lifeline sessions that removed unconscious blocks and old negative energy of which I was quite unaware.

To Ron Ellison, whose Reiki treatment resolved resistant physical issues and enabled me to see my own chakras. And for his Reiki attunements that have enabled me to further heal myself and others.

To my Pilates and Yoga teacher Hallie Love, for the instruction that took me out of chronic physical pain and re-introduced me to the experience of my subtle energy body.

To Dr. Kevin Michaels for giving me back the stability of my spinal column through his chiropractic skill.

To all the friends who have cared about me, helped and

supported me throughout the years, and those with whom I have touched souls.

To everyone who seeks to comprehend the Truth in life and who won't compromise once they have found it, and tries to bring wisdom and help to others.

To everyone who chooses positive over negative despite every reason not to, and tries to do their best to help others, to do the right thing, to achieve something better than there was before, to create love and beauty.

To you all I send my deepest gratitude, love and respect. You keep humanity and hope alive.

# BOOK 1

## The Events and Realizations of a Spiritual Awakening

# Chapter One
# Death and a New Beginning

## Experiencing Life Beyond Death

*Never was there a time when I did not exist, nor you, nor all these kings; nor in the future shall any of us cease to be.* ~ *Sri Krishna, Bhagavad-Gita*

I had an experience some years ago that changed the orientation of my life. Without my realizing at the time, it moved me onto the journey that resulted in my writing this book. As John Lennon observed: *Life is what happens to you while you're busy making other plans.*

My wife Vicky and I were taking care of a dear friend we had known for many years. Allen had been very sick for a while and was now dying of AIDS. One Sunday morning found my wife, myself, and his mother Kathy—an intelligent, no-nonsense, retired schoolteacher—standing around his bed in his hospital room. Allen had had a fever of over a hundred and six the night before, and had slipped into a coma. His doctors predicted that he was very near the end of his life.

The three of us had been taking turns talking to him, although he was unconscious. We said things like: it was OK for him to leave, and that he should go toward the light.

We were doing this because it was what he had asked us

to do when the time came. He had asked us to encourage him to let go of his ruined body and leave it. A book about dying that he had read described the transition in these terms, and we had agreed to be part of this process.

We each told him we loved him but that it was OK to go now, to let go of his body.

Despite an earlier interest in such things, I considered I had never experienced anything supernatural—I had never had an out-of-body experience where I had seen my own body from an external viewpoint as I had heard others describe, or seen ghosts or UFOs. I thought of myself as a pretty grounded, nuts-and-bolts individual.

Suddenly Allen's mother, who was at his bedside talking to him, called to us urgently:

*"It's happening!"*

The three of us immediately gathered around the bed; I was on the left side, my wife at the foot of the bed, his mother on the right.

We all experienced the same thing simultaneously. When we later compared details, what we felt was amazingly similar:

At the level where Allen was lying in his hospital bed— at approximately the middle of our standing bodies—we felt a sensation of energy. It was as if a horizontal field of energy six inches thick was passing through our bodies with particles moving inside it. The closest thing I can compare it to, is to say the sensation was somewhat electrical in nature. I had never experienced anything like it.

Then this energy field moved slowly upward, taking about a minute to reach the top of my head. As it was happening, I felt my friend's presence and personality as vividly as I ever had in all the years I'd known him. I remember being surprised that although he was no longer in his body, his personality—the essence of his particular being, was quite unchanged.

Because he had been sick for so long, Allen's energy had been diminished for quite a while, in the same way someone with a bad cold or the flu can seem to be barely there with you. But now it was as if he had gone from about thirty percent of his personality present to a hundred and fifty percent.

This was all not just an impression or an idea. It was as compelling as if he had suddenly walked into the room completely healthy and laughing and had picked us all up and hugged us. The experience was as fully physical as if someone had firmly gripped my arm and pulled me across to the window. It was like nothing I could conjure up in my head. I cannot be more emphatic about this. This wasn't an illusion. It was as real an occurrence as anything that has ever happened to me.

Then the energy field cleared the top of my head and the sensation of it was gone—and so, too, was the presence and personality of my friend. The feeling was as if he had walked out the door forever. One second his personality was vibrantly and fully there, the next it was completely and utterly gone.

Grief overcame me. Allen's body now looked completely different. I could not define what had changed specifically; he simply looked dead, whereas before, even though he was in a coma, he still looked alive.

I never felt his presence or that field of energy again.

My wife had an additional perception: Although Allen was apparently unconscious up to the moment of his death, his eyes were open. He was propped up on cushions, and my wife was looking into his eyes. At the moment of death, she said, his eyes went from a vivid blue to gray, and his curly hair went from blond to a gray hue.

It was clear to us all that we had experienced the physical leaving of Allen's spirit from his body. As the two had separated, his spirit was large enough to pass through all of us for a brief time as it slowly ascended.

That was his farewell to us.


Before this remarkable event occurred, I had been pretty closed to matters of the spirit for the previous thirteen years.

Earlier in life, I had sacrificed much to follow what I thought was a valid spiritual path, only to end up feeling betrayed and disillusioned. In the anger that followed, I had thrown the baby out with the bath water and decided to become a materialist. I didn't want to hear about spirituality or any of that nonsense. For the first time, I turned my full attention to my new wife and children, a career, making money, acquiring possessions, and cultivating only my closest friendships. I did this with a vengeance, working all the hours I could. My wife did the same, and we achieved much more success than I had ever thought possible in a relatively short period of time.

I was no longer interested in hearing about spirituality or religion of any kind. I was beyond skeptical on the subject— I was antagonistic. I considered anyone who fell for such things gullible and naïve, and since I had been around the block, I was neither.

My life thirteen years earlier had been sadly out of balance, and by entering the real world and having a wonderful family and achieving financial and career success with my graphic business, I had brought one part of my life into balance. I felt empowered, in control of my life and my material world. I was successful in an industry where many millions of dollars were on the line, and art directors and account executives were critically examining my work because I was contributing to such things as films, movie posters, TV commercials, print ads, and music album covers.

And I was doing just fine, with no need for spirituality, thank you very much!

But now suddenly, at Allen's death, it was as if the other side of my life had come knocking on the door again.

After thirteen years of ignoring anything spiritual while I pursued worldly matters, this intense and completely unexpected spiritual experience came as a shock.

I suddenly realized in a few seconds that the spiritual world was just as real as the material one it coexisted with, and that I needed to begin living in both, and learning how to integrate them for myself.

My earlier ambivalence about my spiritual nature had been replaced by an experience that left me with no doubt that we are indeed spirits existing in conjunction with our material forms, and that as spirit, we survive the death of the body.

What had previously been a theoretical concept for me had become a personal experience—and, as a result, a complete certainty. I now felt as sure of our spiritual nature as I was of our physical one. I realized that all human beings are a composite of two entirely different entities: an immortal spirit and a temporary physical body, expressing the combination and interplay of two quite different realms of existence.

It was essential, I knew, to become aware of both sides

of this dual nature, and to nurture them both. I realized that ignoring one's spiritual nature has consequences just as unavoidable as the effect on a person's physical well being of lack of exercise and poor diet. Since that experience at Allen's deathbed, I have found that the pain and violence, emotional suffering, and addiction that is rampant among humanity is a direct consequence of our failure as a species to fully comprehend and act according to our spiritual selves.

Many years later, I was talking with a hospice nurse who had been present at the deaths of over a thousand people. I asked if she had ever experienced anything similar to my sense of my friend's spirit leaving his body.

"Oh yes," she said, "You can feel people leaving. With some people, it is more pronounced than others, perhaps because you are closer to them or for other reasons, but you can feel them leaving."

Another nurse who had been present at the deaths of many patients told me the same thing, that with patients she had an emotional connection, she could often perceive their passing.

In a similar way, the reality that we are dealing with universal experiences was brought home again in an intense conversation with a couple at a party in Santa Fe, when I had described what occurred when Allen died. The husband said to me: "I want you to visit our house sometime. Hanging on our wall is a painting done by a friend of ours—he works at a hospice. It is a visual depiction of exactly what you just described to us."

As time went by, my awareness of my spirit-self deepened, and I began to see that almost everything I did was basically spiritual in nature or had a spiritual component.

And it occurred to me that if we leave our bodies at death, it followed logically that we must enter them at some point before our birth.

Now, the concept that we have souls is thousands of years old, of course, and hardly news to anyone. It wasn't news to me either, but what made such a great difference to me was realizing that we don't have souls, we *are* souls who are experiencing life in a body from a human perspective. Instead of seeing life as if the material world is real and the spiritual world some kind of phantom, my viewpoint gradually reversed. If the world experience of our five senses is only temporary, then clearly *it* must be the illusion, and treating it as completely real is a big mistake which leads to all kinds of problems.

It is one thing to know about something intellectually but quite another to actually experience it. It is like the difference between knowing a small person was inside my pregnant wife and the reality of seeing her give birth to our daughter. Watching as another living human being emerged from my wife's body was one of the most incredible and profound things I have ever witnessed. Despite my intellectual knowledge, the actual experience of seeing the birth took me into a new reality with all the impact of diving into cold water on a hot day. So it is with all the spiritual experiences I have described in this book.

Spirituality is so much more than just the simple fairy story some people dismiss it as, a comforting way to soften the idea of our own mortality. Since my experience with Allen's death, I know it is something far beyond a mere myth we tell ourselves, like a bedtime story for children who are afraid of the dark.

As an exercise, I noticed how I felt internally when I

considered that I was not my body but rather a spiritual being who is temporarily inhabiting my body, and that the spiritual entity that is truly me will continue to exist after the death of my physical body. Just as, after you arrive at a destination, you step out of your car. Just as at the end of the day, you step out of your clothes. The concept felt right; it was uplifting; it sat well with me; it felt true.

On the other hand, when I then considered the idea that I was just my body—the flesh and bones that I could see and feel—the effect was negative and disturbing, and even depressing. It felt as if I was trying to swallow a lie. It didn't feel true.

If you have doubts, try the same exercise. Try noticing what your own internal reaction is to these two opposing ideas.

Exploring our spiritual, non-physical, and non-intellectual selves is what I believe is missing in most of our lives. It is the lack of this experience and awareness that leads to so many human problems and ills. Believing in materialism and disregarding our spirituality is the most fundamental mistake any of us can make in life. Everything that is in error proceeds from that basic false premise—and the chaos of the world around us is the result.

Contacting one's true spirituality, and then living with this awareness every day, brings balance into life along with the sense of peace, joy, wholeness, and rightness that most of us have been missing, despite all our other accomplishments and possessions.

This is what I invite you to experience for yourself in the chapters that follow.

# Chapter Two
# Another Lesson

## The Function Of Suffering

*All life is suffering. ~ Buddha*

*I walked a mile with Pleasure*
*She chattered all the way*
*But left me none the wiser*
*For all she had to say.*
*I walked a mile with Sorrow*
*And ne'er a word said she*
*But oh, the things I learned from her When Sorrow walked with*
*me. ~ Robert Browning Hamilton*

It has been my experience that realizations often came to me when I have been going through a painful experience.

Of course I would prefer that it wasn't so, but it seems that when everything was easy and smooth in my life, I was just happy to enjoy the ride.

I have read about other people experiencing this: a crisis of suffering that leads to a sudden departure from normal thought and perception—a tipping point where what had been accepted as real would no longer suffice—where the soul demands a deeper truth for release from its pain.

I believe this is the function of suffering in our lives. Suffering gets our attention, it breaks through our ego where nothing else will, it pushes us to face things we were sometimes unwilling to when everything was going well. The lesson is always waiting for us in life, if we will just ask ourselves what we are being shown, and pay attention to the answer.

Some people manage to experience suffering while surrounded by material wealth and comfort, while others experience joy despite deprivation and hardship. But if a positive experience can be derived from a negative situation, then that negativity or suffering has been informative and nurturing of consciousness. At the moment of insight, an experience ceases to be negative, and what we thought was disaster reveals itself to be our teacher.

Having an approach to our life that we welcome only positive experiences and we resist and complain about any negative ones doesn't serve us well. Instead it is more helpful to try to accept anything that happens to you calmly, and be open to the lesson you are being brought. If you are able to improve your situation, you can then do so without first filling yourself with negative emotions.

As hard as it was for me at the time, let alone how hard being sick and dying was for him, I was certainly informed greatly by experiencing my friend Allen's physical decline, and eventual death.

In his last months, Allen had several crises in his state of health. He would suddenly say to me: "I don't feel good. I've got to go to the hospital now!" This was his understatement of course. He didn't feel well chronically by then, although he bore his situation with great courage. I never once heard him complain or relapse into self-pity. So when he told me he didn't feel well I knew it was serious.

I would help him into the back of my car with some pillows for comfort and drive him to Hollywood Community Hospital, breaking speed limits all the way. Eventually, the staff would get him stabilized and I would be allowed in to see him, tucked up in his hospital bed with tubes going into him. He would give me a wry smile and we would chat for a while until I was sure he was ok for the time being and he'd say, "It's ok, go home, I know you have things to do. Thanks for the ride."

I would say goodbye, promising to call the following day, and then walk out of his hospital room leaving him alone there. Then I would drive out into the Hollywood night, leaving the horror of my friend's situation behind me with an overwhelming gratitude that I was not in his situation, facing an inexorable death sentence, but healthy, with a life stretching out before me, full of opportunity and promise.

I remember the delicious sweetness of the night air, the ordinary street lights glowing incandescent like Christmas decorations, the luxurious feel of the leather seat and steering wheel of my car as it purred homeward to my comfortable house and my loving wife and family. The fullness of all that I had swept over me and I whispered: "Thank you, thank you, thank you!" up to the night sky. Witnessing his crisis put me into a heightened state of appreciation for my own life and good fortune.

I knew that if I had died that night, perhaps in a car crash on the freeway home, and I was offered in some afterlife scenario the possibility to return to earth for just a short while to see my wife and children, I would have gladly accepted any bargain, any disability, poverty, or loss, and it would weigh nothing compared to a little more time alive with those I loved. Such it seems is the sweetness and preciousness of our existence.

I would hug my wife and children tightly when I returned home safe on those nights.

The lesson being revealed to me was about the magnificence of each moment of existence, if only we can be open to experiencing it, and not take it for granted, or become dulled to it by routine.

But gradually, the routine of daily life with its demands and stresses would take over again and my perception would return to one dominated by humdrum, petty concerns and daily details. The colors of the world would become less intense and my bountiful life would assume the commonplace aspect that I took for granted.

Then at Allen's next health crisis the whole experience would be repeated. This happened five times. Again, my experience of the commonplace was made extraordinary by the prospect of death and the loss of the everyday things that make up our lives.

I was not the quickest learner during this process, but gradually something changed in me: I realized that there was no guarantee of the future. Any day might be the last of *my* life.

Clearly, this life offered ample opportunity for death on a daily basis. I assumed the goodwill and competence of hundreds or thousands of others around me everyday. If one of them failed to perform for a few seconds, I could be gone in the blink of an eye. The freeway with its dramatic tire skid marks, or the daily news, announced how many times a day this was true for other people.

At that time, four people were being murdered everyday in Los Angeles. We had come across one of them when we went to breakfast one morning. A man had been shot to death at a gas station across the street from our favorite deli. His crime was owning a luxury car that a thief was willing to kill for. His body was still on the ground covered by a sheet, waiting for the police to arrive.

So I made a decision: to start enjoying today, no matter what might be going on, because today might quite literally be my last. There were no guarantees of an idyllic future. The only time I had was *right now*.

I also decided to cease living by my achievements. I had been goal-oriented. I would set goals and when I achieved one I would allow myself to feel good. I felt I had earned it after all. The rest of the time I was consumed with working towards the next goal and experiencing a general dissatisfaction about what I *hadn't* yet achieved.

For example, I had been written about in a national airbrush illustration magazine and some of my work had been shown. But the article wasn't solely about me and I wasn't on the cover of the magazine. I felt when I made the cover then I could afford to really feel good about my work. This perhaps was a good methodology for motivating my career, but pretty disastrous for managing my life! It occurred to me that I may never make the cover—so was I just going to feel no happiness or joy or achievement in the meantime?

I decided to start *enjoying the moment, living for today*. Trying to live as though this might be my last day. Allowing myself to be happy regardless of what I had achieved—this was pretty anarchistic stuff after so long a period of grading my happiness on the basis of work ethic and production.

I resurrected the phrase *Here And Now* from my old Buddhist readings into my consciousness. The idea is that all we ever have is this moment, *here and now*. I would mention the concept from time to time but I had yet to fully connect with it. It is one thing to know about something—it is quite another thing to *experience it.*

One morning I was in the bathroom brushing my teeth, and I suddenly noticed that I felt happy. Not just cheerful but overwhelmingly joyful and content. There was a warm glow in my heart. I became a little alarmed. What had I done that would warrant such a delicious feeling of wellbeing? I couldn't think of a damn thing! I just felt goofily happy for no good reason. That moment felt completely fulfilling and I had no desire to search for anything else to satisfy me, I was fully at peace in that moment. I decided to stop worrying about this odd phenomenon of joy for no reason and simply enjoy it.

Something was happening to me—but at this point I wasn't able to connect all the dots.

# Chapter Three
# All Change

## From Looking Outside, To Looking Inside

*Surely God would not have created such a being as man, with an ability to grasp the infinite, to exist only for a day! No, no, man was made for immortality. ~ Abraham Lincoln*

Shortly after Allen's death we moved away from Los Angeles. The city had been very good to us in many ways: providing us with careers that allowed us to raise our children in a comfortable home and enjoy many privileges. My wife Vicky had joined the clothing company of two friends and helped it grow enormously. But when the clothing company was eventually acquired by a Fortune 500 Company, corporate politics and infighting replaced a lot of what had been joyful work for her.

I had a graphics business that was involved with advertising and special effects for film and television that had been enormously fulfilling and rewarding. But I eventually found the professional accomplishments that had previously thrilled me had become matter-of-fact and no longer significant to me. It was another case of discovering what I thought was going to be the stunning climax of everything, actually didn't seem to mean that much once I had achieved it.

Since I can remember, creating artwork of any kind had always been a pleasurable and satisfying pursuit, but I longed now to do personal work and paint more.

I discovered that the act of creating something is in itself magical. Being paid well is nice of course, and also necessary to pay the bills, but it is the work you remember. Life seems to be about finding the balance between what you have to do to survive, and what you really want to do. Someone said money is like air—it's no big deal until you don't have any.

The English poet, artist, and mystic William Blake wrote in the 1700's: *The road of excess leads to the palace of wisdom.* I wouldn't describe my life in LA as particularly excessive, it was even modest compared to others, but I did experience acquiring sufficient material possessions and professional success to notice one day that, as nice as they were, those things didn't provide me with exactly what I had thought they would.

When I was younger, living in a fairly modest world monetarily, I visualized myself one day living in a cool house with a beautiful wife and family, surrounded by excellent stuff, driving a great car, and wearing stylish clothes. I figured that when I had all that, I would feel complete and fulfilled. I had achieved all the things pretty much as I had visualized, which was wonderful. But yet, I still didn't feel quite the way I thought I would. I became increasingly aware that something was missing.

I began to notice there would be a repeated arc of experience that would occur with the acquisition of each new possession. First, there would be a physical and emotional rush of excitement about owning the new object and then, a period of admiration and satisfaction about it that also reflected on me for being such a splendid fellow to own such a thing. Others would often admire my new purchase and I would bask in the reflected glow of the fine possession. But then after a while, it would go as flat as an old glass of beer. The object ceased to do anything for me. It sank into the landscape around me and became just another part of what was normal.

George Harrison, in Martin Scorsese's documentary *Living In The Material World,* describes this phenomenon of realizing that all the success, fame, acclaim and possessions he had earlier so desired, did not provide what he thought they would. And this is from someone who achieved far more than most people ever will. He mentions the tremendous gift that he was able to realize this because of all he had achieved and attained at such a young age, because most people never get to have all the material things they had wanted, and as a result remain trapped in the illusion that they if they could just achieve them then they will be fulfilled.

At first my assumption was that I now needed a new and more wonderful acquisition. The reason I no longer felt excited about my previous prize must clearly be that it was not as wonderful as I had first thought it was. But as time went by, I couldn't ignore the pattern of this experience. I realized that whatever possessions I had, just became normal after a while. I assumed this phenomenon was the same for others around me, because the people I knew appeared to be in a relentless pursuit of more and bigger and better stuff.

So many people around me appeared to be dissatisfied with what they had. The purpose of their lives seemed to have a lot to do with acquiring more. I saw people even exhibit shame if their stuff wasn't as new or as expensive or as big as those around them. Their status and their sense of self worth was apparently connected to the clothes they wore, the car they drove, and the house they lived in and so on.

I wasn't immune to this pressure. I knew it disturbed me in some way, but I wasn't able to completely dissociate from it. I would go to parties and people who had talked to me for five minutes when I had arrived in a Honda, now spoke to me for twenty minutes when I arrived in a Mercedes. My new car apparently made me worthy of fifteen minutes more of their time.

This is not to imply that there is anything wrong with owning beautiful things. Aesthetic objects and beautiful physical forms are also creative expressions of universal laws. Our appreciation of aesthetics in its myriad aspects is a form of spiritual perception. There is definitely a relationship between beauty and truth. However this becomes warped and negative when we *identify* with our possessions: when we confuse our value and worth with that of the beautiful or valuable things that we own.

Another way we can misuse our objects is *by expecting them to change how we feel about ourselves.* When we do this, we do ourselves a great disservice. For that is not, and never can be, their function. How we feel about ourselves is our own responsibility, not that of our possessions, or the other people in our life. Yet the basis of most advertising is to convince us that by acquiring a new product we will experience life differently: the emptiness we are currently experiencing will finally be filled.

Possession thus promises transformation. But this is a false promise. Many people work so that they have the money to be able to shop during their time off and experience the transitory rush of acquisition and increased status. Perhaps one question we should all ask ourselves is: *how much do we really need?*

It is true that when we are starving one meal can make a big difference. I was living in Copenhagen, Denmark, at one point when I was in my twenties, and following a spiritual path that I believed at the time was important. But I was so poor and eating so little, that I noticed one day I could move my teeth around in my gums with a little pressure from my fingers. I was becoming seriously malnourished. A friend took me to an Indian restaurant and bought me dinner one evening and I ate so much that I was in physical pain, because I didn't know when I would eat so well again. I will always remember her kindness.

Similarly I remember standing in the Radhuspladsen waiting for a bus one evening. It was wintertime and a thermometer on a building was registering minus 32 degrees Fahrenheit, plus there was a serious wind chill factor coming up a street from the strait of water that leads to the Baltic Sea. Icy wind was blowing past the statue of the Little Mermaid and right into the center of town. I was wearing a thin coat and I feared I might freeze to death before the bus arrived, I could feel the cold settling in my core. The relief when the bus finally did arrive and took me to my room where I was able to warm up was real; it was the first time in my life that I had glimpsed the possibility that I could actually freeze to death. I had never been that cold before.

So when we experience this kind of relief from physical discomfort we can make the assumption that if a little physical comfort of food or warmth is *this* good, then *more* physical comfort must be much, much better, and so this can become our dominant goal of acquiring wealth and ensuring comfort. But this is just an illusion. Once we get past satisfying the physical basics of enough food to eat and enough shelter to keep us alive and healthy, more physical possession does not significantly change our chronic emotional state.

Luxury can give us a little emotional bump for a while, but from my experience, then we settle back to feeling how we did before in a matter of months. The super-rich are not significantly happier than the rest of us.

I found it was the same with the places I had visited. When I was young, I had an image of the way I would be when I was older. I wanted to be well travelled and experienced in the ways of the world, a debonair, sophisticated middle-aged man who knew his way around, the kind of character you see in old movies played by Humphrey Bogart.

And so I visited some of the most beautiful places on the planet: Italy, France, Switzerland, Greece—I went all over Europe looking for the perfect place that would in some way, change me. But travelling around, wonderful as it was, hadn't made me what I thought it would either.

I couldn't spot what was missing. I just knew that none of the approaches I had taken had got me exactly where I wanted to go in life, and that I still had no idea where or what that was.

There is a saying of Buddha's that applied to what I was experiencing: *You can't get everything you want. It is impossible and you will never fully succeed. Luckily, there is another option: you can learn to control your mind, to step outside this endless cycle of desire and aversion. You can learn not to want what you want, to recognize desires but not to be controlled by them.*

The question to ask ourselves is: what is the experience,

or emotion I believe that owning or having this will bring to me?

If we can achieve that experience and emotion *directly,* then we can bypass our craving for obtaining the physical objects and circumstances we mistakenly believe we must have to feel happy and fulfilled.

Then we can switch our attention to pursuing that spiritual goal, which can actually bring us what we desire at our deepest level. Which all the riches in the world on their own never can.

There is nothing wrong with owning nice things. But there is something wrong with expecting them to do for us what only our own spirit can do.

The pursuit of inner bliss through possession is a delusion. One of the reasons some very successful and wealthy people implode, is that they achieve all they thought they wanted to make them happy, and they discover it still did not make them happy! And they feel very lost at that moment. They either manage to find a spiritually nurturing path of some kind at that moment, or else, in their disillusion, they descend into a self-destructive path that may include drugs, alcohol or other additions. The popular media is always bringing us the latest story of the catastrophic collapse of a celebrity who seemed to have it all.

Why then, as a culture, do we continue to look toward celebrities and the super wealthy as our role models for happiness? Achieving your goals can be more devastating than *not* achieving them, when they are completely materially based.

Especially if achieving that wealth involved violating one's personal integrity because of the exploitation or harm of others. When we prize wealth above our own integrity or our connection to other people by disregarding them and seeing them as simply a means to our ends, or profiting at their expense, we are lost.

At the moment, much of humanity is still locked in the lie that the physical universe can provide all that they desire and need. Because they haven't achieved all the possessions they desire, they haven't experienced the disillusion and emptiness of achieving complete material wealth. They still think if they only possessed *more*, *then* they would achieve their bliss. This is another part of the Grand Illusion.

There is nothing wrong with wealth, so long as it is balanced with a spiritual life. We are spiritual beings having a physical experience, so we need a balance of the physical and spiritual worlds.

At the other end of the spectrum, it is hard to have a spiritual life when one is starving for lack or food, or diseased, or unprotected from the elements. We all need to achieve that point of balance between physical and spiritual.

But the fact is that because we are *spiritual* beings having a *physical* experience, not the other way around, only a significant spiritual experience will be able to satisfy the inner craving we all have deep down for something that will finally satisfy us. That seeking for an indefinable something within all of us that drives us to all the many experiences we have in life, is ultimately the spiritual returning and reuniting with the universal Consciousness from which we came.

We try relationships, love, sex, family, a home, a business, wealth, possessions, luxury, fame, and power—every game we think may finally be the one to satisfy us. Only eventually, after we have played every game there is, after we have exhausted every experience we can have on this planet, do we reach the wisdom that what we are seeking is to reunite with Spirit, Consciousness, or God. That enlightenment is waiting within us, buried beneath the totality of falsehoods and unconsciousness that is the Grand Illusion.

This is the classic theme that appears in many stories of the young person who leaves home to seek their fortune, and eventually returns home to find peace and happiness.

At that time in my life in LA I felt I was plugged into a system that was no longer working for me. It felt like a drum was beating inside me: *Time to move!*

Our children were off to college now, leaving only the youngest with us. It felt like the right time for a change. The question was: Where to go? Then Allen suggested my wife and I go with him on a trip to see Santa Fe, New Mexico. Of course we said yes. We knew it would be his last trip of this kind anywhere.

We loved Santa Fe on sight: The Sangre De Cristo mountains, the architecture, the sense of history and permanence. We knew we would return there. A short time after Allen's passing, my wife flew out to look for houses. A couple of days later she called me to come see what she had found, and I did.

The fourth house we entered I loved immediately. I suddenly remembered many years earlier when I had lived in an old Spanish house belonging to a girlfriend in Marbella on the south coast of Spain. I loved the feeling of the architecture with its beams, thick walls, and Saltillo tiled floor. I had made a declaration to the universe as I stood there in her living room: *One day I want a house like this.* It was a moment of instinctive, vivid intention and desire. That day was now here. I was standing in the very house that I had asked for.

We made our leap of faith. We wrapped things up in Los Angeles and before long we were driving to Santa Fe.

We arrived in our new home appropriately enough on my birthday. And we started our new life. Strangers in a strange land.

We built a horse barn and an art studio. My wife set about raising horses and I set about painting. I started showing in galleries. Then we both started a band. We had both been involved in music when we were younger: me in London and Vicky in San Francisco and Los Angeles.

It seems to me that once you seriously embark on a spiritual quest that life will push you in the direction you need to go in order to learn your next lesson. You find that you are doing one thing but life has other plans. Sometimes a chain of events string together and you arrive magically where you need to be despite your best efforts to control matters. My chain of events was gathering momentum.

As a result of the physical demands of playing music and moving heavy equipment I eventually found myself with continuous back pain. It went on for months and kept me awake at nights. I had broken my back in a bad fall while climbing when I was a young man and old physical problems were being resurrected.

I went looking for help to end the pain and tried a number of things without success.

Then somebody from whom I was receiving treatment steered me towards Pilates and Restorative Yoga. I started following very specific instructions to do things with my body that made little sense to me. When I repeatedly asked my instructor: "Why am I doing this?" She told me: "It would take too long to explain. Just do it and you'll see why."

After three weeks of working with my new teacher, I was

again pain free. I liked the exercises and basic restorative yoga poses like Supta Badha Konasana (Reclining Bound Ankle Pose), and continued the classes, because I was afraid my pain might return if I stopped.

But then an interesting thing started to occur. As I did these exercises, I began to feel sensations of peacefulness, energy, and joyfulness. Something about the movements in combination with breathing and being unusually mindful of what I was doing, was unlocking a new sense of aliveness within me. I found it both stimulating and also disturbing. I wasn't quite sure what was going on with me. It felt as if the ground under me was shifting, as if something was waking up. I started to read about Chakras and subtle body energy. I took some classes in meditation.

Vicky was also getting involved in this too. She went looking for books that would shed some more light on what we were both experiencing. She came back with a book by Eckhart Tolle: *The Power of Now*.

We were entering a new chapter of our lives.

# Chapter Four
# Separation From Ego

## Our False Identity

*The ego is a veil between Humans and God.~ Rumi*

As I started to read about spiritual subjects again, I began pondering the question of *ego* and how it keeps us locked in a mental box.

The term *ego* came into use in the early nineteenth century from the translated work of Freud and Jung. It literally means "I" in Latin. It has since made its way from the realm of psychology to be included into current spiritual vocabulary. Its meaning has changed from being one of the three components of the Freudian model of the human psyche: the *ego*—the organized, realistic part, *super ego*—the critical and moralizing part, and the *id*—the uncoordinated and instinctual part.

In common usage, *ego* means an excess of ego or someone who is self-absorbed or conceited and arrogant.

In modern spiritual usage, 'ego' has a different meaning. Ego could be defined as: *A false mental creation of one's sense of identity, producing an experience of separateness and isolation from other beings and things.*

The ego is in fact a delusion of who and what a person

believes themselves to be, other than simply an immortal, spiritual being. The truth is that as spiritual, non-physical, formless beings existing outside of space or time, we have no identity. But now crammed into the universe of forms, space/time, and especially a physical body who is part of a family and a tribe with no memory of what we were before, it is quite understandable we would think we are part of everything we see around us.

So our *ego*—our sense of identity—is actually a mental construction composed of ideas of who we are based on all we have been identifying with since we were small children. These include all of the following: Our body, our name, our family, our education, our culture, our nationality, our race, our socio-economic standing or class, our profession, the roles we play such as father or mother or son or daughter, our possessions like our house, our car, our clothes—including anything that makes us feel special and important like that treasured watch or jewelry—the skills we have acquired, our achievements that we can casually boast about, the organizations we are affiliated with, our history and our formative experiences, our group of friends, the sports teams we support—that make us feel superior—the qualities we have that we feel proud of—the things about which we become self-righteous and condemn others, the things which we defend to make ourselves right and others wrong.

All these things come together to give us the picture of who we consider ourselves to be.

This is what constitutes our ego in spiritual terms.

Our everyday life reinforces all of this of course. When we look in the mirror there is our familiar reflection looking back at us. Everyone we know identifies us by that face and body and name. We have papers that prove it too: a driver's license, credit cards, a passport, certificates from schools and colleges.

Your government, your employer, your family and friends, your bank, the police force and the IRS are all convinced that this is who you are. If you tried to tell them you aren't, they would consider you are either crazy or up to no good!

So what am I saying exactly about identity? Just what is the big point about ego?

Why is this an important subject?

On the face of it, this may seem like nonsense, but it is simply the logical extension of the principle we encountered in the first chapter—that we are actually all *immortal spiritual beings*, who existed before, and will continue to exist after the death of our current physical body.

Just as I experienced my friend Allen clearly existing after his body died, he must have also existed before he entered that baby body for the first time, before his mother first called him by his new name, "Allen." So in between having a body, he had no identity or form, but nevertheless existed. That is what I mean by having no form or identity.

If you think of yourself existing before and then after this current life and having no physical identity to call yourself but still having the core consciousness you have now, that may make it easier to get your head around.

So we don't *have* souls; we *are* souls, who are experiencing life in a body from a human perspective at this moment. On the physical level all these things that comprise your picture of your ego are absolutely true. But on the spiritual level they are not true at all. You existed before you occupied the body you have now. And you will exist after this body has died.

After your body dies at the end of this lifetime, none of your false current ego identity will be true. All of this life—that seems so vitally important to you right now—will be as important to you as your last life is to you now.

So who are you really? You are actually an immortal, invulnerable, non-physical spirit.

And love, joy, compassion, and your connectedness to universal Consciousness is your natural state.

Believing that we are *only* all of the current physical things such as our name and our body, is to lose sight of who we truly are. It is like being an actor who believes he actually *is* the role he is performing in a play!

It is this false belief of who and what we are, that blinds us to the truth and the experience of who and what we *truly* are. Our attention has become fixated on this temporary, half-truth of our current situation, and so we have forgotten and cannot experience the immortal, real truth that lies underneath. And as a result we have a basically false viewpoint of life.

**We cannot see the ego because we believe we *are* the ego. We believe the ego's thoughts are *our* thoughts.**

And we believe we must protect the ego—"ourselves"—at all costs—and so we human beings lie, cheat, steal, kill and commit all manner of destruction to keep safe that which we believe is us—but which in reality is nothing more than an illusion. And that is the basis of all human insanity.

It is only identification with this ego that makes us experience the world as separate individuals, alone and fearful, rather than part of a cosmic consciousness, connected and nurtured, feeling cradled in universal love.

It is identification with ego that makes human beings insane, and why our history is written in blood and suffering.

When we are identified with our ego, we compare

ourselves to others. For the most part we do not experience our universal *connection* to others, aside from maybe family or close friends, but instead we experience our *competition* with others: Are they *better* than us, more talented, skilled, powerful, better looking, more wealthy? In which case we feel negative emotions like insecurity, jealousy, resentment, fear and inferiority.

Most people have experienced sibling rivalry for example. If we judge ourselves better than someone else we can feel superior, and smug, and we judge them as not a threat, and we can look down on them and feel clever and reassured for a while. But if someone is obviously better than us in some way and we feel inferior, then all the torture of negative emotions can occur, and this can drive people to undermine and attack others who are more successful than they are.

The play, made into the movie *Amadeus,* by Peter Shaffer, deals with the fictionalized jealousy of the court composer Salieri of Mozart's talent, which drives him to arrange events that bring about Mozart's death. This is a study of the universal theme of someone who is completely ego-bound, descending into madness despite all their great talent and accomplishments, because they cannot let go of the obsession to compare themselves with another. In this case with one of the dominant musical geniuses of his time.

This is a large part of what keeps us separated and isolated from becoming one with God, Goddess, Spirit, Presence, Yahweh, The Almighty, Father, The Supreme Being, Brahman, Vishnu, Krishna, Allah, or however you refer to the universal Consciousness of which we are all a part.

I need to make the point that there is no judgment intended in using any of these terms, they all refer to the same entity. Please substitute the one you are most familiar and comfortable with whenever you see one of them used in this book. There is only one universal Consciousness, regardless of the name we use.

Separation from Ego—like all the aspects of spirituality described in this book—is an *experience*, not just a concept. The concept comes first as a signpost towards you having your own experience, after which no discussion is necessary because it will be part of your personal knowingness and wisdom. There is therefore no point in making *decisions* about this subject on a mental level *before* it becomes an experience. It will be your ego that is making these decisions anyway—and it is certainly not eager to embrace a line of of thought that will lead to its own disolution!

So, as with all the new concepts you encounter in this book, try to comprehend the concepts without judgment, so that you can try to have the experience.

The great trick of becoming spiritually awakened is recognizing and maintaining awareness of the paradox of our situation as a human being: we are each truly a timeless and non-physical being, who cannot be harmed and cannot die, yet we are experiencing a vivid physical existence where everything is continually changing, and the vehicle we are using to have this experience—our body—is mortal and can easily be harmed in a thousand different ways.

We know for certain that one day we, and everyone we know and love, will surely die as the current physical form we now recognize. And to the extent that we are *identified* with this physical world and our current physical body, is the extent we are filled with fear about the potential loss and death of all we love. This fear of losing what is actually only a temporary illusion is what cripples us and renders us powerless to cause all that we could, *if* we were able to maintain the awareness of what we truly are: immortal, invulnerable, and part of God, with all the wisdom and power that implies.

Achieving Christ Consciousness or Enlightenment, is done by removing all the false beliefs and unconsciousness that cloud the truth of what we really are. It is a reductive, not additive, process. The first step of this is separating, and staying separated, from the false identity of who we believe we are—*our ego.*

This is the beginning of our sanity, the beginning of our true spiritual journey. This is the beginning of viewing the world without great distortion.

If you are having a hard time separating yourself from the person who looks back at you in the mirror, consider this: you were just as convinced that you were the person staring back at you in the mirror last lifetime too, and in all your previous lifetimes. And yet, now you may not be able to remember any of them. And even if you can—how significant are those identities to you now?

The point is to be able to be fully present in this life *without* being identified with the face in the mirror and believing the illusion is real. *Then* you can really be free to play the Game of Life to the fullest and still remain conscious. The paradox is: the less identified we become, the freer we become, and the more intensely we can engage with life because we have no fear to hold us back.

A point of clarification regarding the Conscious and Unconscious mind: there are not literally two separate compartments to the mind. There is one mind, with some parts that are conscious—meaning of which we are aware—and parts that are unconscious—of which we are unaware. But with work and attention we can transform these unconscious aspects of our mind into becoming conscious.

The Conscious mind pertains to those parts which are logical, with positive emotions and thoughts, and with positive beliefs about the world that are based on accurate or scientific knowledge.

The unconscious mind consists of several things, including: reactive, knee-jerk, illogical responses; negative emotions, based on painful past experiences which have not been fully looked at; and negative beliefs that are based on incorrect and uninspected information or assumptions. In this book I refer to the totality of spiritual unconsciousness as *the Grand Illusion.*

As we bring the focus of our attention and consciousness onto the unconscious mind, one part at a time, its negative energy is transformed into positive energy, and it then becomes part of the conscious mind. Remember that the law of conservation of energy in physics tells us that energy can neither be created nor destroyed. But it can be transformed by having its vibration changed, which is what happens when we bring about an increase in consciousness to a part of our mind that was previously unconscious.

Not included in this definition of the unconscious mind are the parts of the brain that run the thousands of automatic body functions of which we are quite unaware.

The ego belongs to the unconscious mind. And as we become aware of its falsehoods, bit by bit, we separate from it and gain in consciousness. As we do spiritual work, the unconscious mind shrinks, and so there is more conscious mind. As old, encysted negative energy is transformed into positive energy we experience more life force, vitality or *prana*, *chi*, *qi or ki*—all words in different languages for the same entity.

As with many spiritual truths there is a paradox at work here: the usual response to the idea of separating from all that we think of as *us*, our ego, is to think: "Oh no! If I do that I'll be nothing at all!" In fact the reverse is true—the more we realize that we *aren't* all we see around us, the more of our spiritual essence becomes available to us. We are in truth far more than we currently believe ourselves to be. As a result we begin to experience everything with far more depth, vibrancy and connectedness than ever before.

We are like someone who started playing a game of Monopoly, but who has forgotten they are playing a game, and now believes the game is real life and that this Monopoly board, the pieces and play money, is all there is. We have forgotten our real world, and our false belief in the little Monopoly world keeps it hidden from us. Being identified with the physical and the temporary causes us to lose the viewpoint of the immortal and the True.

As we awaken from ego, we begin to experience our connection to everything around us.

Being in this life with the awareness and viewpoint that all is temporary, and that we are actually here having experiences which enable us to learn spiritual lessons, allows us to experience the full richness of existence, free from fear and isolation. When we see that there is truly nothing to lose, our fear of loss evaporates.

This life can be thought of as watching a thrilling movie, from which we can learn lessons, but at the end of the "movie"—when this body dies—the lights will come up and we go on, unharmed and still existing.

Having an atheistic belief that that there is no God is simply symptomatic of being identified with ego. While you are strongly identified with ego you cannot experience God. Once you no longer identify with ego, then experiencing God becomes unavoidable. But this is an *experience*, not a mental concept that can be proved or argued cleverly by theologists and others.

Spiritual experience is the revealing of Truth, and this is beyond the realm of mere intellect. As Osho says: *The answer to a fundamental question is an experience not a sentence.*

When you are experiencing your connection to your own spirit and universal spirit, you feel held and nurtured by the universe around you and fear melts away. You experience the love that is your natural state.

Love is not an emotion incidentally—this is who you *are* when the mind ceases to dominate your consciousness. This state is sometimes referred to as *bliss*. You cannot experience this love and fear at the same time. It is necessary to separate from your ego delusion to experience your natural state of bliss.

When you put your attention back onto the unconscious mind again, and believe the lie of the temporary ego identity, you will close down your access to this state of bliss.

You may be intellectually well aware of the concept that you are a spiritual being, and yet still remain plugged into that which keeps you fixed in the false viewpoint of ego identification.

This is not an intellectual idea that you read and understand. This is a process of *transformation* that involves your active participation.

Until you have *experienced* separation from your sense of ego identification, you are looking at everything through a false lens, and you will remain locked out of further spiritual progress. This is why separation from ego is so important. This process of separating from ego is the real beginning of one's spiritual journey, the door to spiritual evolution. Because once you have stepped through this door you have the opportunity to see everything as it truly is.

Before this step, the lens of ego will have distorted everything you have seen. You will have been viewing things around you through a veil of illusion. Although you may have had moments of clarity, eventually ego identification can lead you back into insane and destructive or deluded behavior. Even if you have had the insight of separation from ego, it is always waiting for a moment of stress to reduce your consciousness so that it can reassume its former position of control.

The ego is the most insidious mechanism because it does not present itself as something separate from ourselves which we can easily locate. We start off completely identified with the thoughts we think. We believe at first that our thoughts are us, that we are our thoughts and they are true, that they tell us about the nature of reality, that they describe the world around us, that they are the most we can know, and that they hold the key to all our questions, and that we can think our way to wisdom. We cannot even detect that something alien to us has taken over all our thoughts and motivations, because we falsely believe we *are* our ego.

But when we start to simply observe our own thoughts, we gradually start to experience a transformation of consciousness: we realize that we are not our thoughts, and they are not us.

We realize that just because we thought a negative thought, this does not make it true at all. We see eventually that all our negative thoughts are untrue, and they are just loops of negative energy that repeat over and over and that we have been in a dream, hypnotized and controlled by these thoughts for a very, very long time, lifetime after lifetime.

We separate from them, and see them for the out-of-control mental mechanism that they are. We wake up from their deceptive and tyrannous domination, and we bring them under our conscious control, we become the master of our own mind and start to train it to be focused where we wish it to be, we change our negative thoughts into positive versions.

We see that we are not part of the physical universe at all, that we are just here for a while, to learn the lesson that life brings us. And we finally start to live in peace, with a calmed mind.

The paradox is that the more we cling to our sense of ego identity, the more we try to reinforce our feelings of how special, how different, how important, how individual we are, the more we close ourselves off from that which our souls desire—connection to the source of Spirit from which we came and of which we are always a part whether we can perceive it or not: a wave in the Ocean of Spirit.

## My Experience

My experience of ego separation took place unceremoniously in a Whole Foods Market one evening as I was grocery shopping. It may have been in the cereal aisle…I was thinking about the subject of ego and identification as I was pushing a shopping cart around.

I kept spotting all the things I had added to my own sense of ego over the years. I was remembering practicing how to move my hands and standing and moving in ways that I considered to be more manly and less childish at around age thirteen, when something extraordinary happened to me:

I suddenly saw all of these things I had identified with since I was a child like a big structure around me: all kinds of bits of stuff, tied together like pieces of wood with string, that formed my fortification, my crab's shell of defenses that was all about me, protecting me from the outside world, that I had been making since my childhood. And then I had the sensation of the whole contraption lifting off me and away up into the air.

I found I was now seeing differently. I could suddenly see my surroundings in the market without actually focusing or having to move my eyes to do so. Not all the way behind me but to the sides quite a way. The boxes and packets of food appeared to be glowing as they sat on their shelves.

I was experiencing an overwhelming sense of love, connection and appreciation for everything around me. I felt as if a skin had been peeled off me and that I was now experiencing everything first hand, in a way that was overwhelmingly intense. I couldn't focus on shopping anymore and I found myself going over to the flower section.

The blooms in front of me that were normally just ordinarily beautiful, had now suddenly become amplified into such achingly exquisite aesthetic living creations that I could feel completely, using only my eyes. I stood there lost in a communication of gratitude with these incredible creations and their dazzling colors and forms.

I suddenly realised that I was now weeping with joy in front of the flower section of my local market, and that I just might appear crazy. Abandoning my cart, I stumbled out into the night before someone noticed the nut job on aisle fifteen and alerted security.

I got into my car and drove away, but quickly discovered I was unable to focus properly on driving with much degree of safety. I pulled into a parking spot and saw with some alarm that I was next to a police car! Although I was absolutely sober, I felt impaired physically as if I was under the influence of something. My perceptions had shifted in an instant from the normal rational world, into an overwhelmingly beautiful and exquisitly blissful realm that I longed to remain in, but in which I feared I would have had an accident if I had continued to drive. I sat in my car for about half an hour and gradually I felt more in control of my body and grounded, and I was able to safely drive home.

This is why I suggest doing the exercise at the end of this chapter when you are in a safe, quiet place, and by yourself, free from interruptions. And definitely not when you have to drive your car!

By the next day, I was seeing the way I was used to again, but my viewpoint of who I really was, had totally changed. I cannot guarantee your experience will be as dramatic as I have described. Maybe it will be much more so. We are all individual in how we experience these things, but the basic spiritual laws apply to us all.

Like all the extraordinary experiences I have had, after a period of adjustment I was able to assimilate them into my everyday life, and the extraordinary became ordinary again, but a very different kind of ordinary. I no longer believed that I was all of these other things and it was an experience of great relief and freedom. There seemed to be fewer things to worry about or that were able to hook me into negative emotions. I noticed that if something did hook me, I came out of it so much faster than I used to.

This experience was not the end of the process of

becoming separate from my ego—merely the beginning. It is a continual, daily practice to stay free and conscious, some days one is more successful than others. When we engage in this work we are starting to undo a habit of many, many lifetimes of delusion, and each day offers new triggers that seek to hook us back into the delusion, and becoming aware of each one is a spiritual practice in itself.

### *Exercise:*

Write down a list of all the things you consider make you who you are.

You are looking for all the things that seem to make you different from others, that make you unique and special.

Start from the present: your name, body, profession, family, culture, nationality, possessions, societies you belong to, sports teams you support, and so on.

Then move back in time, listing your education, fraternity or sorority you belonged to, clubs, teams, hobbies, activities etc.

You are looking for everything that makes you feel a sense of identity and defines you—everything that makes you feel special, bigger, more powerful, proud, and confident by your association with it.

It could be buying a car, a house, a pair of shoes, special jewelry or a watch—for women designer purses seem to hold that power sometimes! Anything that was significant in making you feel special. Go back to your earliest memories of being aware of yourself as a member of your family. Perhaps you had special toys or clothes that made you feel special, or heroes with whom you identified. Perhaps you felt you must adopt certain beliefs or attitudes in order to be accepted and OK.

When you have made your list, meditate upon the fact

that you existed *before* any of these connections were made, before any of these things were true. And that you will continue to exist after none of these connections exist, after your current body is dead and in a grave or cremated.

So who are you really, without any of these temporary identifications?

If you are stuck on something—being a particular race or gender for instance—it may help to picture yourself as the opposite:

If you are a man now imagine being a woman—but still being you inside. If you are a woman imagine being a man. If you are white now imagine being black, if you are black imagine being white—but still you inside. Whatever you are now, imagine yourself as the something else, or the opposite, but still you inside.

Imagine yourself as a timeless, immortal being who is living this life temporarily from a human perspective. Because that is what is actually happening.

Imagine that you have lived many lives before, with many faces and identities and families—when you looked in the mirror, another face was looking back—but it was still essentially you inside. If this is foreign to your present belief system, just observe how this concept makes you feel.

Eventually, you should be able to detach yourself from the concept of ego. Maybe this will be dramatic—maybe not.

Notice if you now feel more connected, and less separate from those around you.

Once you have achieved a viewpoint of separation from your ego it will require continual work not to become seduced back into feeling identified, separate, special, and isolated.

Good luck!

# Chapter Five
# Tribalism—The Collective
# Ego Consciousness

Separating From Group Consciousness—Beliefs And
Manifestation—Personal Ethical Responsibility

*Now this is the Law of the Jungle—as old and as true as the sky.
And the Wolf that shall keep it may prosper, but the Wolf that shall
break it must die...the strength of the Pack is the Wolf, and the
strength of the Wolf is the Pack.* ~ *Rudyard Kipling*

*The individual has always had to struggle to keep from being
overwhelmed by the tribe. If you try it, you will be lonely often,
and sometimes frightened. But no price is too high to pay for the
privilege of owning yourself.* ~ *Friedrich Nietzsche*

The phenomenon of ego identification has an aspect that
we should examine specifically: that of identification with a
group, or several different groups. This can be defined here
as *Tribalism,* or *Collective Ego.* This can include your family,
community, nationality, a professional group such as the
American Medical Association, the Bar Association, or the
Teamsters, the Military, a sports team—or all of the above,
and many more.

A group of people or tribe can have its own consciousness,

or more specifically things that they agree upon and identify with, and therefore have become their reality. We hear terms like "corporate culture" or "military culture" which describes a specific way of thinking and what is considered normal and the way things are done in those worlds.

Certain countries or cultures have attitudes towards other countries or cultures, based on historical experiences. One race or socio-economic group can have attitudes and generalized beliefs about another group that are passed on from parent to child, regardless of whether these still have any truth to them or not. Racism and prejudices are kept alive in this way, and children can be fed lies along with food, shelter and love, and so separating true from false can become very difficult. The fact that an individual from a particular group may embody none of the stereotypical traits they supposedly possess can be absolutely overlooked because of prejudgments.

This subject deserves its own chapter, because even if you are successful in separating from the concept of ego identity as described in the previous chapter, if you still are unknowingly identified with cultural attitudes and beliefs, you will encounter difficulties.

Reality is that which we agree is real. This changes from culture to culture and from one time to another. Some things which used to be real now seem ridiculous to us. For instance, most of us take for granted these days that slavery is not a good idea, that the world is not flat, that the earth is not the center of the solar system or the universe. Most people believe in the principle of evolution, even though that may be only part of the entire story. What is *true* is a gradually changing landscape of accepted reality, and if you subscribe fully to the group's consciousness, then you will evolve at the same rate as the group.

We evolved and survived in tribes. Individually, human beings are not big or strong enough to exist in competition with lions, tigers, bears, or a host of other ferocious predators. But by employing intelligence, communication, organization, strategy, and the development of weapons to compensate for the lack of fangs or claws, tribes of hunting men became a force to be reckoned with in the primitive struggle for food, and eventually managed to rise to the top of the food chain. But we only achieved this *as members of a tribe.*

We are therefore social creatures. Belonging to a group is deeply rooted in us. So separating from the group mind and developing an individual consciousness is no simple task.

And it is not achieved without struggle and some suffering, for the tribe is very interested in protecting the tribe and in its continued existence. The tribe believes that if it dies, all the individual members will also die.

This is the essential point of this chapter: it is important for each of us that we identify how much of what we believe and think is just "group think" that we have adopted, sometimes at a very early age, that we are not aware of. How much of our beliefs, attitudes, reactive responses and feelings are not really ours at all, but just what we have absorbed without realizing it, as we did our language and our accent?

This involves a process of self-examination, where we look at and question all that we believe, think, and feel about other people and other groups of people who are not like the group we were raised in. Those who look or think or behave differently than we are used to.

This is important because until you go through this

process, you will have negative beliefs, attitudes, feelings, and thoughts about other people and situations *that are not really yours.* They will be part of your mental machinery that goes through life with you and influences your experience— *but in fact they belong to other people!* Not only will you not experience life and other people directly, but you will have an unconscious filter that will color your perceptions.

**Anything the mind accepts as true becomes a law in the subconscious and manifests in the world of the one who accepted it.**

This can happen as a vulnerable child during a time of emotional stress, but it will stay with you for a lifetime, unless you deliberately do something to consciously transform it from negative to positive.

If you have grown up in a particular society, and especially if you never move away from that society, you can spend your whole life unconsciously playing a role in life, just like a part in a play, complete with attitudes and reactions, which is part of your ego identification, and this can take a *lot* of work to spot.

When one is identified with tribal consciousness then what is good for your tribe is "good"–regardless of the damage caused to other tribes. It is the mentality of the Mafia: "Protect family and the group—but everyone else is "fair game." In tribal consciousness patriotism is good, and under the banner of patriotism, nations can go to war with each other and good men can kill other good men. There is nothing wrong with pride and love of one's own country, *as long as* it is not an unconscious identification that is willing to deny another pride and love of their country.

Once we escape identification with our group and start to

think individually, we are able to look at things from a human and global perspective, and we realize that the parents of our enemies weep just as much when their children die in wars as we do for ours. We become less vulnerable to the propaganda that governments engage in to demonize those they cast in the role of enemy, and when we look with an unbiased eye into history we often uncover the events that caused another group to regard our group as an enemy. And we move past the childish viewpoint that our side is always right, and "they" are always wrong.

If you wish to progress on your spiritual journey, disengaging from group identification and group consciousness is a vital part of that journey, a giant step, and one which takes a considerable amount of courage. Then you will be free to access the truths of your own awareness and you will begin to be able to follow your own internal compass of what seems real or unreal to you. You will be able to think freely.

You will cease to need the group's approval. And you will cease to need a middleman to interact between you and God. You may then decide that you agree with a particular group's ideas about a certain subject once you have examined them on their own merits, and not just because you were told to think that way when you were young. The only authority you will respond to is your own, based on your own experiences.

The tribe will not take kindly to the news that you have decided to leave it and strike out on your own in order to pursue your own spirituality. You will be rejected as selfish and crazy if you become too vocal about the subject. Your spiritual journey is something best undertaken quietly. And yet this separation of consciousness is an *essential* step from the consciousness of spiritual childhood to spiritual adulthood.

It is essentially the point where we assume spiritual responsibility for ourselves *alone,* and no longer ask for permission or approval or absolution from another human being. We no longer require another to act as intermediary between us and the universal God consciousness of which we are all a part, if we can only wake up from our delusions to be able to experience it.

The tribe has always told you that selfishness is a bad thing. The behaviors that are commended by the tribe are of course those that serve the tribe: self-sacrifice for the good of others is noble and applauded. The soldier who dies in the service of his country; the fireman who runs into a burning building to save a child; the nurse who ignores the risk of personal infection to look after a sick patient; the parent who works two jobs and scrimps and slaves to raise their children and give them a better life—these are the heroes of our society.

These are the models that we are taught to emulate in countless movies and television shows and the tribe applauds them. I am not saying for a moment that all these ideals and actions are not laudable and courageous and valuable.

I am saying that there is a missing component in all of these scenarios that does not receive the same amount of concern from the tribe—and that is you. It is more productive to *live* for something than to *die* for something.

Be very wary of anyone who wants you to nobly sacrifice yourself, so that *they* can be better off. That is a scam some of us have been falling for a long time and it is time for it to cease. You deserve to be included in a good survival solution. Heroes may die in the movies, but they actually live to make their next film, and are well paid in the process.

I salute the courage and self-sacrifice of brave men and

women who have put others before themselves throughout history and knowingly paid the price. I mean no disrespect to their memory. They are far more evolved than those whose code is cowardice and selfishness, and who place their own survival above their integrity.

But it is time for us all, including brave men and women who live with a code of honor and knowingly risk their own lives for the sake of others, to evolve further to the point where we can live in peace with integrity and courage and with kindness to each other.

It is time we ceased to allow ourselves and our best motivations to be manipulated by a calculating few, who cynically wave the flag of patriotism and honor in order to simply forward their own special interests by cloaking them in marketing's most unassailable subjects of country, family, duty, courage, apple pie and motherhood.

Before we rush off to grab our rifles and sacrifice our lives or those of our children to armed conflict, we need to examine very carefully whether or not the latest threat to our respective national security is actually what is being sold to us, or whether it is just another piece of shabby deception. It is time we become immune to the jingoistic rhetoric combination of patriotism and religion, and cease our kneejerk responses to violence in support of the tribe.

Instead we should become very educated, informed, suspicious, and aware that acting peaceably and compassionately to our neighbors is every bit as patriotic, and a darn sight more religious or spiritual, a way to support the tribe.

The men and women who work hard and honestly to raise a family with kindness and love and produce children who are also kind, productive, and treat those around them with respect and care, are also heroes—for this is not something that is easily done. It requires courage and persistence over many years.

Being a parent while supporting a family is the hardest thing I have ever done in my life—it took every bit of strength that I had, I often felt I was clinging on with my fingernails—running a business, doing homework with my children, visits to the doctors, creating a home while still finding time to create a relationship, you know how tough this all is, even though Superdad and Supermom may never be action heroes on the big screen.

You cannot be responsible for your own life and your own spiritual development without including yourself in every equation. Self-sacrifice, by definition, does not include you in the equation. If you are truly here in a body on this planet to learn and raise your consciousness, then like the passenger in an airplane who is instructed to first put the oxygen mask to their own face before they put the mask on to their children's faces, first look to your own development. Then you will be in an empowered position to help others. You cannot give away that which you do not first have yourself.

And like so many statements in this book, this is not an invitation to miss the point entirely and in this case become self-centered, callous, self-indulgent and ignore all the responsibilities you have heretofore undertaken. Indulging your personality and ego is not the same thing as evolving your spirit.

As incarnated individuals our own spiritual consciousness is our own individual responsibility. Separating our consciousness from that of all the groups that we may currently belong is an essential part of assuming that responsibility. For then we can be acting with our own consciousness, and not because the group told us that is how we are meant to think.

Just how many beliefs do you hold that you have never inspected or questioned? How many attitudes towards the world and other people and indeed yourself were inculcated into you at an age when you trusted adults and believed all they told you? Especially the adults who were kindest to you when you were vulnerable and small. If your parents were racist or xenophobic then you were given these attitudes along with the essential food, shelter, and love and the bonding that small children have to their parents.

It is the task of every adult to eventually see their parents realistically as human and flawed, rather than unassailable paragons of perfection and emulation. One can still love the good in anyone, while not being blind to the reality of their shortcomings. Perceiving short- comings in a parent does not equate to family disloyalty to those who gave you life and nurturing.

Forgiveness of others and yourself becomes part of this process of disentangling yourself and your beliefs from the family and culture in which you were raised. Honesty of perception is not disloyalty.

Fear or distrust and rejection of outsiders who look or speak differently are part of the history of tribal survival. In Stone Age societies survival may well have depended on adapting these rules in order to ensure the survival of the family and the tribe. But this is no longer the Stone Age, and to continue to keep these attitudes is now counter-survival.

In the same way there may have been a tribal bias against

homosexuality because every child was needed to keep the family and tribe strong and ensure its future. Therefore every union, to be useful to the tribe, should produce a child. Male children were prized above females in some societies because of their superior physical strength that made them useful to hunt animals or raise and harvest crops.

We no longer live in those times. We need to drop our prejudice against those who do not look like us, those who do not share our ideas, our culture, our sex, or sexual orientation. Men and women are not the same, but they are definitely each other's equals. And one does not have to look very far for examples to see all the gay people who have been very successful and made huge contributions to our society. The idea that *only* your tribe and those who resemble you can make valuable contributions to human society is demonstrably untrue.

If you harbor beliefs like this, it is time to do some research, get out more and encounter doctors, scientists, musicians, artists, athletes, writers, engineers, inventors, teachers, dancers, filmmakers, architects, and builders of every race, color, creed and sexual orientation.

No one society or culture holds a monopoly on genius or stupidity. As we drop our identification with our tribe, we cease to have a vested interest in trying to prove any stereotypes to be true. *Tolerance arises within us naturally as we lose our false beliefs.*

**You have the task before you now to start questioning and inspecting every belief you now hold, to see if it is in fact really so, or whether it is an uninspected idea that is part of a tribal belief system that you have simply adopted.**

Here is a useful tool to help track false beliefs: Whenever you encounter a negative thought, emotion or belief, notice the red flag and investigate the falsehood that lies beneath them. You will always find one. False beliefs cause suffering in your life, and are another part of the Grand Illusion that stands between you and your awakening to your true spiritual nature.

### Truth and truth

I wish to make a make a distinction here between truth and Truth: How we view the world around us is subject to change as we learn more about the nature of the physical universe. Truths that change are *relative truths*. Einstein's Theory of Relativity became challenged by quantum physics. Then along came String Theory, which will very possibly be replaced by another explanation of how the universe is structured as scientists discover more.

The Truths we are discussing in this book, however, have been true since human culture existed and will still be True thousands of years from now. They are *Absolute Truths*. For example: the Truth that you are an immortal spiritual being will never become untrue.

**Identification with the physical world in all its aspects is what reduces our consciousness and brings us suffering.**

Living one's life *consciously*, involves letting go of all one's identifications.

Paradoxically, knowing that one is *not* all the things that one is intimately engaged with in life and knowing one's attachments are temporary heightens one's experience of being alive and does not diminish any of it as you might think at first. It is identification with the things of life that make them appear dull, monotonous, routine and lead us to feel fear, isolation, dissatisfaction, and frustration. The more we cling to our possessions and the comfort zone of what we mistakenly believe ourselves to be—the more these feelings increase. Conversely the more we open our hearts and experience love—the more connected to others and life around us we feel. And in that expanding connection to love and the nurturing spiritual universe, we find our fears and feelings of isolation evaporate.

There is a wonderful analogy in the film *The Matrix*, when Neo takes the red pill and awakens from the group perception of reality to the real world. Fortunately, the consciousness to which you are awakening is for more glorious than the reality to which Neo awoke.

The awakening from unconscious tribal group-think to individual awareness involves the taking back of your self-determinism from all the affiliations and loyalties you have made, often unconsciously, going back to childhood. Are these really *your* thoughts, attitudes, values? Or are they the inherited thoughts, attitudes or values of your tribe? How many tribal prejudices and biases are you unconsciously holding onto right now?

It is not a simple process to fully unravel this tangled skein, but it is an essential one to undertake. For as long as you have unexamined tribal agreements you can be easily hooked back into the unconsciousness of tribal ego behavior and put back to sleep.

We can then quickly snap into an *Us Versus Them* mode of thought: our tribe versus their tribe. Using another filmic analogy: the scene in Kubrick's *2001* where the tribe of vanquished apes violently take back the watering hole from the other ape tribe who had earlier driven them out, by the first devastating use of animal bones as weapons, perfectly describes this primal behavior that waits dormant within us all.

That reverting to tribal allegiance and the bonding of men to a team ready to commit violence against another tribe is a powerful motivation—which aside from brief periods of peaceful creativity, pretty much describes the entire history of mankind.

We see this mechanism exploited and released at events like football matches. Usually it occurs peaceably, but not always. Sometimes those caught up in tribal unconsciousness are bound together by nothing more threatening than the manipulation of an inflated ball around a grass field and wearing the colors of their team, and yet they resort to violence.

When you feel yourself ready to go to war against another nation after listening to a particularly inflammatory news item, realize that you have just slipped into tribal consciousness.

Those who are completely identified with their tribe are sleepwalking through life with *only* group consciousness. Their awareness is the awareness of the tribe and so their awareness will only evolve at the rate of the tribe.

Shifts in group consciousness are often brought about by individuals who are not identified with their group and are thus able to perceive and think individually. Their consciousness is above that of the group and they start movements that eventually result in the group's collective shift of consciousness, which then becomes part of the status quo, the new group reality.

These individuals are often ridiculed, resisted and sometimes even ultimately destroyed by the group in the difficult process of changing its awareness. The process could be likened to changing the course of a massive ocean liner: its enormous inertia takes a while to affect a change upon it.

We are familiar with the travails of Galileo Galilei at the hands of the Catholic Church when he tried to demonstrate the factuality of Copernicus' treatise that the Earth revolved around the Sun based on direct observation through his telescope. Because this concept directly contradicted the dogma of the Church that the Earth was the center of the solar system, he was put on trial, forced to recant under threat of torture and placed under house arrest. Later he was recognized for being a visionary.

Military organizations use time honored techniques in basic training to cause a shift away from any sense of individual identity to a group bonding that will result in troops who will obey orders in battle regardless of personal danger or destruction of life. For practical purposes obviously a non-cohesive army wouldn't function too well, but that might be the point given the utter destruction and cruelty of war.

The personal toll on men who join an army, trusting their commanders to make decisions for them that are wise and just and that they can live with in later life, is often extreme. The statistics of soldiers who have enormous difficulties returning to normal life after serving in battle or who become suicidal, is an indicator of the damage we do to our young men and women by involving them in war. More US troops died from suicide in 2012 than in combat.

It is time for our young men and women to stop willingly dying for the ambitions of politicians who stay safely behind the line of fire, while banks get rich funding both sides of the latest conflict, and the purposes of multinational conglomerates are achieved.

Politicians thrive on our laziness to think, failure to

examine issues and our loyalty to the party line and our patriotism.

A vital part of our children's education should be the examination and development of personal ethics, not to inculcate them into any particular dogma or religious viewpoint, but to allow them to question how they feel they should act in all kinds of circumstances and then examine the likely consequences of those actions based on real-life information.

If you already feel like an outsider or a misfit and not part of society in general, as I had, then this is actually a gift. Circumstances have already separated you from the tribe and your task of awakening from tribal consciousness may be much easier as a result.

### Feeling tribal

When you find yourself thinking in generalities about *those people who always act that way,* or if you feel another group threatens your group, you are in a tribal mode of group identification. When someone criticizes your country or group or its actions, if you personally feel insulted or affronted and feel impelled to retaliate first rather than examine the facts, you are in tribal identification. If somebody looks different from you or comes from a different culture and this in itself disturbs you, or if you feel that others who don't look and act like you are inferior or wrong, you are in a tribal identification.

Once you separate from this identification, you will find that others who look different or come from different backgrounds no longer disturb you. And you may discover that such people will relate to *you* in a far more accepting way than before.

### Racial And Cultural Identities

Racial and cultural identities are particularly hard to let go of. If you are a member of a racial or cultural group that has suffered considerable abuse and cruelty in the past such as African Americans, Native Americans, or Jews then you probably identify strongly with this group, but you may also carry with you the collective suffering and injustice of the group history—even for things that you personally have not experienced.

This is a big trap because you will then devote a large amount of energy to feeling resentments and victimization surrounding this painful subject. Casting yourself in the role of victim because of group identity or indeed for any reason and dwelling on self-righteousness and moral indignation is always disempowering and leads to a lack of consciousness.

A friend of mine told me his experience of working with a group of Native American shamans, who despite working with spiritual issues, shared a strong resentment toward white men for what they had put Native people through. Now although their grievances were totally justified regarding the horrific abuses Native peoples had suffered, their lack of forgiveness was very unhealthy for them personally. My friend, although not Native himself, took on the same attitude of resentments for the personal injustices *he* had endured, and the result was his emotional collapse, until he started to *forgive* the abuses he had received and then he recovered. This became an enormously instructive lesson to him about the healing power of forgiveness, and why he had the experience.

This is another example of taking on a consensus attitude as part of one's ego identification.

It is time to let go and heal. There is no final value in playing the role of victim; no matter what initial rush of power it may seem to give you.

*Exercise:*

List out all the groups to which you belong or of which you consider yourself a member. Review the agreements you have made to each group. Go back to the earliest: your family, school, sports teams, and so on. List the loyalties you agreed to each. Examine all these agreements to be a tribal member in the perspective that you are also an immortal spirit.

Examine the attitudes and beliefs you have in your deepest heart about those who are not part of your family, group, tribe, race, and culture. How do you really feel about those who are members of a group or race who oppressed your race or group in the past?

Note any that you feel distrust for as requiring work—be it forgiveness, or just the recognition that it isn't happening any more and that it is time to let it go and start living fully in the present moment.

# Chapter Six
# Here and Now

## Focusing Our Attention Fully On The Present Moment

*Do not dwell in the past, do not dream of the future, concentrate the mind on the present moment. ~ Buddha*

*The establishment of inner harmony is to be attained neither in the past nor in the future, but where the past and the future meet, which is the now. When you have attained that point, neither future nor past, neither birth nor death, neither time nor space exist. It is that NOW which is liberation, which is perfect harmony, to which the men of the past and the men of the future must come.~ J. Krishnamurti*

The moment of the most profound spiritual transformation of my life came at the time of my darkest distress. Alcoholics and other addicts refer to hitting bottom before a life change that leads to recovery. It seems there is a similarity to the mechanics of insight here. I do not believe suffering provides the only portal to spiritual change by any means, but it happened that way for me. Suffering seems to do us the service of giving us the focus that can result in insights.

My particular experience happened at a time when both

my parents were on their inexorable decline towards death. My father had entered hospital first after yet another small stroke occurred as he was climbing the stairs. He had fallen back and cracked his head on a table and was knocked unconscious. When I entered my parents' house, I saw the ominous blood stain on the carpet at the foot of the stairs that marked the violence of the incident.

Not too long after, while waiting for a friend to drive her to visit my father in hospital, my mother's hip had simply collapsed. The bones had crumbled as she stood in the hall-way, leaving her immobile on the hallway floor.

Fortunately, her friend had arrived on time and called the ambulance. Without this extraordinary piece of good timing she would have laid on the floor of the otherwise empty house unable to move or contact anyone. She might have died there before anyone found her.

I had moved to America three decades earlier. My relationship with my father had been stormy and competitive from the earliest of times. I had nevertheless visited England and seen my parents regularly over the years. Now they were sick I had been flying with my wife to and from England and America as these events unfolded, and our hospital visits were now to see both my parents. Ironically, they lay close by each other but separated by an entire hospital floor, one above the other.

When we weren't at the hospital, Vicky and I spent most of our time trying to sort out the chaos that had become my parents' house. A series of small strokes had gradually unplugged the logical connections of my father's once intelligent mind and caused a descent into a world of confusion. His once neatly filed papers had been shuffled into a jumbled mess, mixed in with junk mail and the remains of an old packet of peanuts. The lid of his bureau had been ripped off at some point because apparently he couldn't figure out how to use or locate the key.

My wife heroically helped me piece together what had become a detective story of their records so I could take over administering their finances. Then we started to clean up as best we could. But the house had become a reflection of my parents' infirmities, depression, and dementia. For several years my mother had strongly, even violently, resisted my trying to fix, clean, or sort out anything in their house when I would visit as I had done in the past. The childhood home that had been as neat as a pin, warm with my mother's love and filled with my father's music had gradually become something from a nightmare.

It seemed something within my mother had snapped and her only response now was to have nothing change in her world. The result was that everything was now falling apart. The garden that once been filled with lovingly tended flowers in the summer was now so overgrown it resembled a Grimm's fairy story, complete with a fox living among the weeds which stood five or six feet high where the neatly mown lawn had once been.

The house was very depressing to enter. One wall was damp where plastic siding that had been put on incorrectly now trapped water. Moth larvae could be seen moving in places on the wool Chinese carpets under sofas. Fungus was growing on part of a ceiling where the roof leaked. I felt I was entering a Steven King novel.

At first, I had resisted this change in my mother. My father asked me if I would help by cleaning up. I told him of course I would. But he would not let me get a technician in to fix the oven that my mother complained would not work, even when I said I would pay for it. I finally brought an element and fixed it myself much to my mother's disapproval.

She was terrified of the microwave oven and when a car alarm went off in the street she rushed into the living room convinced that it was about to explode.

I tried locking the door to the bathroom and cleaning it as she banged on the door and called for me to stop the whole time.

I cleaned the kitchen with my right hand while I held her at arms length with my left as she told me to stop over and over. I was no longer allowed to clear up the garden. No matter what needed to be done, they would, between the two of them, prevent it. My father would have nothing fixed because he considered himself able to fix everything as a matter of principle, whereas in truth he had not been able to fix anything for some years, and he was unwilling to pay for anyone else to fix anything, although he had ample money to do so. It was like trying to play a game of chess where every move I made ended in checkmate.

In years past when this family madness was just starting, my old friend Thomas would pick me up from their house in his car and I would climb in and weep from the frustration and impossibility of it all. He had wisely tried to counsel me: "You can't change them. This is how it is." But I was unable to accept the inevitability of my parent's descent into this kind of incapacity. It felt like watching them drive slowly off a cliff and being unable to intercede.

I don't recount any of this family drama to elicit sympathy. I am setting the stage in terms of my frame of mind at the time when I had the realization that changed my life for the better. I was desperate, and desperation can open the mind to something new. For me this was a perfect storm of family issues. Not only were both my parents dying but also in my father's case there was a whole lifetime of unresolved antagonism and failure to establish peace between us, despite all my best efforts over the years.

My mother was deeply depressed and systematically refused all help. For most of my life I had been able to energize her and lift her out of depression by just visiting her. But now I was failing to reach or help her. I was failing in my self-appointed role to be her savior.

They had simultaneously elicited and refused my help with their affairs and tied my hands in all practical matters. My childhood home had disintegrated into chaos in front of me and I had been blocked at every attempt to renovate and fix it up. I had never felt so disturbed and impotent in my life. It felt like a continuous nightmare from which I could not wake up.

I was staying with dear friends but one day the routine of the house and the hospital visits had finally got to me. It was a Saturday evening. I had sat with my father, feeding him his dinner, because the man who had once been the strongest man in my world, whom I had once feared the most, could no longer lift a spoon. When he finished eating, I said goodbye, kissed his forehead and told him I would return the following day. He smiled. Considering his helplessness, my father had become quite cooperative and even cheerful these days. He had always possessed a kind of mad dog courage and it served him well now and he showed no self-pity or fear at his condition. My resentment against him that had burned in me for so many years had left and been replaced by empathy and caring as I saw how dependent and childlike he had become.

Early on in my hospital visits to my father, before my mother also had to be admitted, I had brought him a portable CD player and a pile of his favorite jazz music. As he lay in bed, I turned on the player and put the earphones on his head. The instant he heard the music he started to weep. My mother started to panic: "He's getting upset! Turn it off, turn it off!"

I told her: "No, he's crying because he loves it so much. Let him listen. It's healing for him." Even though his brain had been pulled apart by the many strokes his music still went straight to his spirit. Music was his religion. It was where he found peace, love, and comfort.

Music had been the bond that held our family together. It could reach both my father and myself, bringing us together after we had fights when no words could reach us. I arranged to have his favorite music—jazz and classical—playing in rotation during all his care until the day he died.

Then I had gone downstairs to my mother's ward and sat by her frail emaciated body, which seemed to vibrate with distress and unease. It made me scream inwardly to see her suffering and be powerless to help her. Earlier I discussed her situation at length with her doctor and he told me that they were encountering the same thing that I had for some years—she refused to take any medications that might help her. They could not force her to take any medication against her will unless she was declared mentally incompetent and placed in a mental institution. I told the doctor that I considered that the violence of such a course of action would do far more harm than good and I would fight any such attempts with every resource I possessed. He told me not to worry, that he agreed with me and that although she may be depressed her cognitive faculties were intact as established by a psychological test. He said their hands were tied also and he felt frustrated by being unable to help her beyond the hip replacement and tending to her nursing. I knew exactly how he felt.

The hospital wanted a plan for her care before they would release her when it came time. I tried to be positive and nurturing but she would let me do nothing for her or provide her with anything. Not even a cup of tea. It seemed there were no solutions. I purchased new clothes for her and threw away the old threadbare and torn ones she always insisted on wearing. She had caused such a fuss when I gave her new slippers and a robe that I lied and told her the hospital had lost her old clothes and the Red Cross donated these new clothes. Her look told me she wasn't buying my story but at least she didn't complain. At home I found her wardrobe full of clothes in excellent condition that she simply would not wear. Perhaps it was symbolic in her wanting her life to be over that she refused to engage with it by putting on new clothes.

I asked her what she wanted do when her hip was healed—now that the house was empty I was eager to get everything that was wrong with it fixed up. Could I go ahead with that? When she left hospital did she want to convalesce in a nursing home until she was stronger, or would she prefer me to arrange nurses to come and visit her at the house once it was fixed up? I could move her bed downstairs and have a downstairs bathroom built for her. She just sat looking into space with no response. I pressed her, explaining that the hospital staff needed to know and they were demanding a care plan from me. Suddenly she raised up on one arm, looked at me and with a violence and intention that shook me, said in a low, forceful voice: "I just want to die!"

It seemed that the woman who I had always been so close to, who I could always cheer up and get a smile from since I was a small boy, had become completely unreachable. I finally kissed her and said I would come back the following day and walked out of the brightly lit hospital ward. I walked into the deserted stairwell and, as had become my custom recently, I wept.

When I pulled myself together, I walked out into the night, found my car and drove away. I drove to a big parking lot and went looking for something to eat. I walked around. It was cold and raining and the streets looked greasy, dismal, and deserted. The shops were closed and it wasn't a night to be out if you didn't have to be. It appeared I was in the wrong part of town because I couldn't find the welcoming glow of a restaurant anywhere.

Frustrated I returned to the parking lot and I was walking towards my car when things started to fall in on me. In the deserted, cavernous grey concrete parking structure I could feel the desolation and grief taking me over. I felt I was going to lose control of myself somehow, as if I was about to be swept away in a rushing current. Then I thought: "Come on! You've got to get a grip!"

I suddenly remembered reading a line in Eckhart Tolle's masterwork, *The Power of Now*: *To contact your spirit and come into the present moment, put your attention inside your body.*

Standing alone in the cold empty parking structure, I did just that.

Suddenly I saw all the places where my attention was simultaneously stuck: to my mother in her hospital bed, to my father in his hospital bed on the next floor, throughout the depressing chaos of the house that once been my childhood haven, in the inhospitable streets all around me, in my emotions of grief and despair that resided somewhere in my mind.

All the pictures of these locations hung in the air around me for a second. And then I experienced something like the moment in Star Wars when the jump to hyperspace is made and the stars stream by: In a rush of streaming light, my attention was released from all these different locations and it came together and crashed into my heart. My attention had been instantly gathered up from these scattered fragments of my mind where it had been trapped and suddenly it reassembled in my heart.

In this moment, I became un-hypnotized from watching and believing the thoughts, painful emotions, and dramatic moving pictures that my mind was ceaselessly generating. I awakened to the present moment around me *without* the influence of my mind to color everything. Nothing in my mundane circumstances had changed one bit—what had changed utterly was my perception of it.

Suddenly freed from the stranglehold of my mind's continuous chatter, the universe that I now perceived was completely transformed: I believe I staggered, as my heart seemed to explode with relief and an almost unbearable emotion of love flooded out of me and engulfed me. Tears streamed down my face: I moved in less than a second from the pain of overwhelming despair to absolute joy and serenity. I felt held by the space in which I stood. The parking garage was no longer stark and foreboding.

Instead I felt surrounded by a nurturing and comforting love that I was a part of, just as it was a part of me. I was no longer isolated from the world. Now I felt it to be a natural part of me and I part of it. I had come home to the natural state of things.

I instantly saw the explanation of the biggest mystery of my life: how in the past I would experience moments of heaven when I felt a blissful serenity and sense of exquisite joy of the perfection of existence, and then inexplicably something of which I was unaware would shift. A door seemed to close and I was dropped back down to earth feeling alone and caught up in mundane normality.

The explanation was simply this: the focus of my attention had been stuck on my thoughts, emotions, beliefs, and pictures about the world around me. It was stuck in the disturbing and unresolved incidents of the past and in my fearful projections of the future. It was stuck there for so long that it seemed normal. I had no idea this was even occurring. I did not question my mind. It had free range to do as it pleased. What it was doing, was creating new thoughts, feelings, and pictures of the world every second. I would watch and accept everything my mind offered me without considering for a moment that all of this stuff might not be true! One moment, it was in the past. The next in the future and then it was in the present. It was like a fly that buzzed around randomly.

Sometimes I would have whole conversations with myself in my head as I walked down the street. I could be having whole arguments with myself about a particular subject that concerned me, or I might be re-enacting a past incident that had disturbed me. But as I never said any of these things out loud, nobody else knew. I looked as normal as the next man—however normal that is. This is how almost all of us operate. We walk around doing our jobs and looking after our families but with our minds running amuck, running the show. Running us.

If you doubt me, ask yourself if you have ever walked

or driven somewhere and arrived but had no idea how you got there, having consciously noticed hardly anything. Our mind is so clever that we can drive a car on autopilot and hardly notice or remember anything afterwards, because we are simultaneously focused on the internal mental dialogue that we are consumed by.

Thoughts about our job, a movie we saw, a date we are going on, a conversation with a friend, what to eat for dinner—on and on. Anything but the actual world around us, moment by vivid moment.

Sometimes we get so preoccupied with our thoughts we end up at the wrong location entirely. I might have intended to drive to the grocery store but find myself in front of my daughter's school instead because that route was so programmed into my mind.

**In the instant of my awakening, I had simply gathered up all my attention that was being trapped in my mind, and brought it completely and totally into the present moment.**

What I realized completely at that instant was that: *We are not our thoughts or our mind. We are the one observing our thoughts and our mind.* The focus of our attention is under our control and will, and it directs the gaze of our spirit into this physical world. We can choose to consciously focus our attention on to the present moment around us and end the tyrannical reign of our mind. We can consciously subjugate our mind to become our servant and we become its master. That is the correct relationship. When our mind runs our lives we experience suffering because it presents a version of reality, which is full of falsehoods and illusions.

71

All that we need to do to awaken and transform our lives completely is realize this and practice shifting the focus of our attention from our mind to the present reality that surrounds us so that this becomes the new habitual way we live.

When we become conscious and awaken from the hypnotic grip of our mind, we begin to experience our own spirit, and our natural state is love, compassion, kindness, connectedness to universal consciousness and all life.

All that ever occurs is in the present moment. The past no longer exists; the future has yet to exist. The simple practice of continually focusing our mind fully onto what we are doing in the present moment will make it come alive with a tremendous intensity.

When we find ourselves day dreaming into the past or future, if we continually gather our attention back up again into the present moment 100%, no matter what we are doing, this becomes habitual, and the drama that our mind projects will gradually fade away, and what replaces it is a sense of aliveness, contentment and connectedness.

This whole process of transformation of attention focus may take some time to achieve before it becomes the new, normal way of living, but as it is occurring you will experience the noise and drama and negative emotions of your mind gradually calming down, and the peaceful, loving joyfulness of your true spirit replacing it.

That is what had happened to me in an instant, with staggering intensity. At the moment this occurred, I was still in an ugly, bleak, concrete box of a parking lot on a rainy night, and my parents were still dying. I was still cold and hungry; nothing had changed in the external world that moments before had almost brought me to my knees with despair.

But now in this new moment I was able to accept the fact that my parents were dying. It seemed to be a part of the natural order of things. I was no longer fighting with God or the universe about the situation of their lives. I was able to accept reality without internal protest.

I steadied myself as best I could, and with great care, because I was having a little difficulty doing normal things in this heightened state. I carefully drove myself to a restaurant.

Whereas I was unable to find one before, now I found one immediately. I parked and went in, sat at a table by myself, and managed to order something. If anyone had looked in my direction they may have thought a beaming, crazy man was having dinner. Tears ran down my face as my heart continued to flood with gratitude and overwhelming love.

I realized I now held the key for which I had been searching much of my life. It was as simple but as profound as shifting the focus of my attention out from under the heel of my monkey mind, and into my body, and into the present moment.

Suddenly Jesus' teaching made sense: *The Kingdom of God is within you.* Luke 17:20-21 KJV. I felt as if I was in God's presence, as if I had entered heaven. I wanted nothing more than to have this experience forever—I was bathed in exquisite joy and love.

Although I had understood the concept intellectually, and then read an entire book on the subject—Eckhart Tolle's *The Power Of Now*—I was not able to *apply* the principle of coming in to the present moment and it remained just an intellectual concept, until a moment of crisis and despair on a rainy night in a London garage. These same principles have existed throughout spiritual teachings for thousands of years.

This is the Hamsa, So'ham technique of the Kashmir Shaivites. People have rediscovered it every generation for centuries—focusing your attention inside your body, and especially on your heart.

My experience was one that mystics have written about throughout the ages, something that has been experienced by many other people. It is certainly something that *can* be experienced by *everyone*. Once I comprehended it I recognized this truth being recounted everywhere.

The Persian poet and Sufi mystic, Rumi, said it this way: *Remember, the entrance door to the sanctuary is inside you.*

Again, I cannot stress this enough—the difference between the *mental concept and words* and the *experience* is beyond calculation. I wrote this book because of my three pivotal experiences: my friend Allen passing through me at the moment of his death; my separation from ego in the supermarket; and this experience of overwhelming bliss at a time of previously overwhelming grief. It was these experiences that motivated me to read everything about spirituality and mysticism I could lay my hands on to intellectually understand what had happened to me that had revealed the existence of a new world to me.

Sometime later I saw a You Tube video of a lady named Jill Bolte Taylor. She has a book entitled *My Stroke Of Insight*. She is a neuro-anatomist who some years ago suffered a stroke that she describes had the effect of shutting down her left brain hemisphere—the side of the brain that thinks lineally, methodically, logically, and analytically. It is the part of the brain that takes details from the present moment and relates them to incidents from the past and events that will be happening in the future. It is also the part of the brain that creates the endless stream of monkey brain chatter about what it thinks constitutes reality. It makes judgments about what it perceives in the present moment. It also deals with language and numbers.

As a result of her stroke, Jill Bolte Taylor had the experience of being conscious but with just her right brain functioning: the right brain collects data from the world around us through our senses in the present moment only and makes them comprehensible to us. It looks at things as a whole; it is also concerned with creativity and intuition. She is a scientist who directly experienced her spiritual nature.

Her experience sounds very similar to mine: her mind's chatter stopped; she felt expansive, huge. She experienced euphoria, free of the emotional baggage and stress of her life—she said she felt she was in nirvana. She felt energy in her and around her and felt connected to the energy. She was so connected in fact that she was unable to discern where "she" ended and the world around her began.

In that last respect our experiences were different: I was still aware of what was "me" physically and what was the rest of the physical universe around me, and where one ended and the other began. She lost that differentiation. I definitely wouldn't have been able to drive my car at all if my experience had gone that far, I was having difficulty as it was.

In her neuro-anatomical model, my left-brain had apparently ceased having a strangle hold on my attention, and the focus of my attention had gone into a right brain dominated mode.

Fortunately, I was able to have my experience without having a stroke.

There are some who are involved in brain research or psychology or psychiatry and also believe we are purely physical machines and discount the existence of any spiritual component to us, and they are pinning all their hopes that eventually their science will solve all of mankind's emotional and behavioral problems at a physical, psychological, and mental level.

However, I am talking about *consciousness* in this book, not brain anatomy, as I have no illusions we will solve any of our emotional or behavioral issues through the physical study of the brain, no matter how valuable this science is. To change consciousness, we need to address our spirit, the *user* of the physical machine that is our body, not just our body, or just our mind.

Interestingly, my previous spiritual experiences had occurred often when I was engaged in *creative,* non-analytic experiences: painting, playing music, being with people I loved, and so on. This may have been part of my instinctive motivation for following this path rather than going into the sciences, which also interested me.

This also explains my observation of very well educated people sometimes tending to become bound by their intellect. People who have extensively trained and exercised their left brains can tend to have a very analytical experience of the world, and if they are stuck in that then someone with a very right brained view may appear incomprehensible to them. And it is also why engaging in right-brained activities such as playing music or painting is good for left-brain dominated people, and visa versa. I found when I was playing music and painting that playing chess felt very therapeutic and physically delicious to me. This switch of focusing on the other brain hemisphere helps to balance the brain.

You, the spirit, are experiencing the physical universe

as a human being, via the filter of your brain. Your brain creates *mental equivalents* for the swirling conscious energy of which the physical universe is composed, which you then experience as solid matter, and "reality."

I have tried to stress throughout this book that you will get nowhere if the Truths in this book remain at an intellectual level. The point is not to just understand these concepts. One must put them into operation and experience them personally for them to take effect.

Your mind is the *problem* here. *Not* the ultimate solution. Although ironically your mind is the tool that will enable you to grasp the concepts that will allow you to break free from the control of your mind, and contact your spirit and the present moment. You are going to perform the trick of using what is wrong, to fix what is wrong. You will then achieve a whole new way to exist in the world: awake, present, and in contact with the bliss that is your natural state.

Experiencing life continually in the present moment and free from the tyranny of our minds is a huge step on our spiritual journey. Living in the present moment is an evolution in consciousness and a complete change in what it means to be alive. It is not just an *interesting* idea. Like many things along the spiritual path, the key is subtle and very easy to miss but the implications are great.

You may have become used to important destinations and directions in the physical world being big, better, bright, loud, impressive, clearly marked, well lit, shiny, advertised, "as seen on TV", with fireworks and marching bands and cheerleaders and klieg lights. If you expect the signposts to the spiritual world to be the same you will drive right on past them. They are subtle, quiet, specific, and simple. They will not reveal themselves to you because you are important, wealthy, well connected, socially powerful, or famous. Or just think you are.

The Gospels of Mark (19:24) and Luke (18:25) tell us: *It is easier for a camel to go through the eye of a needle than for a rich man to enter the kingdom of God.* Not because there is anything wrong with wealth. Just that wealth can facilitate self-indulgence, preoccupation with pleasures and material distractions, and reinforcement of ego. All of which can render the subtle sign posts to the spiritual world all but invisible.

Being poor is no guarantee of awakening either—we can be so distracted by just trying to make a living all the time that we can miss the whole point of our lives. We need to become less distracted. We need to pay attention in order to find these important signposts.

In the past, I would have glimpses of this state of bliss of being completely in the present moment for short periods and then they would be gone. I never understood the simple mechanics that brought them about or that ended them. Sometimes I would focus on my surroundings so intently that I would become unstuck from my thoughts and instead experience the world directly, with my mind in the background. That's when my surroundings would almost glow, they would appear so vivid, and the normal familiar things would appear exquisitely perfect. I would lose any desire to be anywhere else: I was instead content to stay where I was for eternity. It had magically been transformed into bliss.

These moments were the gold of my existence. They were what I longed for in life. The sense of loss when they would end was frustrating and saddening. I had been trying to understand how these moments came and went since I was a young man. They occurred sometimes when I played music, when I was painting, when I was with friends, when I was in a beautiful natural setting, or when I was with a particular girl. I had made the classic mistake of attributing my change of state to those *external* elements.

Now I saw it was an *internal* experience. It was the way I was responding to those external things that caused the experience. But I was causing it myself, albeit quite unaware. I was always experiencing *my own response* to the external world.

The person listening to a beautiful piece of music may be moved to tears. And yes it is the music they are appreciating. But it is their appreciation that they are experiencing. If they could not perceive the beauty in that music then nothing would happen for them. Another person sitting next to them and hearing the same music might feel nothing.

If the tree falls in the forest and no one is there to hear it does it make a sound? No. A sound is the effect of disturbances in the air striking an eardrum that our brain interprets and our spirit appreciates. In the same way the radio waves make no music until there is an antenna and a radio to receive and interpret them, and then we can hear the music.

*You* are the source of your own emotions. The world is one thing—and often out of your control. But how you experience the world is, or can become, *under your control*. And you can select the version of reality that you wish to experience by your own thoughts, emotions, and beliefs— but that is a subject for another chapter.

The shamans of the Amazon have long used a substance derived from plants called Ayahuasca (or "iowaska") which translates to "spirit vine," to bring about a change in consciousness which reveals the spiritual dimension. This drug has a different purpose than recreational drugs when they are used to mask or distract the user from an uncomfortable reality—the purpose here is to gain direct access to reality, and thus an increase in consciousness, not a decrease. Author Graham Hancock has written the book *Supernatural* about this subject.

None of my mystical experiences were the result of drugs, I have no personal experience of this approach and so have no judgments. What ever works to increase consciousness works.

As I said: that night in the garage I was still in an ugly, bleak, concrete box, and my parents were still dying. I was still cold and hungry. Nothing had changed in the external world that moments before had overwhelmed me with despair.

It was my *perception* that had changed and allowed me to instantly change my experience from despair to joy, love, acceptance, and peace. The mechanics of the secret I had sought for so long seemed so simple now: when my attention became spread over my life, my emotions, and thoughts like butter over a piece of toast, I experienced life as stressful or dull, or during times such as this crisis, as overwhelming.

When I collected my attention out of my mind and my environment and focused it into my body, I came into contact with my own spirit and with universal spirit or Consciousness, that many call God.

I sat at the table repeating to myself so that I never forgot it: *This is all I have to do, to go inside: Here I am always, inside.* I realized that I did not have to learn to love. Instead I just had to clear away the accumulated debris and junk of the ages that clouded and covered over what was already there. This was my natural state: love, joy, and peace.

And so it is with all people. This is accessible to everyone who can become free of the restrictions of living a second-hand version of reality that exists within their own mind, to live fully and first hand in the vibrancy and love and connectedness that exists in the present moment.

Here and Now.

# Chapter Seven
# A Further Freedom

## The Beneficial Mechanics Of Regression Therapy

*The real voyage of discovery consists not in seeking new lands but seeing with new eyes ~ Marcel Proust*

That night, I drove to my friend's house in a state of elation and the feeling that I was at the center of the universe. My heart continued to be flooded with an overwhelming emotion of love and a sense of connection to an encompassing and nurturing world around me. Although I was by myself in the car, I had never felt less alone in my life. Each moment was completely fulfilling to me. I had none of my usual desire to be anywhere else, or to do something else, or my usual craving for entertainment. I noticed I was able to see the road ahead of me without really focusing on it specifically. It was the same increase in visual perception that I had experienced in the food market during my earlier experience when I had my first experience of separation from ego.

I had a slight concern that I would lose this magical state. I had realized that I had approached this blissful state many times earlier in my life, although never to this extreme, but it always ended and I never understood why. This had always been a huge loss to me and the entrance in and out of the state had remained a complete source of mystery that I had been attempting to solve for decades. I had walked down some blind alleys that had promised to explain all this to me but up until now all had failed to do so. It seemed so much more profound than could be explained by the common phrase: "I'm just in a bad mood today." All I had known up to this point was that certain kinds of activities *sometimes* resulted in this kind of state, but it would always cease at some point, and always out of my control.

This time was different in that I had never felt this degree of intensity before. I had more certainty that I would not lose the state, as I now felt I understood very clearly how to access my own spirit at will.

I woke up the morning following my transformation and got ready to return to my parent's house to continue the enormous job of clearing things up and deciding how to best approach the house's many problems. I have never been one of those people who greet the day by leaping out of bed full of life and eager to grasp the world with both hands. Since I can first remember, I usually felt best shortly before it was time for most people to go to sleep—a night owl. So I washed and dressed that morning in my customary early morning fog. But when I got into my rental car, before I drove away, I put my attention on to my heart. I felt it flare awake like a furnace ignition from a pilot light and I was instantly back in the blissful state that I had fallen asleep in the night before.

My life during the next days became one of sharp contrasts: I found that by keeping my attention focused on my heart throughout the day, I could stay in my state of bliss even as I attacked the grisly problem of the work on the house. All I had to do to bring about a complete transformation in how I felt in my daily life was to *deliberately shift the focus of my attention away from my endless steam of thoughts and onto my heart inside my body, and I would connect to my own spirit.*

The moment I did this, I completely stopped identifying with my own thoughts; just as earlier I had ceased identifying with my mental image of who I thought I was—my ego. I no longer believed myself to *be* my thoughts. Nor did I take any of the negative ones that seriously. Just because I thought something or felt a negative emotion about something, *I no longer believed it must be true.* It was just something else that my mind was generating among an endless stream of thoughts and images. These were not reality. They were an inner model of reality, and my personal, internal mental version of what was out there—quite a different thing!

There may be positive thoughts I had that were not true also, but they didn't seem to be toxic to me. I didn't believe fantasy ideas like I could fly—which might lead me to jump out of a high window. Having a generally positive view of life seemed to be working for me, in as much as when I felt good about things and expected things would be OK, they generally seemed to work out OK, so I stopped worrying about the positive beliefs.

Clearly it was the negative ones that were toxic and caused problems for me, and required my immediate attention. Positive beliefs usually seemed to *work*, and so were useful, whether based on fact or not. Don't misunderstand this: I am not say that in scientific matters facts cease to matter if you think positively—never assume anything, including: *well that beam will probably be strong enough to support that load,* or *we probably have enough fuel to get there and don't need to fill up as we enter the desert,* and similar specific physical world issues. Always find out for sure!

I am saying that a generally positive attitude is a great advantage, and seems to help things run smoothly.

As time went by in the weeks and months ahead, I found myself questioning my thoughts and beliefs to see if they actually matched with reality or not. I discovered that many of them were complete nonsense that evaporated in the clear light of examination. I could clearly see now what is wrong with us as human beings: We have become hypnotized by our own minds. We have failed to realize that our minds—incredible calculation machines—are continually producing a stream of mental equivalents for what they interpret as what is going on in the world around us.

And if they are missing information, *they just invent it!*

This worked pretty well in bygone days when you might be chased by some large, hungry animal with enormous teeth and claws. You had to make split second decisions that meant the difference between life and death. Then, your mind was making assumptions based on past information to help you get away from danger. Such as: *Yes, I believe I can jump that ravine, or swim in that fast moving river, or climb that tree, to elude my pursuer; this looks like a better escape route than that, based on my past experiences.* If your assumptions have been correct in the past and helped your survival, you might tend to believe that your future assumptions are also going to be correct, and so making assumptions may become a habitual way of operating in life. You might routinely fail to distinguish between that which you have assumed, and that which you have investigated and verified to be true or false.

However, now we have decided to be in the business of pursuing truth, making assumptions must be a practice of the past, as we are now going to operate only within verifiable facts that we know to be true to the best of our ability to investigate them. If we cannot verify something, however, we acknowledge that, for the time being, we just do not know. And meanwhile we can hope for the best.

### Darkness Returns

When I visited my parents in the hospital, it was hard to see them in such a pitiful condition. After each visit, I was able to lift myself out of my anguish by continuing to keep myself focused in my body and my heart never failed to flicker back to life.

Until one day: I had left my parents after my usual hospital routine and had kissed them each goodbye. I walked into the deserted stairwell and wept. A grief stronger than any I had ever experienced in my entire life descended on me. It had elements of utter despair and an overwhelming heaviness that was so strong that it actually made it difficult to walk to my car.

Somehow I managed to drive home, trying all the way to anchor myself in my body and come out of the grief. This time nothing helped however and the awful feeling remained with me.

When I arrived back at my friend's house, I excused myself and went into an empty room where I wouldn't be disturbed. I sat down and collected myself. I couldn't ever remember feeling such heaviness or such a strong emotion of desolation and despair. I tried to think what had brought this emotion upon me and why it was so overwhelming this time. It occurred to me that what I was feeling went way beyond what was appropriate for the situation I was going through.

Even though both my parents were dying, I had been

dealing with the experience. This on the other hand felt like some kind of primal human suffering.

I decided to try using a regression technique, which I had used in the past on others and myself in doing therapy sessions. This technique is a way to release emotional charge from painful incidents in one's past by re-experiencing the incident with a therapist and gradually facing whatever was initially too painful to remember about the original experience. If one is able to look at and accept what happened in the incident, its negative power disappears.

The underlying principle is that we are only negatively affected by those experiences in life that we are unable or unwilling to accept as they are occurring. This is entirely a subjective matter based on what each person can experience and accept, and which he or she rejects as being too awful to accept and process. In other words, a loss or experience that might reduce one person to a fetal position on the floor, might not affect another person in a lasting way at all. This is not to say that the other person may not experience emotion or is unfeeling or callous. But that their willingness to accept the reality of a situation or loss is much greater.

Their internal resistance to experiencing what is happening is far less and so they are able to face up to and accept what is happening as it happens or shortly afterwards. They are therefore not left with a residue of psychic trauma which requires cleaning up later with some kind of therapeutic or spiritual technique or practice.

Incidents that we can't process as they happen, leave emotional scars that stay with us as emotional landmines waiting to be brought to the surface by an experience that is similar in some way. As time goes by, we may lose track of these traumatic past incidents and be unaware of their existence.

We can, in therapy sessions, confront painful experiences in the past by fully recalling and re-experiencing them, and so one becomes released from the pain locked in the past experience. Sometimes it is necessary to find an earlier time a similar thing happened because these can hang together on a connected string, the earlier feeding emotion to the later ones. As I had previously done quite a bit of this kind of work in the past with others guiding me and then by myself, I felt I might be able to resolve the heavy emotion I was now experiencing. I wouldn't recommend trying to do this by yourself. It is easy to become bogged down and overwhelmed by the emotion, unless you have a therapist with you, or unless you have had a lot of experience doing this. I am describing what I did next, to show the possibility, and how the mechanics of this works.

It occurred to me to ask myself a question: *What incident could have been responsible for this emotion?* I instantly saw a mental picture: it was of a primitive man in a forest in the black of night. It was cold, raining and he—who also seemed to be me—had no shelter, no fire, no clothing, no weapons, and no companions. The figure was hungry, completely alone, and desperate. There was no sense of a family waiting somewhere in a warm cave to return to. The sounds of animals hunting were nearby and there was the possibility of being torn to pieces at any moment. As I let the image become as real as I could to fully experience every nuance of it, it seemed that if ever a human being felt desperation, isolation, overwhelming fear, and hopelessness, this was it. It also seemed to be an archetypal early human experience. I ran through what I could see of this incident a couple of times and the emotion I was feeling had lightened somewhat but it was still strong.

I asked if there was an earlier incident containing this emotion. I immediately saw another picture. I was a little concerned as it appeared by its content that it might be later in time, but the emotion suddenly felt even stronger in this incident so I felt as if I was still on the right track. It appeared to be around a thousand years ago perhaps, in a European village. An old lady was sitting alone in a small hut, quite the most appalling looking creature. She was very fat and her skin was covered with open sores and boils. She had stringy, greasy, grey hair. She smelled revolting. She was hideously ugly in her features and she was weeping.

She lived on the outskirts of the village because she was an utter pariah. For a reason I couldn't determine, I knew she was hated within the village; no one would talk to her. She had no friends or companions. She was a lonely and completely desolate individual without any hope. And that was the emotion I was feeling. I let the image sink into me as I tried to examine every detail of it, and experience everything this wretched creature was living. This image also seemed to be an archetypal experience of human suffering, rejection and isolation from all other human contact.

Suddenly the energy and emotion that had been sitting on me so heavily, lifted, and in an instant was gone! My relief was enormous. I felt normal again, light and happy. Literally, if I had been carrying around an armchair that was tied to me for the last hour and a half and someone had just cut the straps and lifted it off me, the resurgence of my energy, strength and mood could not have been any stronger. This terrible feeling had left me as quickly as it had come on.

Running these 2 past experiences was pivotal for me.

Something about the experience of my parents' suffering had brought this negative energy into my awareness with devastating force, and then it left me in an instant after my examination of these two incidents.

After I had run these incidents, a tendency I had to an emotion of "beautiful sadness" or melancholy, which I had often experienced throughout my life, even faintly tingeing moments of joy, disappeared completely. After this, and my other experience of coming fully into the present moment, and maintaining my attention in the present moment, I was no longer aware of negative emotions of sadness affecting me that had no direct cause in the present moment. I felt healed from my past.

This is another example of: *The truth shall set you free*. (John 8:32 KJV) Viewing what you see without any reservations, judgments or flinching, and going to the earliest incident on a chain of similar events, will enable a troubling event to discharge and cease to have any negative effect on you. The significance and details in any particular incident is unimportant and should not be challenged. What is important is locating negative energy that is impinging on you, and then releasing it.

Some modalities, for example Reiki or Qigong, release negative energy and change it to positive with no significances involved at all. You don't need to know the specifics of what caused the negative energy in order to release its effects. Work is done at a spiritual energetic level, deeper than intellect.

The Eastern embraces the concept of reincarnation. Buddhism and Hinduism include that the final goal of spiritual evolution is to release each spirit from the necessity to be endlessly reincarnated in physical form. The fact that we are here, in a physical body, and very much identified with the physical universe with all the problems that it causes us to experience, is evidence enough that we have spiritual work to do.

Finding an approach, or a number of different modalities that are successful in helping you deal with your own issues, is a personal matter for you to investigate and decide. The good news is that there are many things that work, and different approaches work better for different people. There is no one, *right way*. Whatever works for you, makes you feel better, releases negativity and increases positivity, and increases consciousness, is valid therapy or spiritual practice.

We are all on our own separate journeys. Just because someone is not on your same path does not make it wrong for them, so don't make the mistake of judging another's journey.

Be tolerant, and focus on your own journey, and let others be responsible for theirs.

There are many ways out of the darkness of the Grand Illusion. How we come into the light is unimportant, all that is important is that we find the light.

# Chapter Eight
# I Have Seen Such Beauty

I have tried to describe the experience of being fully in the present moment, heart fully open, drowning in the love and beauty of pure existence, but mostly my words seem to me like empty, repetitious superlatives.

I have repeatedly stated that spirituality is an *experience*, far beyond mere thought.

In the same way that any human experience, such as falling in love, or losing a loved one, being completely moved by a piece of music or other art, the birth of a child, or any other life experience that is so intense that you are completely taken over and feel it with every fiber of your body and being, this far exceeds a mere mental concept of the same thing.

This poem is the most successful description I have so far been able to make of this experience, written with an open heart, flooding with love:

I have seen such beauty through my eyes:
The sky on fire with blood red sunsets
The ocean pink and purple
Glowing wave caps
Foaming onto the sand beneath my feet

Tide pools and seaside caves
Full of salt water mysteries and childhood magic

Tall trees in soft green forests
Shimmering leaves
Sunlight dappling down
To ferns and moss floors
Carpeted with bluebells

Clouds of cherry blossoms suspended in air
Timeless
Then raining down pink and white
Around me

Waterfalls cascading onto glistening rocks
With stones waiting like jewels
Beneath flickering fish

A girl with delicate neck
Smiling eyes and coral lips
Wet with kisses soft as sin
Naked nymph wrapped in lace
Lovely limbed
Smooth skinned
Round like precious fruit

I have looked into the eyes of a newborn child
Godlike, pure spirit
Untainted by life's rough ways

I have heard such sounds through my ears
Rivers of melody

Notes and harmony
That tore open my heart
Sent my spirit soaring
Aching for life
Eager for the dance
Pulsing rhythm through my hands and feet

Birdsong at dawn
A symphony of singers
Life force manifested
In sound

I have felt such love in my heart:
Giving and receiving
My heart flooding
Overflowing
The dear ones I hold in my heart always
Who have touched me with kindness,
Wisdom, caring, laughter
Or passion and sweetness,
On my journey
I will think of you with tenderness and gratitude
As I draw my last breath

But all these words are pale echoes
Of these experiences
For to live fully
To be here now
To feel intensely
Vivid, rich, open
Not dulled down by routine

Or closed up by pain
Or settling for mediocrity

All this is a hero's quest
A lifetime's striving
Not easily won
But to do otherwise
Is a lifetime wasted

# Chapter Nine
# The Grand Illusion

Immortality—Ego—The Present Moment—Grand Illusion Defined—Spiritual School—The Internal Compass

I have now described the 3 major experiences that transformed my life and allowed me to exist for a period of time in a reality beyond the normal, and experience what has been described as bliss, heaven, nirvana. This despite very emotionally devastating circumstances.

To reiterate, these were:

**A) Awareness of spiritual immortality**—the experience at the death of my friend that we continue to exist after the death of our body.

**B) Separation from ego**—which allowed me to experience connection to a spiritual matrix which surrounded me and of which I was a part. While I was in this state the physical world around me became vibrantly beautiful, and I felt connected to everything around me and filled with love, and at peace.

**C) Coming completely into the present moment**—my attention shifted completely from my mind onto the present moment around me. The experience of this last state resulted in me being filled up with love and joy beyond anything I had ever experienced, I felt connected to a divine presence that surrounded me, I had no fears or anxiety. My heart continually felt ready to burst with love and joy. This state continued for weeks, despite the daily difficulties I was dealing with as my parents were close to death.

My instinct was to retreat to somewhere quiet and isolated where I could just remain in my state of bliss and investigate and savor it without being disturbed by the slings and arrows of outrageous normal human existence.

But I was unable to do this, and had to continue to deal with a normally heartbreaking situation, as well as reinter the busy world of my business and family.

I also realized that this had a profound purpose for me, because I was now able to observe first hand, what took me *out* of my state of: bliss, love, joy, fearlessness, and glowing beauty of the world around me, and back into the normal human state of: stress, anxieties, fears, anger and other negative emotions, thoughts, intentions and beliefs.

Because I could clearly see that although I had been given the gift of accessing a blissful state of existence long enough to know with certainly that another far more desirable state of human existence was possible, I didn't possess all the skills needed to stay in this state as I encountered all the normal stresses of everyday life.

But I now had a tremendous incentive to learn what these were—because my life had shifted into a black or white experience—it felt as if I was either standing in the sunlight in an idyllic and peaceful garden where everything was just as it should be, or I had been shoved out into a grey world where the wind was always blowing and the wolves of uncertainty were howling.

Cataloguing what took me out of my peaceful, loving,

joyous state, and what worked to return me there again, became the rest of the content of this book. I studied the mechanisms of how we enter, and then eject ourselves out of, our internal peace and contentment, into our colorless, dull and mundane world of stress or even nightmares. It was clear that this was an *internal* change, because the physical world around me had not changed, but how I was experiencing it and was able to deal with it, changed completely.

I saw clearly that spiritual awakening is a reductive process—the *removing* of the layers of unconsciousness that hide from us our own natural spiritual state which is love, joy, compassion, tolerance, kindness, peace, connectedness, creativity, aesthetics.

We don't have to learn these—we *are* these qualities naturally once the unconscious layers of *memories of painful history, guilt, false beliefs, negative mind constructs, negative emotions, thoughts, intentions and deeds, judgments, and deluded attachments and identifications with mind and the physical universe* are removed from clouding our spirit.

I needed a name for this rag bag of sorry cosmic junk that we cling to and drag everywhere with us and so cause ourselves endless suffering—and I came up with the *Grand Illusion*—and so the title of this book. That is its definition.

## The Habits Of Transformation

In order to edit this book down from its original size— which rivaled the phone book—down to something more manageable, I will next be describing those principles we need to practice in our daily lives to align ourselves with the spiritual architecture of the universe which has always, and will always, govern us all, as simple *daily habits*, which I have gathered together in Book 2.

These are the principles we need to *apply* in our daily lives in order to bring about a positive transformation of our Consciousness.

These are the habits I applied and continue to apply in my own life. They will work for anyone who sincerely tries to apply them in their own life.

These are the habits which will open the doors of heaven on earth to us—or if that phrase has emotional connotations for you: bliss, nirvana, paradise, ecstasy, joy, peace, serenity, tranquility—choose which ever suits you best. They are all referring to the same thing.

Just as the words Universal Consciousness, Spirit, Presence, God, Goddess, Supreme Being, Yahweh, Father, Krishna, Brahman, Allah, Jehovah, are just a few of the many names used all over the world and throughout history for the same divine entity.

Please insert the one you are most comfortable with in the text when we discuss this. No judgment is inferred in my choice.

As I have mentioned the principles we are discussing in this book are universal and apply to all people at all times, as does gravity, which is also part of the architecture amongst which we exist. As we learn to apply these principles in our lives by making them habitual, we will be able to experience and then return to inner peace, contentment, love and joy, even as we travel through one life experience after another.

I should make the point however that happiness is not the *goal* of life—the evolution of our consciousness is. Happiness is a side benefit when we get things right, it is the way we know we are doing or thinking about something in the right way.

In my experience things tend to go in cycles: you encounter a lesson, if you sort it out successfully your reward is a period of happiness and smooth sailing. Until the next lesson shows up, and the process starts again. You might look at someone who is in the middle of lesson number 50,206 and he might seem an awful mess from the outside. And compared to someone who has just completed lesson number 10 successfully who looks great you might think they are nowhere. But you don't see the big picture. That is why we shouldn't make assumptions and judgments about other people, because we are not standing in their shoes. Your job is to focus on your life, not someone else's.

This process is never static, it is constantly changing until it is completed, and you become enlightened, and that day will come if you earnestly pursue a path towards it.

The purpose of life is to experience lessons that give us an opportunity to learn spiritual lessons. Whatever else we think we may be doing—having a career, running a business, raising a family, changing the world—we are actually in Spiritual School.

Yes all those other things are true at one level, but underneath that level it is still all about lessons in Consciousness. So we each are given life experiences that will assist our consciousness.

Sometimes these are hard and very difficult or painful to go through. But even though you may not be aware of it while it is happening, you have agreed to it.

And just because someone is going through something very hard such as a death by cancer or some other painful disease, this does not mean they are being punished or that this is evidence of some earlier wrong doing, or that they have failed. Don't judge others like that. It simply means there is a lesson waiting for them in that experience that can raise their consciousness.

A life that is luxurious and perfect but from which the person learned nothing, may have been great fun, but it was a waste of a lifetime when you view it as one of possibly many thousands. The wheel of life and death and rebirth will continue as long as necessary for each individual, if we learn nothing in a life we have just extended the time our entire process will take because we haven't moved forward in gaining Consciousness.

The only thing you will take with you at the end of this life are the lessons of consciousness learned, or consciousness lost, or those issues you have yet to deal with.

This is what you will take with you on your journey into your next life, if you are to have one and do not attain enlightenment in this life, on and on until you have no more lessons to learn.

At that point that you do attain enlightenment, you will have graduated from the School of Life, and you won't have to return here anymore, unless you choose to do so in order to teach and help others.

So if you don't like a life experience you are having, pay attention and learn your lesson *now* so you won't have to continue to have to experience it.

This is how we change the curriculum of our experiences. If we fail to learn a lesson the same experience will circle around for us again and again, until we do. Once we learn all we need to from an experience it will cease to show up in our lives.

We exist within a paradox of pre-ordained experiences which we agreed to, but we still have free choice on how we deal with them. How we deal with them is the factor that can change our future curriculum.

We are never given something to endure that we are not strong enough to handle. How we choose to react to each situation however is our free choice. We can moan and complain, we can get mad and curse God and blame others and hate the world, we can become closed off and bitter, or we can pay attention and have a moment of clarity and great awakening and align our consciousness closer to the architecture of the universe.

The choice is always ours. Our free choice is a great gift that can never be taken from us. And the moment we move into greater alignment with the spiritual laws of the universe we will experience an internal peace and joy that surpasses any pleasure or entertainment the physical world alone can offer us.

As we get better at noticing our internal energetic response—positive or negative, to everything we do and experience, we discover a valuable tool that we *must* cultivate. I call it our *Internal Compass*.

If we pay attention, we can become aware of our positive or negative internal energetic reaction to everything, and we can use it to judge what is helpful to us and what is harmful.

This is our flashlight in the darkness. It is our infallible compass pointing us towards the one true north of enlightenment and Truth as we make or way through the labyrinth and out of the Grand Illusion.

# Chapter Ten
# An Introduction To Your Chakras

## The Functions Of The 7 Basic Chakras

*Before enlightenment - chop wood, carry water. After enlighten-*
*ment - chop wood, carry water. ~ Zen Buddhist Proverb*

*All truth passes through three stages. First, it is ridiculed. Second*
*it is violently opposed. Third, it is accepted as being self-evident. ~*
*Arthur Schopenhauer*

We touch on the subject of chakras in this book and so this
chapter is an introduction. The subject of chakras is a large
one with a great deal of information about it. The history
of this knowledge stretches back thousands of years, first
mentioned in ancient Hindu text about 1500 B.C.

In the same way that it is useful to know about the
anatomy and biology of your physical body, it is useful to
know something about your energy body. You are the owner
of one of each, and they are your vehicles with which you
navigate your human experience in the physical universe.

The subject of chakras is the subject of the anatomy of
your energy body. Your energy body—also known as the
light body or etheric body, is your connection between
your non-physical spirit that exists outside of space/ time,

and your current physical body, which exists entirely in space/time.

It is this energy body that you take from lifetime to lifetime. It enables you to contact the memories of your past lifetimes, even though your old bodies died long ago. Included in it is the old energy of the past events that remain unresolved and are still able to affect you negatively.

Part of your spiritual work is to resolve and release this energy so that it can no longer affect you in the present moment—like selectively emptying a suitcase of the cosmic junk of the ages that you keep dragging with you wherever you go.

Keeping your attention in the present moment helps to keep this toxic energy from coming into play, but until it is cleared, this energy remains a potential source of disturbance to you.

Your energy body resides in and around your physical body. How far around differs from person to person and according to circumstances that may be impacting an individual from moment to moment. This energy body extending outside of your physical body is what is referred to as your aura, and which some psychics can see or perceive.

You may be able begin to see this energy yourself. Take your hand right now and spread your fingers. Around each finger for about a quarter of an inch is a slightly blurry transparent field. It will be more visible against some backgrounds and light than others, so if you can't see it immediately, move your hand around in different light and against different backgrounds. Seeing it is a bit like seeing heat coming off a road except it doesn't shimmer.

We tend to perceive that which we believe we should be able to perceive and visa versa. Once you can see your own energy around your hand you can practice seeing the energy around other people. Seeing auras in color is a matter of perception of energy which is not ordinary visual light spectrum energy.

It is this energy body that you are contacting when you put your attention inside your physical body. Your energy body is a portal to your spirit.

I had some practical experience with my energy body which became explosively real to me during the incident described in Chapter Six—*Here And Now*, and my subsequent opening of my heart chakra as a regular practice which we will address in Habit 13.

But I had never seen my chakras and they were to some extent a theoretical concept to me until I was receiving a treatment from a Reiki master.

As he started the treatment and laying on of hands he asked me what I could see.

With my eyes closed, I suddenly saw a circle that appeared to fill the space within my head that was slowly revolving clockwise and it had an appearance of something like liquid marble. At first it was a magenta color, then purple. These were rich saturated colors. The Reiki master asked me to tell him if the colors changed. He moved his hands and the color changed to blue, then green, then with a yellow blob streak mixed in as if someone had poured paint onto a revolving wheel.

He removed his hands and asked me what I could see.

The colors disappeared. I told him, "Nothing—the room is fairly dark and I have my eyes closed!"

He replaced his hands and I could see the colored vortex again. I told him, "They're back!"

I realized that I was able to see my chakras by the energy

he was flowing into me through his hands. This is not a standard Reiki experience—it may also happen for you or it may not. Reiki will however always be a beneficial experience.

I had seen colored charts and descriptions of chakras that were colored, but I had assumed that was just a conventional representation that had come about over time.

Now I realized that *these are the actual colors of the chakras as seen by the psychic vision.*

They *are* the colors of the rainbow in the visible spectrum.

I had just seen the first five.

These are the recorded data centers of your history, a fact that alters the concept of what and where you mind is. Your physical brain, as well as being the instrument that creates equivalents for the five physical senses whereby you experience the whirling bundles of energy of which physicists tell us the physical universe is constructed, would appear to be the interpreter for thought between your consciousness and your memories while you are in your physical body.

But it is not where your all memories are stored. Which explains how you can access memories from past incarnations, as you take your energy body with you from incarnation to incarnation.

This understanding brings a fuller meaning to the saying: *Wherever you go, there you are.*

This information also changes the perspective for anyone contemplating suicide or seeking to escape their pain by taking drugs or alcohol or other distractions: this is all pointless delaying of the inescapable—you need to confront your issues and the sooner you start the sooner you will get through it. Delaying this or creating more mayhem that affects others negatively will only dig you in further and give you more to work through later on. That is a better incentive for living virtuously and causing others no harm than I can think off.

And that describes my personal attitude to spirituality—I have no desire to be holier than thou—I simply have no desire to suffer more than I need to. I enjoy feeling good.

Regardless of your physical circumstances, your spiritual circumstances will remain the same until you do some useful work on yourself. Living in a bigger, more beautiful house, driving a more fabulous car and wearing designer clothes or getting plastic surgery, will not change your spiritual condition. They merely provide a fun distraction for a while.

The function of the different chakras is to record and store all the information of our existences, especially those experiences that we are unable to process as they occur and which leave behind a negative residue. The kind of category of experience in which you are involved determines in which chakra it is stored.

Let us go through each of the main seven ones and see what their domains are:

**First Chakra:** The root chakra. Located at the base of the spine, points downward towards the earth. Each of these chakras are funnel shaped, starting off smaller then widening as they proceed from our bodies. Color: red. This chakra is involved with feeling grounded in the world. Energy from the earth enters here and through the soles of your feet.

This chakra is to do with standing on the earth and establishing a firm base from which you can build your life. It controls whether you feel secure; your confidence about handling yourself in the world; this influences your ability to attract money and have a fulfilling career; all your beliefs that you have learned from your family and the society in which your grew up with all the cultural attitudes and beliefs that went in deeply before you had the intellectual ability to question anything. This is where your tribal agreements are stored, your relationship to groups. All your beliefs about the physical universe and your relationships to it are also located in this chakra, as are your issues of separating yourself from the tribal ego or group consciousness to be able to develop your own individual consciousness.

You may need to work with these elements until you are able to live stably and successfully in the world. These are the roots from which the tree grows into the world.

If you have received a great threat to your physical survival you may have experienced it in your bowels which relate to this chakra. This is recorded in literature as a human response to this kind of distress, such as facing death or loss of a great deal of money or similar experiences. Drumming helps the energy of this chakra.

**Second Chakra:** The sacral chakra. Color: Orange. Location: points horizontally out from your body in front and back around the level of genital organs. All your chakras point out horizontally like this at different locations in your body, except your first (points downwards to the earth) and last (points upward to the sky.) Your sexuality and ability to experience pleasure from sex without guilt, shame or other negative emotions, and any issues regarding this subject are related this chakra. Sexual abuse issues reside here. Our desire to merge with another human being and create is here.

This chakra has also to do with family, children, friends. Your relationships to individuals, rather than groups, are here. You must resolve any past issues with any of these matters for the health of this chakra.

**Third Chakra:** Solar plexus chakra. Color: Yellow. Location: points horizontally out from your body front and back around the level of the solar plexus, above the navel.

This chakra has to do with your sense of self, self-esteem or lack of it, your integrity and issues to do with becoming centered, or needing approval or permission from others in order to feel OK. If you feel unworthy, powerless, indecisive, victimized by life, or have frequent stomach issues, these are related to this chakra.

Your intuition about your survival enters here. That is why we talk of your "gut feelings" about whether things feel safe or not to us, whether we trust people or not, whether we feel we should do something or not. You have most probably had this experience yourself and in this exact location of your body. That was not coincidence—or indigestion! We need to learn to listen to signals from this area, pay attention and act on them.

**Fourth Chakra:** Heart chakra. Color: Green. Location: points horizontally out from your body front and back around the level of the heart.

This chakra has to do with your emotions, your ability to feel them, or not. This is where you feel love, and this is where you feel a broken heart. You have most likely felt stronger feelings in this part of your body than other chakras. Of all the chakras, the effect of this one is the most recognized in western culture. We even celebrate Valentine's day with hearts seen everywhere.

Issues of loss, grief, upsets you have had with people, long term issues and loneliness, are all recorded in this chakra. If you tend to sabotage your relationships with fears about commitment, reliance on others, or distrust, this comes from unresolved issues stored in this chakra, and these are the issues you need to handle to clear this chakra. If you feel you do not deserve love, if you feel you cannot love others or trust them, if you cannot feel love, all these issues are stored here and must be cleared up so that you can freely love others and love yourself.

**Fifth Chakra:** Throat chakra. Color Blue. Location: points horizontally out from your body front and back around the level of the throat.

This chakra has to do with issues about your will or lack of it, or being stopped. It also has to do with your ability to express yourself. If you feel you cannot express yourself easily and effectively or that no one will want to listen to your opinions, this stems from issues in this chakra.

If you feel you have been stopped and cannot exert your will this can result in difficulties expressing yourself adequately. Issues with this chakra can manifest as a sore throat.

We start off exerting our will over others in group situations. Then graduate to directing our control to ourselves as we become centered and no longer spiritually dependent on a group. The old German army had officer trainees work with big horses to grow their will. Until they were in control of their 1500 pounds of power with a brain the size of a walnut, they weren't allowed to be in charge of large groups of men.

**Sixth Chakra:** Head or third eye chakra. Color: Purple. Location: points horizontally out from your body in back and front around the place in your head forehead just above and between your eyebrows. Otherwise known as the 3rd eye.

This chakra involves your intuition, or knowing things without direct, physical information, your intellectual wisdom, and your mind. This is the chakra that contains your inner compass to guide you to good decisions. The things you believe relate to this chakra. Clearing out false and negative beliefs so that your intellect can come into line with your will and your heart is part of your work in this chakra.

Your mind deals with what you already know and have experienced from your past, and what new accurate information you can access. Your third eye brings you information about your future, so it is important that these two work together, so that you can make guided and helpful decisions. If you have been too skeptical and untrusting of your intuitive information, you may have ignored or disregarded it in the past—you may even remember times when this happened: you had a feeling about what was going to happen but which you ignored, and then it happened. "Being psychic" starts by trusting the information or "knowing" that you get from this chakra. As with anything, once you take a leap of faith, it will become easier and stronger with practice.

Understanding wisdom intellectually and being able to exert your self-control and intention to bring it into effect as you act in the world, is aligning your sixth chakra with your fifth chakra which will result in your emotional fourth chakra also coming into line. When what you think, do and feel are all in agreement, you are becoming balanced.

When I was very young, maybe three or four years old, I first noticed that if I pointed something at the space just above directly between my eyes, I could feel a dull ache there. This was my first awareness of experiencing my energy field as a tangible entity, although at the time I had no idea what I was experiencing.

All the work we do to remove false beliefs, to learn to think clearly, sanely and logically, without bias or prejudice, to learn to respond positively and without old negative patterns of negative reactivity, and replacing ignorance or superstition with scientific information—this is all part of the rehabilitation of our 6th chakra.

As we clear more unconscious falsehoods from our intellect we become more open to intuitive intelligence, creative inspiration and wisdom.

**Seventh Chakra:** the crown chakra. Location: points upwards from the center of the head. Color: violet or white as in all the colors combined. This is the point where life energy enters the body.

This is the chakra of spiritual enlightenment and awareness that is beyond intellect and mind, although such awareness may be able to be expressed in words that resonate with those who share the experience. This is your connection to spiritual matters and to Universal Consciousness or God. When this is strong you feel connected to God or the universal Consciousness, you feel watched over and you can experience gratitude easily for all that is in your life. When this chakra is weak or closed you will feel alone, not connected to God or abandoned by God, and maybe unworthy of spiritual help. Issues in this chakra may manifest as migraines and headaches.

As a meditation: Visualize divine golden light entering in to your crown chakra and filling up the inside of your body. Be aware of your internal energy as you do this.

If you lay in a spooning position with your partner, taking

turns to be in front and behind, you may be able to detect each other's subtle energy fields running through each of you. When I first met my wife and we lay next to each other, our connection was so intense that this experience of energy was very tangible to both of us, and so we knew for certain these fields existed many years before we started learning about the anatomy of the field.

Yoga, Qigong, Tai Chi and Reiki are all ways in which one's energy body and chakras can be addressed, experienced and made healthier. This has both a spiritual and physical beneficial impact on us.

When these direct approaches to energy healing are used in conjunction with the spiritual practices outlined in this book, the combined effect is transformative. We need to practice all of these principles in order to achieve balanced progress. If we just do energy work but remain ignorant of the spiritual laws, we will continue to create more negative effects to have to experience and deal with.

Yoga has a practice of spinning one's chakras clockwise through visualization to energize them. I found it released negative energy in me.

Illness manifests first in the energy body and eventually arrives in the physical body, so issues we have in our energy body are much easier to deal with before they show up as disease in the physical body.

I was used to dealing with things on an intellectual level by talking about them, taking them apart and examining them logically and so releasing emotional energy. But when I had acupuncture, or did yogic spinning of my chakras or had Reiki, I was amazed that toxic emotional energy itself was released without me having to think about anything specific at all. That was when I realized that subtle energy could be worked with by itself, without having to first attach a specific significance to it.

Once you comprehend the Laws that are outlined in this book and align with them, you see that going into the details of each little deviation from them that brought about a particular problem are no longer important. You become released from being stuck to the details of day-to-day dramas.

As an example: one day many years ago I arrived at my acupuncturist's office in Santa Monica California fuming mad. I had come straight from a meeting with a teacher who I considered was behaving like an imbecile and attempting to victimize one of my children who at the time had chronic asthma. This teacher rejected all my attempts at introducing scientific information or a letter from my daughter's doctor to resolve the situation. My inner "protective parent" had been challenged and I had been unable to shift my mood for an hour since on the drive over.

My acupuncturist, a former neurosurgeon from New York, checked my pulses and quickly sizing up the situation, inserted two needles: one on either side of my forehead. To my amazement my anger immediately vanished! I hadn't spoken a word. He answered my look of incredulity with the matter of fact statement: "It's just trapped energy, and we just released it."

It was experiences like that one that made me a believer in our internal subtle energy body as something as real as my liver or spleen. I looked at his NY medical certificates hanging on the wall, next to his acupuncture certificates and asked my doctor why he did acupuncture now instead of neurosurgery? He said it was because he got better results and as a result he was far more satisfied with his life.

The revelation to me was that we *can* address our internal subtle energy and enable it to flow again and release emotions *without* any significance or thought being involved.

It is important of course that we learn our lessons of spiritual cause and effect in order that we cease making the same mistakes which keep us mired in the consequences of suffering.

# BOOK 2

## The 20 Habits of Spiritual Transformation—Awakening From the Grand Illusion

*We are what we repeatedly do. Excellence, then, is not an act, but a habit. ~ Aristotle*

# Prologue

Aristotle told us that *we are what we repeatedly do.* Psychologists tell us that a new positive habit only takes 21 continual days of repetition to create.

It is not so important what we *think* about philosophic ideas if they just stay in the realm of mental theory; it is *what we put into practice* so concepts can become experiences in our own lives that matters. This is how concepts become internal wisdom.

For that reason, this second book is designed to bring about a spiritual transformation in the reader by adopting *new habits of behavior* that will align them with the universal spiritual laws. Laws that always apply to all people in all places; laws that are part of the very fabric of the universe, woven into it at the moment of its creation.

So that through practicing these habits, we begin to live in harmony with the architecture of the universe in which we exist.

By doing this we start to experience inner peace and joy and love, which is our natural state of being.

Practicing these habits will put us on the path to enlightenment.

And practicing these habits will enable us to maintain and return to the new states of being that we achieve, because it is the *violation* of the spiritual laws that puts us back into the world of our mind's creation, closes down our heart once opened, closes down our connection to and love for others and the universe around us, and makes us return to negative emotions.

Don't be overwhelmed that there are too many habits listed to keep track of. They are introduced in a logical order, and they are interdependent, so as you start to do them and experience benefits from each, they will begin to join together as one comprehensible whole in your mind, because they are in reality all just aspects of one consciousness, and the whole subject will become instinctive and natural, because it is.

Referring back to the contents list will eventually be enough to help you keep track of them. Once you experience something working for you in life it becomes part of your internal wisdom, no longer something external that takes effort to remember.

The principles behind these habits are not new; they have appeared as enlightened teachings throughout the history of humankind, although some of them were only taught in secret organizations until fairly recent history. They are as old as the universe itself.

What is new is presenting them together in this particular way as this accessible approach to attaining consciousness.

In dealing with spiritual matters, we are attempting to describe in words that which cannot be fully described in words. We are trying to comprehend *with* mind that which can only be experienced *beyond* mind. Therefore all these word are inadequate, they are not the territory itself, only a map to help each individual find and experience the territory for themselves—beyond words or mind.

This book can only act as signposts to help you on your journey of personal experience and wisdom.

So first be *open* to trying new concepts in your life. Then be *pragmatic*: always notice what works for you in life when you apply it, what produces a positive result or emotion, only then adopt that as part of your personal wisdom.

And reject that which does not work for you when you have actually tried it, what fails to produce a result or gives you a negative result or emotion, no matter who tells you that you must believe something.

If you can be very honest with yourself and others about this, despite any outside pressures, then in this way you will develop the wisdom of your own experience, based on true integrity, which no one can take away from you.

This is a very fortunate window to spiritual wisdom that we are living in, during the Age of Aquarius. It is not an accident that you are holding this book.

Do not waste this opportunity after countless years to finally become free of the Grand Illusion.

Is this a lot of work to do? Yes. Is that any reason not to start? No.

Like everything else in life, you will experience positive benefits in relation to the effort you put into doing this work, and you will experience positive changes that will spur you on to more.

Is it important to do this work? Yes.

There is nothing more important and rewarding that you can do in your life than awakening your own consciousness.

We have been lost in a labyrinth. You are finally at a point after many lifetimes where you have the opportunity to walk through a door to all that your soul desires.

# 1st Habit of Transformation: Staying Conscious of Your Spiritual Nature

## Remembering What You Are—And What You Are Not

*There are many paths up the mountain but the view from the top is the same. ~ Zen proverb.*

*Unthinking respect for authority is the greatest enemy of truth. ~ Albert Einstein*

*Whether you believe in God or not does not matter much, whether you believe in Buddha or not does not matter so much; as a Buddhist, whether you believe in reincarnation or not does not matter so much. You must lead a good life. ~ The Dalai Lama*

The **First Habit** of transformation is to always keep in mind, that despite whatever is happening around you, that **you are an immortal, invulnerable, spiritual being**.

Remember that you are *not*, in essence, a part of the physical universe; that you exist outside space/time, although you are having a very convincing and involving physical experience right now.

Remember that your current physical circumstances, including your body, are temporary and will change, your physical form will die but you will always remain.

Remember that nothing can really hurt you, and you cannot really lose anything.

Do not allow yourself to be overcome with grief or loss or fear. These are all the result of illusions, and all take away our strength and power to create positively.

Staying conscious of this awareness allows you to be fully *in* the world, but not overwhelmed by negative emotion such as fear because you are aware that you are not, at your core, *of* the world.

Your body is your vehicle that allows you to have this physical experience in linear time and three-dimensional space. It is your space suit, your *avatar*.

Remember that this life is nothing more than a very real and very convincing, illusory, temporary situation with the purpose of providing you the opportunity to learn spiritual lessons. It is not an *illusion*—there is definitely something there—but it is *illusory*—in that it is not at all what it appears to be.

Think of it as a high definition movie or a top grade fair-ground ride. The movie or ride will come to an end and you will exit this life and continue your journey quite intact as the *core you* that has always, and will always, exist. And there will be no sense of loss as you reconnect with your natural spirit state—quite the reverse. There are many people who have had near death experiences and then come back to life, and were able to describe a state so loving and nurturing that they lost all fear of death and wished to communicate this fact to others.

This also isn't a new idea—in fact it is one of the oldest— in ancient Vedic texts the physical and mental world is described as *maya*, the illusion or dream which vanishes on knowledge of the fully Conscious self.

Leading quantum physicists are now telling us the same thing—that the physical universe is *illusory*, that what it *appears* to be to us through our five senses as interpreted and modeled as equivalents of physical reality in our brain, is not really what is going on.

We know there is *far* more space than matter making up the most dense materials on our planet, and the reason that objects do not fall through each other despite all this space is that they have energy fields that repel each other. So you are actually hovering very slightly above the chair you are sitting on, a minute distance away from it, as the energy fields of your body and the chair repel each other.

The mathematics of String Theory tells us that there are *many* dimensions of space—existing right where you are at this moment—not just the three we move in and perceive. Other scientists have even proposed the concept that the universe is holographic in construction. The picture of the universe will no doubt continue to change as science pushes further, but what we do know for sure is—things ain't the way they seem to be.

We spirits have become entangled with physical *maya*, or illusion, over a long period of time, which veils our true self. And it is time for us to wake up from these illusions. To the extent that we have become identified and attached to the illusory, temporary and constantly changing physical universe, is the extent to which we suffer.

We are continually telling ourselves and believing lies about what we are: That we are human, physical beings, that we are our bodies, that we can die, that we can be hurt, that we can experience loss.

It is the false *attachments* and *identifications* that we as spiritual beings have with the physical universe, and with our history in the physical universe, that keeps us unconsciously imprisoned here, returning lifetime after lifetime. And these come from the *basic* illusion that we are something we are not and can never be—part of all this physical stuff around us.

Not that this realization puts us at odds with the physical world, for it too is an expression of Consciousness. It is conscious energy, and we need to embrace and accept the reality of our situation as human beings because this is where we will learn our lessons of Consciousness.

And this is the paradox we must come to realize: To be able to be fully *in* the world, but not *identify* with it, because we are not *of* it.

That is why always keeping in mind what we truly are in our essence, is so important.

The solution to all our suffering starts with awakening from these lies which cover the truth that we are actually immortal, invulnerable, spiritual beings who are having a temporary and very convincing physical experience in our current life.

This is not a radical concept—it is at the basis of every profound spiritual teaching in humankind's history.

Our awakening and our path to enlightenment is the *taking away* of our illusions, one by one, and so we gradually come to the realization of our true nature, our God consciousness, buried beneath all the illusions, falsehoods, attachments, and identifications that we have been accumulating for eons of experiences.

Once we awaken to this truth of what we are at our essence, and our true relationship to this life we are currently experiencing, we are able to gradually learn to navigate this physical experience with internal peace, joy and love, despite all the reasons the physical universe may try to convince us otherwise.

This is the purpose of the habits outlined in this book, and why they are so worthwhile adopting. You have waited a long time to reach this opportunity to awaken. It would be a great shame to waste it.

Our spiritual and physical existence is governed by unchanging laws which are a fundamental part of the structure of the universe.

The habits outlined in this book, if practiced, will bring us into alignment with these laws and the architecture in which we exist. When we align ourselves with and learn the spiritual laws we put an end to our suffering, in the same way a small child learns not to put its hand into the fire and not to bang into hard objects.

There is only one consciousness in the universe, appearing in a myriad of forms.

You and I, at our core, are expressions of this same consciousness. At our core, your consciousness and mine, is not just similar, it is identical. What makes us appear separate to each other is our separate bodies and minds. There are billions of bodies and minds on this planet, all plugged into the same universal consciousness. On the surface they appear to be individuals, but at their core they are all one spiritual Consciousness.

This is the meaning of the teaching that *we are all one.*

This is why it has been taught again and again that we should do no one any harm, why we have been taught to love one another, and treat each person as we would have them treat us—because what we do to another, we do to ourselves. In truth, we are all one.

It is the degree of our individual unconsciousness,

existing in each person—the extent of our personal entanglement with delusion or *maya*—that allows different degrees of this pure Consciousness to shine through in us. And so one person appears to be an evil psychopath, another a saint, depending on how great or how little is the extent of their individual unconsciousness that masks their basic wisdom, their basic consciousness.

Each person has the potential to dissolve their unconscious delusions and become enlightened. And that is the purpose of your life here on Earth. We are all enrolled in a School of Consciousness. And our lives are actually a curriculum of opportunities for us to have realizations of Consciousness. That, despite whatever else you believe you are doing with your career and pursuits and your family and friends, is what you are doing here.

In essence, you are spirit, you are not physical matter.

You are a spiritual being having a physical experience, and it is helpful to keep that in mind.

It is an error for us to see spirit and physical matter as opposite ends of a polarity and thus opposed to each other. We are all expressions of the one universal Consciousness or God, so we should feel no antipathy towards the physical universe which is also a creation and manifestation of this universal Consciousness—but spirit and matter are not the same thing.

The world needs to feel real to you in order for you to take it seriously enough for it to *reveal to you the issues you have not yet dealt with*. When life stresses us, our fears and hidden negativity are revealed to us in a way they are not when life is comfortable.

This is the stuff we are here to deal with, to transform from negative to positive and so dissolve and finally become free of it. This is why, instead of seeing life adversity as something to complain about when it happens, we should embrace it and look for the lesson in it for us to learn as soon as possible. The faster we learn it, the faster our life will change for the better, the faster we can graduate from Life School.

Our school curriculum here is interactive—as we learn our lessons of consciousness, life ceases bringing us the same experience. There is no longer any point because we have learned the lesson contained in that experience. And we are no longer broadcasting to the universe that we need that experience.

In other language: We are no longer attracting that experience to us.

It is this same reason that life must appear serious to get our full attention and involvement, that most of us don't remember what we were doing last lifetime, or the agreements we made about what experiences we would have in this lifetime before we reincarnated.

If you were raised Christian in the West you may have trouble with the concept of reincarnation. This isn't a big issue because firstly, there is nothing in this book or practicing the habits that contradicts the original teachings of Jesus, or any of the teachings of the other enlightened ones that show up in the great religions and philosophies.

There are some existing contradictions in the Bible between the Old Testament that exists today, and the teachings of Jesus in the New Testament. This led Thomas Jefferson, 3rd President of the United States, to create his own Bible, consisting only of the teachings of Jesus, and disregarding the rest.

Secondly, *what we think about philosophy* is nowhere near

as important as *how we live our lives*. We are going to attempt to go beyond mind and its thoughts into experiences of the spirit. If there are parts of this book that seem far-fetched or a stretch to accept or agree with, that is fine. Just put them on a shelf for future consideration. You could practice all the main habits of this book and still receive great benefit from them if you were an agnostic or atheist.

Being focused on the Present Moment, Forgiveness and Acceptance and the other habits all work, regardless of what you currently believe about life. This book is not asking you to believe anything—it is asking you to practice certain principles in your life, which I am referring to as *habits,* to see what happens to you: Do you feel better or not?

Don't get hung up on particular labels or cultures— spiritual truth is universal. It doesn't matter where it comes from or who said a particular truth—a truth is still true no matter who says it.

It *is* of paramount importance however that we live kind, compassionate, loving lives and cause no further harm to others.

If you have got this far in this book, chances are that you are an old soul with many life experiences who may have the feeling that you have been on this fairground ride many times before. So it is time to know, and keep in your mind, the truth about the illusory nature of life, in order that you may fully awaken.

# 2<sup>nd</sup> Habit of Transformation: Staying Focused on the Present Moment

*I am not what happened to me, I am what I choose to become.* ~ *Carl Jung*

This practice alone will transform your life. It will make the world around you come alive. It will reduce the anxiety and stress you feel. It will enable you to start living in the actual world around you, instead of the 2<sup>nd</sup> hand, mental version of what you *think* and reactively feel about the world around you.

It will take you out of being hypnotized by the endless chatter of your mind into being awake. It will help calm your mind down and make it become your *tool* instead of your *master*.

Become mindful: focus on what you are doing while you are doing it 100%.

Be fully aware of everything you are doing without letting your mind think about other unrelated issues. Become aware of the energy of the universe of which you are a part *in this moment*.

We all have to do mundane things such as run errands, cook food, clean up after ourselves, while pursue our careers, and interacting with our relationships. The temptation is to distract ourselves from the less interesting parts of our life and seek entertainment whenever available.

However, if instead you put your full attention on each task, no matter how mundane, and do it as well as you can, then performing each task becomes a spiritual practice in itself, even though the task appears menial, what the Zen Buddhists refer to as our " chopping wood, carrying water" work.

Regular daily life becomes transformed into a mindful meditation in this way, and our "monkey mind" that is completely out of our control, which is the reason we demand constant distraction and entertainment in the first place, will gradually calm down and start to come under our control, especially when we combine this with daily meditation.

**Instead of distracting yourself to take your mind *off* of the mundane things in your life, try the opposite—try focusing all your attention *on* them and doing them as well as you can.**

You will experience a change in the quality of your life and you will start to sense the spiritual nature and energy comprising your environment and the objects around you. The Buddhists refer to this as living *mindfully*.

Don't allow your mind to wander. Don't daydream.

Unless you have a specific task to perform such as: recalling information, reviewing what happened in order to figure out how to do something better next time, confronting a past painful incident to release painful memories with a therapist, or making future plans—then always keep your attention fully on the present moment.

Anchor your attention inside your body. What works best for me is to focus on my heart and feel the energy there, because this is the strongest perception I have of my subtle energy body.

Each time you complete a task that requires your attention, focus your attention back onto your heart, even if it is for a few moments, and notice as you breathe, the energy in your heart.

This continuous refocusing of your attention inside your body will anchor you in the present moment and help you not wander off into the realm of mind and the endless, random thoughts which will hypnotize you back into unconsciousness.

This is a very important part of this second habit.

Inside and slightly around our body is our energy body. By placing our attention inside our physical body and onto our energy body we are accessing a portal to our spirit and this brings us into the present moment.

It has been said: fear is having our attention on the past; anxiety is having our attention on the future. If you are experiencing having your attention fully on the present moment, with your heart open—and we will talk more about achieving that—then fears and anxiety melt away. You are instead able to be in the present moment with a sense connection to the universe around you. Then you are able to deal with whatever is happening in the present moment.

Bringing your attention completely into the present also means letting go of the delusions of mind: letting go of the past. Letting go of your history as something that defines who and what you are, or what you can become in the future. Letting go of past hurts; letting go of past guilt; letting go of all past injuries that demand revenge or resentment; letting go of all efforts to try to change the past.

Notice that in this moment none of those things exist, unless you are in the middle of an actual present time crisis.

But usually we are not in the middle of a crisis—and we find that *in this moment* life is actually manageable, if we can separate from our out-of-control *thoughts* and *feelings* about our life.

Often the problem is not life itself; it is our negative thoughts and emotions about life that are actually upsetting us. If we can calm those down and realize that the past *is no longer happening now,* we can cease to recreate it in our heads along with all our negative thoughts and emotions about it.

This is why we can sometimes be better at handling other people's problems than our own—because we aren't weighed down by any of the bad emotions connected with the situation—so we can clearly see: "Oh, all you have to do is this, then, this, then this..."

This is often how a good life coach is able to help a person navigate an otherwise overwhelming situation.

To be fully in this present moment is to be free of all the delusions and baggage of the past, free of the noise of endless, repetitive, compulsive, random, negative, thinking—and only using your mind to perform the tasks you are choosing to. Experiencing instead internal calm, peace, joy, love, and connectedness to the vibrant conscious universe around us. To be able to live in this way is an evolutionary step of existence for humankind.

This is the goal of this habit of transformation in this book.

Simply continually re-focusing your attention back on the present moment and inside your body is an extremely powerful and transformational spiritual technique.

# 3<sup>rd</sup> Habit of Transformation: Remaining Separate From Ego

Remember What You Truly Are—Don't Compare Yourself To Others—The Right/Wrong Trap—Avoid Identifications—Avoid Conflicts—Maintain Humility—Practice Patience—Avoid Compulsive Controlling—Let Go Of Your Story

As we discussed in Chapter 4, separating from your ego is an enormous step that opens the door to spiritual awakening.

Because before you start to separate from your mentally constructed false identity of ego, you have been viewing everything through a false lens of identification, and this delusion colors everything.

What makes this separation such a rare event in human history is that before it happens, we are so identified with our false, mentally created identity that we believe *we are it,* and we believe the thoughts our mind creates from the belief and viewpoint of our ego, *are our thoughts.* We cannot perceive it as something other than our own self, because we completely believe that *we are it.*

The illusion is therefore perfect and so we are locked into it, until, once presented with the knowledge of the illusion, we work to separate our true essence from all that we are not.

The exercise in Chapter 4 is designed to begin the process of separation from Ego.

It may take some work to achieve a shift in perspective. It may happen quickly.

But once achieved, Ego separation is not a one shot event by any means—even if you have been fortunate to have experienced a very dramatic separation by focusing deeply on this subject.

This is an entanglement of spirit and physical matter that has been a habit of thousands of lifetimes. You are now attempting to establish a new habit of consciousness that stays out of this entanglement of false identity and this will require constant vigilance. I do not know of any spiritual task which is more difficult and where you will be faced with more ways to become tricked and re-ensnared back into unconsciousness.

You can even become egotistical about being more spiritual than others! You can even become egotistical about not being egotistical because you are less egotistical than everyone else!

So let us consider ways to avoid these traps and remain separate and conscious, so that your ego doesn't reassert itself and identification doesn't take you over again completely once the light of consciousness has shone into you:

**A) Remember** you are not your body, your name, your family, your education, your culture, your nationality, your race, your socio-economic standing or class, your profession, the roles you play such as father or mother or son or daughter, your possessions like your house, your car, your clothes—including anything that makes you feel special and important like that treasured watch or jewelry—the skills you have acquired, your achievements, the organizations you are affiliated with, your history and your formative experiences, your group of friends, the sports teams you support—that make you feel superior—the qualities you have that you feel proud of.

These are simply the temporary associations you have in this life. This doesn't mean you cannot enjoy them or love them. They are part of the wonderful dance of life that you are currently involved in, so embrace them. It means do so *consciously*. Don't be identified with them or believe you ARE them.

You are that which is aware of your life but that has *no identity*. The spirit behind the physical space suit you are using to experience your life.

Remain aware that everything is constantly changing, and be in this moment.


**B) Don't compare yourself to others**. As in: are you better than them, worse than them? Are others cleverer, more successful, more talented, wealthier, better-looking, taller, skinnier, better dressed, happier, more accomplished, more spiritual etc. etc. or less so than you?

No matter what you have been told, life is *not* a competition. You are here on your journey to learn your lessons, what others are doing or can do does not alter that.

Do whatever you decide to do as well as you can, that is integrity. On some days you will be better than others, on other days you will be worse. That is never the point. As long as you do as well as you can right now and you have tried your best, that is all you can do. Be content with that, don't worry if others can do something better.

Even if you are the best in the world at something, this will only be for a short amount of time—and a whole a lifetime is only a short period of time—and then someone will come to replace you. You are on *your* journey, not *theirs*. We play the hand we have been dealt as well as we can.

We are not more important or less important than anyone, because *at our essence* we are all exactly the same—all sharing the same universal Consciousness. Our social standing, our possessions, our achievements, our education, our income, the size of our house or anything else right now, or lack of them, means nothing beyond just that. They do not make you more or less important, more superior or inferior. They do not make you more or less entitled.

They do not change your consciousness one bit. If you can keep that in mind it will help you to stay out of your ego.

### C) Don't make yourself right and others wrong.

Life is full of dualities: Right/Wrong, Good/ Bad, Black/ White, Hot/Cold, Full/Empty, Learned/Ignorant, Healthy/ Diseased, Just/Unjust, Legal/Criminal, Strong/ Weak, and so on.

The opposite ends of each of these sets of dichotomies or polar opposites provide the basis of the many games of human experience. We can be a policeman and uphold the law and oppose criminality, or be a criminal and oppose policemen. Or become a doctor and oppose disease, or become an opposite: for instance someone whose goal is to spread disease through germ warfare. The fireman fights fire—the pyromaniac starts it. We can become a teacher and oppose ignorance. You can think of hundreds of these life occupations that forward one thing and also oppose its opposite.

When we become identified with any of these sets of opposites, we lose consciousness.

We lose consciousness whenever we identify with *anything*. So when we identify with one side of a pair of dualities this can become a part of our mental ego construct. And we will want to be right about our side and oppose the other side. When we argue from the viewpoint of our side and oppose the opposite side it makes our ego feel stronger and our ego takes us over.

This has nothing to do with the validity or logic of an argument. It has to do with identifying with ideas—part of a mental viewpoint about the world. We can have a valid argument but still become unconscious and taken over by our ego as we are self-righteous about it.

So avoid being right and making others wrong for the sake of inflating your ego as you pursue your life goals. Don't argue for argument's sake. Don't have to win an argument so you can feel superior if you win. Don't do *anything* to feel superior to someone else. That is ego.

Let others have their beliefs, do not try to change them by argument. You cannot shift anyone's perception about spiritual matters in this way. No one sees beyond their horizon. We can only perceive what we believe is there. We see what we believe and we get and experience in the world what we see.

If you tell someone about something that is beyond their perception they will not be able to perceive it, they will think you are trying to trick them or that you are deluded. All you will get is their scorn and derision.

Only suffering or some other profound life experience can crack their ego and open their perception, and this happens to us all in the fullness of time.

Only if someone is open and asks you for Truth is it worth telling them. Even then the ego will try to put up a fight, because the energy we have put into creating it has inertia which fights against its undoing: *Who is he to tell me anything? I don't agree with that, I think this instead... Well that's just his opinion...*

Another important aspect of being right and making others wrong, is that this mechanism will cause you to hold onto and recreate past hurts in order to show someone that you have been wronged by them, and so you are right and they are wrong. "Look what you have done to me! See how much you have hurt me! Say you are sorry! Say I am right and admit you are wrong." This is the anatomy of so many fights, especially between couples.

Your ego is therefore demanding you to play the role of victim and hold onto your resentment and the negative energy memory of a past hurt that you could otherwise let go of completely. Once you ditch being a slave to having to be right and making others wrong, and practice forgiveness of other's unconscious behavior, you can recover from life's hurts so much faster, once you grasp this mechanism and cease to be fooled by it. Because you no longer have a vested interest in remaining injured.

**D) Don't become identified with your life roles**. Whatever role you decide to play in life, make sure you are doing so *consciously*. Don't get lost in believing you *are* the role. Whether you are a doctor, a banker, a scientist, a musician, a teacher, a mother, a father, a son or daughter, there is a huge difference in consciousness between *doing* something and believing you *are it*.

Keep in mind that we have all played many roles many times. In the family dynamic we have all been a mother, father, son, daughter. If you are a father or mother now, just do the job as well as you can right now, but realize your child is only your child for a brief while until they are grown, you do not own them just because you gave them their body, then they are an adult who may be far more intelligent, educated and accomplished than you are. Don't stay stuck in the "I'm the parent you're the child" mode when your children have become adults. If you have made being a parent part of your ego construct and you cannot let go of this you will experience lots of conflicts with your now adult children.

Do you see just how insidious the ego mechanism is? So does this mean we cannot do *anything* in the world? That we cannot take *any* effective action to improve situations? We cannot assist *any* movements to help benefit humanity or the planet?

Of course it doesn't. It does mean however *remain aware* of the trap and don't become egotistical about what you are doing. Don't become self-righteous or indignant or smug or vindictive about what you are doing. Don't wish any opponents harm. Remain conscious!

**E) Avoid conflicts for their own sake.** Conflicts help us to define the ego, they make it stronger for a while. The ego is always hungry for new conflicts.

Consciousness on the other hand, comprehends *all* dualities, all points of view, but is identified with none.

Practice seeing both viewpoints in a dispute. Practice seeing the other person's point of view.

Then if you need to negotiate, you can find a resolution that benefits both sides—because if your ego isn't involved, you don't have to "win" and make the other person "lose."

Without ego involved, you can use logic and intelligence and research to find the best possible solution for all parties.

Keep in mind that the ego loves conflicts, it loves fights and drama, because it has a chance to be right and make the other person wrong. It becomes defined by arguments, the ego is the opposite of oneness, of connection with others unless it is our team against *their* team. Ego is the *reason* people feel individuated, alone, separate, lonely.

If you encounter someone who is addicted to drama don't get drawn into their issues—even if you help them solve one they will immediately start to create another. That is how you spot the addiction—they never end

The egoic person is always *looking* for conflicts so he can feel that brief energizing of their ego through the conflict of *them* against the *others*, when they are always *right* and the others are always *wrong*.

For example: when you drive your car without your ego being involved, it doesn't matter if someone overtakes you, it doesn't matter who's car accelerates faster, who's car is better, or cost more. You are simply using your car as a mode of transportation to get from A to B, not using vehicle to enhance your ego, so conflict and negative emotions disappear from your driving.

And so it is with everything in life

**F) Maintain humility.** Feeling entitlement, feeling better than others, feeling more important than someone else, all this is ego. No one is more important than anyone else because we are all expressions of the divine. At our core we are all part of the One Consciousness or God.

Remember this when you interact with others, whether they are someone "important" or powerful, who can do things for you, or they are opening the door for you or bringing you your food, or cleaning the toilets. Treat everyone with respect, politeness and realizing that a part of God is present in them.

By all means know what you know and perceive what you perceive about others, and when you see unconsciousness help the person if you can, or avoid it or protect yourself as necessary.

But don't condemn others or feel superior, that is ego moving in.

Don't assume that your culture is superior or only your way of life, or your belief system is correct and you have the only path to truth.

Don't be condescending to others, this is ego.

Don't allow your successes and accomplishments to become part of your ego, and convince you of your superiority, infallibility and entitlement. When this occurs the paradox of what is apparently positive becomes negative. Power, fame, wealth, education and accomplishment can then result in spiritual unconsciousness.

This is the meaning of Jesus' teaching: *For it is easier for a camel to go through a needle's eye, than for a rich man to enter into the kingdom of God.* Luke 18:25 KJV.

There is nothing intrinsically evil about money, fame and power, but all make it very easy for ego to enter in and take us over. When we own more than others, and can hire others to do our bidding, or are far more educated or accomplished than others, it takes a person of great awareness not to fall into the trap of believing that they are therefore intrinsically superior to others.

Lord Acton's observation: "Power tends to corrupt, and absolute power corrupts absolutely," is a warning to us all to not allow our good fortune to overcome our integrity, and cause us to become lost in our ego, and so incur the karmic consequences.

Remember that your situation in this lifetime isn't

permanent, it lasts for a very short period of time. Don't confuse status or skill with consciousness. Caravagio was one of the greatest painters who ever lived, yet he killed a man over an argument about a tennis game. Intelligence, accomplishment, power and wisdom are not synonymous.

An unconscious person trapped in their large ego will not recognize a wise person, they will only recognize someone who also has a large ego.

**G) Practice patience.** Avoid expressing anger. Don't let negative emotions take you over. Don't have tantrums, stay calm. Don't swear and shout. Be polite, be respectful of all other people and their viewpoints. Then you will earn people's respect, and quiet words will be more effective than screaming and anger, which alienates people.

Don't become lost in false beliefs like: *this shouldn't be happening, they should know this already, this should be different or faster...* all these are violations of acceptance of reality, and in behaving self righteously and expressing negative emotions you will slip back into ego and unconsciousness.

**H) Don't compulsively try to control everything.** I clearly remember the moment a situation was developing where I normally would have tried to control it to make sure everything resolved properly. Instead a small voice somewhere in my consciousness said: *let it go—let them sort it out on their own.* And so I did. I resisted the impulse to control the situation despite my misgivings—and guess what happened? Nothing at all. The situation resolved itself just fine, the world went on spinning and didn't fall off its axis.

That was a huge revelation to me—I didn't have to control every situation in life for things to work out OK.

I am not saying be lazy, irresponsible, or uncaring, but differentiate between the things you really *need* to control—such as your car when you are driving down the road—and things that other people can take care of competently because this is their business to handle, without your involvement.

If you realize you have slipped back into an ego viewpoint, just start over until you have made the adjustment and de-identified from ego again. There is no failure or shame in this, you are a pioneer in the evolution of human Consciousness.

**I) The Ego will attempt to block and sabotage your attempts to become conscious**. Consciousness means the death of ego. It will give you thoughts like: "I already know all that" so that you dismiss truths—meanwhile you may not be *practicing* them at all. I gave several people Eckhart Tolle's *The Power Of Now* to read, and they dismissed the whole book by saying "I already know all that, there is nothing new there," but they were not practicing any of the principles that would have helped them greatly.

Repeated reading of enlightened writings can eventually break through the mind and ego to the level of spirit and become a realization and personal wisdom.

A friend told me he re-read part of an enlightened text for years before the wisdom finally made it completely past his ego into his spirit. The psychologist may tell you that you need a healthy ego to function well. Having confidence and certainty about what your know, your skills and your ability to handle things in life is not the same things as ego in the sense of the word I am using.

**J) The gift of aging**
It may help to see aging as a gift rather than a curse,

because in truth it is, when it comes to escaping from ego identification.

When we are young and free of disease, physical problems, aches, pains, strains and wrinkles and filled with endless energy and with time stretching out in front of us, it is very easy for us to become lost in identification with our wonderful body.

The more beautiful, handsome, strong and fit, talented and intelligent it is, the more we love it and are willing to believe that this is *us*. When success, wealth and fame is thrown into the mix, the trap of identification is about perfect. Even if we don't think we are attractive when we are young our body is such a powerful entity we can easily identify with it. Only the most aware can awaken from this identification of ego to look for something spiritual.

But as we age our body starts to let us down. We look in the mirror and are no longer delighted. Aches and pains and other physical issues also contribute to our disenchantment. As our mortality becomes real to us, as we know more and more people who have died, this can present is an opportunity for introspection, searching and finding truth. This can be the time in our lives when it is easier to de-identify with our body and our ego. This is the gift of aging.

### K) Let Go Of Your Story

When we believe we need our story—our history, our accomplishments, our trials—to define us and tell others who we are, we tie ourselves into our mentally created ego construction. If we let go of our story and focus on what is happening right now, we free ourselves.

One of the things that can happen when we lose a dear friend is we feel bereft because we have lost someone who knew our story so well. Just have them around reinforces our identity because they know *our story*. So as well as losing our friend we can feel we have lost a part of our identity.

Years ago when I met someone new I felt like I had to tell them my story: *Look—this is who I am.* Relationships with girls would largely be about an exchange of stories. When that was over, so often was the relationship!

All these aspects of maintaining detachment from ego are much easier said than done—but they *can* be done. It is achieved the same way as anything is done—by making a decision, and then through intention and persistence, adhering to a workable path of action.

# 4ᵗʰ Habit of Transformation: Accepting Reality

What Acceptance Means—The External World Is A Mirror Of the Internal World—Always Create From The Positive Version Not The Negative—The Law Of Acceptance—Acceptance and Causing Change—Don't Judge Life With Human Logic—Handling Great Loss.

*Receive with simplicity everything that happens to you ~ Rashi*

*What you resist persists. ~ Carl Jung*

*Amor Fati—Love your fate, which is in fact your life. ~ Friedrich Nietzsche*

*We cannot change anything until we accept it. Condemnation does not liberate, it oppresses.~ Carl Jung*

*If something is wrong, fix it if you can. But train yourself not to worry. Worry never fixes anything.~ Ernest Hemingway*

Let us first define what is meant by *acceptance*. As with several of these principles we will be discussing, I quite misunderstood it at first when I came across it.

Reality is what is. We often come across something in

life and internally instantly judge it—reject it—think it is wrong—feel it should be different—think it should not have happened—want it to have it to have happened differently.

These are all thoughts and judgments about reality that fight with what is—whether we say them or think them or just feel them. And the more we attempt to impose our *thoughts* of *what should be*, onto *what is*, the more we attempt to alter reality, in a way that can never succeed, and the more we suffer.

Our own energy that we are directing to try to change a reality that cannot be changed by thought and feeling simply comes back at us and hits us, and we feel this as the pain of suffering.

Let us be very clear about what we are doing: we are energetically causing our own suffering, moment by moment, every time we disagree with reality.

The opposite of this is *acceptance*.

**Acceptance** is the internal realization that change has occurred, with no reservations or disagreements at the level of thought, emotion or intention, or energetic attempts to hide from or retreat from that truth in any way. Acceptance does not therefore cause any energetic slap back or suffering.

Just as the aikido or judo master does not resist the force of another by meeting force with force, he lets it continue as it comes towards him, steps out of the way and redirects it to his advantage by throwing his opponent.

Just as the fir tree does in the snow storm: unlike the oak, it does not resist the falling snow. Instead when it becomes heavy enough its branches bend and the snow falls to the ground and the branches return to their place. But the oak is strong and rigid and it resists the snow. If the snow gets heavy enough the oak branch will break.

In the same way, if we let the energy of life pass through

us with no resistance but pure acceptance, then we are not negatively impacted by it.

Buddha said: *Pay no attention to the faults of others, things done or left undone by others. Consider only what by oneself is done or left undone.* This is on a personal level—OK if someone has failed to shut the door of the car you are driving you need to get them to shut it before you drive onto the freeway.

But on a personal level what others do and say about the world around them, including their opinions about you, is all a projection of their reality, which you are not responsible for and, at a basic level, is none of your business.

If you cease to require other's approval to feel OK about yourself, if are maintaining your own integrity by your own actions and responsibilities, and if you let go of demanding that reality match your mental picture of expectations, then the world flows through you and by you without impacting you negatively on an energetic level.

Which means you will be able to maintain your inner peace, once you have attained it. The negative words of others can then be seen with compassion to be a result of their fears, but they pass you by without disturbing your inner world.

Now when I first heard about all this, I confused *acceptance* with being *ineffectual* and *powerless* to do anything in the world or make things better.

This is a mistake, a misunderstanding and not what we are talking about.

Acceptance in no way implies apathy, being ineffectual, being helpless or hopeless to improve situations, make things better or succeed.

There are paradoxes throughout each spiritual journey because we are trying to unravel layers of falsehoods while still staying afloat and paddling our canoe down river.

One of the paradoxes is: if you wish to change something effectively, first accept it as it is.

There are four ways of responding to any situation in life: 1) To like something and be happy with the way it is. 2) To dislike it but do nothing. 3) To dislike it and change it. 4) To dislike it and then completely accept it the way it is.

And life falls into 2 categories: A) The things we can change and B) The things we cannot change.

A real life example of something we can change: 1) We move into a room and like the color it is and so we leave it as it is. 2) We move into a room and it is purple, which we dislike, but we do nothing and we continue to complain about the color. 3) We move into a room and it is purple, but we prefer taupe. It is a simple matter to buy some paint and change the color of the room. 4) We move into a purple room, which initially bothers us, but we grow to accept it so it no longer bothers us.

These are all examples of things we can change if we decide to and follow through. Or not.

But in the case of a loved one dying this is an example of a situation we cannot change. We can either fight the reality of the change that has occurred by thinking that they should not have died and spend the rest of our life being upset about it, or we can accept the fact they have died and be grateful they were in our life at all, and get over our initial grief. The choice is clearly ours whether to accept reality or whether to suffer.

Always, when we try to fight reality we lose. Because change is inevitable.

The entire physical universe can only exist through constant change and motion—down to the tiniest particles. So for us to exist in this universe and yet to internally resist its change *in any way* is to experience suffering in some form or another.

It seems to be a common human trait to desire positive things to stay the same beyond when it is time for them to change, and to desire negative things to cease before they have run their course.

Perhaps because we are at our core timeless, we have an innate desire for things to stay the same that have to constantly continually change so that they can even exist. How many times have humans expressed the desire for a perfect moment or situation to last forever. When we invest in this thought and then things change as they always must, we inevitably experience a pain of loss.

In both cases we are arguing with reality.

Reality is what is, and when we learn to accept fully *what is* and align ourselves with reality, and accept it without internal resistance, then we cease our internal conflicts with reality and can come fully into contact with the present moment.

If we wish to change our reality on the physical plane and cause ourselves no internal energetic distress, we must first accept the reality of *what is* with no internal resistance, then change it on the physical level if we wish to in a way that causes no harm.

If something has happened that we are unable to change however, then we must learn to accept it if we wish to be free from suffering.

The process of acceptance requires you to separate from all the versions of how reality *should* be, but aren't, that reside in your mind.

*That shouldn't have happened.*

*If only he had done that instead, everything would be ok now.*

*Why don't people do this instead of that?*

*They should not have said that.*

We must be willing to fully embrace the ever-changing dance of the physical universe and enjoy what we love when it occurs, always in the complete understanding of its impermanence. In this way we will not cause ourselves unnecessary suffering.

The problem that I had with the concept of acceptance for a long time was—*well if you just accept everything, then nothing gets changed for the better—you just become passive and ineffectual.*

This is what I finally realized: you can do whatever you think you should do in life to make things better. Internally accepting reality *first* doesn't prevent this.

If the house is on fire I strongly recommend you call the fire department immediately and do what you can to put it out, and get everyone to safety and save your valuables. That would not be the time to sit cross-legged and accept the fact that everything you own is burning up!

The fact is, there is *always* something that needs to be done in life. And there probably always will be. That seems to be how life is constructed.

As Winston Churchill observed: *Life is one damn thing after another.*

But usually the house isn't on fire.

The fact that things need to be done, and that negative situations need to be improved, is not in dispute.

We are talking about having a spiritual awakening: a *satori.*

And it has to do with experiencing the reality in front of you, without compulsively engaging in the unconscious mental activity of judging and criticizing and arguing with it at all, and then trying to substitute your mental model of how you think things should be, or comparing it with memories of apparently similar past events.

Otherwise you are one of those people who walk around complaining constantly how everything should be otherwise than it is: *There are too many cars on the street, things aren't as good as they used to be, the food in the restaurant is wrong, the portions are too small, other people should behave differently, she shouldn't have said that, he should not have done that, foreigners should all go back to their own countries, that movie was boring, those paintings weren't that good, that team is useless, even the weather is too hot or too cold...*

It never ends. They are so busy complaining they rarely enjoy anything for very long. But by being the one person in the universe who knows how things really should be they are inflating their ego a little bit each time, until it deflates and they need to find fault with something else.

Is this important?

Yes—because it takes an enormous amount of energy to do this all the time. And it produces nothing except upset. They are shooting themselves in the foot by their continual fight with reality. Reality always wins.

And doing this keeps us locked out from being able to experience reality in all its magnificent brilliance, without the endless babble of our mind about *"how things should be,"* getting in the way. They never connect the dots between how negatively they think and how negatively they feel. Because they place all the blame *out there*. Do you see the mechanics of how this works?

The distinction that took me so long to grasp is that: yes we should take whatever actions seem right to us to improve the world around us—*but there will always be something else in our world to fix.* That is how life is constructed—you will never get to a point where you have fixed the last thing and now everything is perfect and it will stay that way, until we fix ourselves.

**Our external life is a mirror of our internal life.**

So are you fixing the world? Or is the world fixing you? And by that I mean affecting you negatively.

**The point of us being here is not to fix the world, but to fix ourselves.**

And by *fixed*, I mean of course that we awaken from our mind-dominated experience of our life, and instead experience the real world around us and our natural state of peace, love, joy, compassion and connectedness to each other.

Once *we* become fixed, *our world* will follow suit. Our external personal life experience reflects our own personal internal spiritual state. The external world is a mirror of the internal. As long as mankind is functionally insane, the world will reflect this by being in turmoil.

The idea that we must first fix the world and then that will fix us is a misconception. It is the wrong way around: A false perception of cause and effect.

Hence Gandhi's saying: *You must first become the change you wish to see in the world.*

Or the mystic Rumi: *Yesterday I was clever, so I wanted to change the world. Today I am wise, so I am changing myself.*

Quantum physicist and author Dr. John Hagelin is of the same opinion. His statement about it is: *Only Higher Consciousness Can Transform Our World.*

When we finally have this experience of complete acceptance, when we surrender to *what is* without internal resistance, we are consumed by an engulfing sense of peace and overwhelming love that flows through us.

My response to this experience was a desire to do nothing but go somewhere quiet and just experience this bliss and gratitude for everything around me, nothing more.

To then try to deal with the world and fulfill the obligations I had was very difficult and the last thing I wanted to do. You may also have difficulty balancing your earthly obligations with your desire to simply remain connected to the divine, but you may be motivated to make your life much simpler than it was before.

Eventually, as you learn to function while inhabiting all these modes of consciousness described in this book AND handling the world competently, well then you will have become a mighty spiritual force! It is much easier to detach from the world and go to a retreat and go on your spiritual journey and not have to deal with the many pressures of life, and there is no judgment intended if that is your choice.

But to be able to handle and master the levels of the physical world at a high level of intellectual complexity and all the difficulties and stress that it can throw at you, *and* also become and maintain spiritual consciousness *at the same time*, is to become the graduate of a master class in spirituality. I believe that is the course that many of us are enrolled in, who are here on Earth at this time.

If something has happened in the past that you spend a lot of time and attention regretting and wishing that you or someone else had done something differently—how is this producing anything useful?

If this was, for example, a case of some procedure that should be changed to keep people safe from a repeat of an accident in the future, and you have the information that can change this—then by all means communicate so others become informed. Write a memo, a procedure, a book, give an interview, get a law passed—whatever means will best serve to produce positive change and awareness.

If you feel you did harm to others and this is weighing on your conscience, then do something constructive to make up for what you did until you feel you have made up the damage and you feel the burden lift off you.

But to do nothing constructive but just to regret something in the past is pointless, and actually destructive to you. In order to regret the past you have to mentally recreate the past. This leaves you locked in your own mental world and out of present time.

The past no longer exists, so you are obsessing about what amounts to an illusion.

Meanwhile the real world is passing you by.

**This is about ceasing our internal mechanism of resisting reality.**

Fix that *first* so you are embracing reality, and *then* go on and create the world positively as you see fit. Then your actions will be aligned with the universe of what is.

Then you can change the world around you *without* it first changing you negatively.

When we are willing to do whatever life requires of us, that does not cause others harm, no matter how difficult, we will have ease in our lives. But when we resist every difficulty, we will experience our lives as very hard. It can be the same life, but our acceptance or resistance in how we approach it, changes our experience of it completely.

### Don't Judge Life By Human Logic Standards
We need to be able to look at the world from a non-human, non-ordinary everyday life perspective, in order to fully grasp what is going on around us. This involves an act of

imagination to detach ourselves from our present situation, and sit somewhere up in the clouds for a moment as it were, and consider this: life is not the forward march of humanity's progress throughout the ages that we have been taught it is.

Yes the history about humankind is true, although it may be missing some chapters, but what is *really* going on is the continual reincarnation of spiritual beings who are coming back to experience life in a myriad of different ways in order to experience, and thus learn, things that will assist their spiritual evolution. We are all in Spiritual School.

Yes you can spend your life healing the sick or feeding the hungry if you wish, and that is a laudable thing to do, and you may gain many insights from doing that.

It is good for us to help others, and it will help balance any outstanding karma we have for past harm we may have caused others. But you will not finally resolve the problem of there being hungry and sick people in the world. Why? Because being hungry and sick is the lesson that some people need to experience in order to become more conscious. And so that condition will continue in the world until no one needs to learn a lesson from that experience.

That is not a reason not to try, because there are lessons for those who are being saved, and for those who do the saving, but be aware of what is really going on here, so you are not overwhelmed by the failure of your own expectations.

Even if all world hunger and all disease was wiped out completely as a situation on planet earth, those who have created the experience of having negative things in their lives will experience the suffering they have created for themselves in some other way.

Just look how many wealthy people living in luxury still experience great hardships.

What I am saying is that the mechanism of cause and effect still remains, and the world will not change for good until people change, and cease to create negativism through their thoughts, beliefs, emotions and intentions. That is why you pursuing your own consciousness is the best thing you can do for the world—we are all connected and the enlightenment of one more being impacts us all.

There will continue to be wars until no one else needs to learn that killing others in wars is not a solution to anything. There will be no peace in the Middle East for example, until the people living there awaken to the fact that killing each other is pointless, non-productive, and only leads to suffering. And at the point they have learned that lesson they will simply stop killing each other.

**The state of the world is a mirror for the state of humanity.**

They will wake up one day collectively and say: "You know I'm really tired of all this killing and bloodshed and suffering. How about we just go talk to those other people and see if we can work things out peacefully. Let's try forgiveness instead of revenge."

Until that day, a bomb lands somewhere and blows things up and their response is: *Revenge! I must go blow someone up in response!* And off they go again. Good luck trying to bring about peace between people who have that consciousness.

An enlightened man from that region in the Middle East wandered around telling people not to kill each other but to love their enemies instead, about two thousand years ago, but still not many people there are listening.

Every sacred teaching worth its salt teaches love, not violence.

Know that if you involve yourself in the cycle of revenge you only trap yourself into further suffering.

If you forgive, you are creating positive energy in a negative situation, and so you release yourself from this cycle of suffering. Your positive energy will return to you.

Instead allow the karma of the person who committed violence to catch up with them.

*You* do not have to try to act as their karma by committing revenge in order for justice to occur; the universe will do it for you impersonally, because every piece of energy each person puts out into the universe simply returns back to them, and if it was negative, negative returns to them.

Acceptance and non-resistance of reality, on a personal level, enables you to detach from the group drama that is continually unfolding around us, so that you may evolve, so that you may raise your vibration level and your consciousness by aligning yourself with the laws of the universe.

You will then experience what *you* are creating for *you*, in your life, through your positive thoughts, emotions, beliefs and intentions. You can then become a bubble of consciousness and peace and love and connectedness in a sea of dysfunction and unconsciousness. And from *that* consciousness you will be able to bring light into the lives of those around you.

If, however, you internalize all the pain and drama of all those around you, you will stay at their level of consciousness, and no one will be helped. You must first climb into the boat yourself in order to help pull others into the boat and save them from drowning. This is not selfishness. This is becoming personally empowered in order to be able to help others.

**You cannot give away what you do not possess.**

It is important also to realize that if you are engaged in a worthy cause, such as feeding people, providing the homeless with housing, or providing healthcare to the sick, always think of it from the *positive* direction, of providing food, housing and helping people to be well.

Never the negative version: *Fighting Hunger, Fighting Disease, Fighting Poverty, Fighting Terrorism,* because then you are focused on the negative and so you are actually helping to create more of it in the world. *Creating Peace* is the positive version, *Fighting Terrorism* is the negative version, and they produce quite different results.

So when we look at the world around us as a workshop or laboratory where people are learning life lessons in order to become more conscious, instead of a place where people are experiencing random terrible things and suffering unjustly, then everything looks very different to us.

Then we can accept reality without guilt, or the compulsion to fix everything and everyone—that compulsion is only a function of guilt or ego.

We cannot look at a scenario where people are born into a terrible situation and judge: *Well that is not fair, that is not right, a loving God would not allow that!*

I would say to you: you simply don't have the full picture to be able to judge what is right or fair or useful to those who are having that experience, and trying to do that isn't helpful to you or them.

If you want to go help them, that is fine, there will be a valuable lesson in the experience for those you help, and for you who is doing the helping. But there is no value for you to argue with reality and decide: *That shouldn't be that way.*

I invite you to try complete surrender and lack of inner resistance to a situation for yourself and observe if it makes a difference to how you experience the situation and if it also alters how others act. The phrase that works to open my heart in stressful moments is this: **In this moment, everything is as it should be**, and as I feel myself relax without internal resistance, then I act to do that which seems the most beneficial for all.

So the law of acceptance is in effect: *That which you accept, resolves.*

*That which you resist, continues to affect you.*

Or as Carl Jung observed: **What you resist persists.**

This applies to our past painful memories. When we try to pull away from them, not face them, or believe they are too awful to look at, they continue to haunt us.

If we need to continue to see ourselves as a victim and need to make ourselves right and make others wrong by the harm we suffered, and we need to use it to boost our ego, saying: *"look what they did to me—feel sorry for me! I am special!"* Or if we refuse to let go of the past and accept it is no longer happening to us in the present moment, and if we refuse to let go of guilt or anger, or the desire for revenge, then our pain will persist.

So you see how we are causing our own suffering by our own choice in these matters. And that we do have a choice whether to continue to suffer or not.

We have to ask ourselves: would we rather be right, or would we rather be happy?

When we confront our past demons fully, if necessary going back on a string of similar traumas to the earliest one with a trained regression therapist, when we look at everything without shying away from it, when we accept everything that happened, they resolve fully and past, trapped negative is transformed into positive. The truth sets us free, and we are released from further pain from that incident.

We have no need to continue to see ourselves as a victim,

and no need to be right and make others wrong by the harm we suffered, or refuse to accept the past is no longer happening in the present moment.

By facing what happened fully and accepting it—we become set free of its effects.

The law of acceptance is:

**That which you accept, resolves. That which you resist, persists.**

Now that you have read the mechanics of how this works, it will be pure self deception on your part if you choose to continue to wallow in pain and self pity, rather than seek healing. **We always have free choice.**

If you can allow each event that is unfolding around you to be as it is, without being invested in the outcome, without internally demanding that life be a particular way, then you will experience a huge relief and peace about being there.

Once you are free of expectations you can just experience what is happening without experiencing the negative energy created by the difference between *what is* and what you think *should be.*

*I let go of all expectations. People, places and things are free to be themselves, and I am free to be me.~ Louise L. Hay*

Similarly, if you can accept and allow another person to act the way they are, without automatically superimposing all the judgments about how they *should* be behaving, you become freed from a great deal of stress and reactivity. Once you start to do this you may be able to perceive the fear that is motivating the unconscious behavior that was bothering you in the first place, and so understanding and compassion replaces resistance and annoyance.

Now I understand, for example, if you are running an airline it is important that the plane land on time and in one piece, and as part of maintaining your integrity you should do everything you are responsible for as well as you can at all times.

All these laws are interconnected and interdependent, so don't make the mistake of misinterpreting one to try to contradict the other. So within that paradigm of practicing responsibility and excellence that is part of your Habit of Integrity, allow life to unfold as it will without superimposing your mental version of expectations onto it.

The world is a giant laboratory for us to practice acceptance of realities that we may think are insane but over which we have no control. The path to insanity is to mentally fight with reality. The path to inner peace is acceptance of it.

If you wish to change the world, or if you wish to change yourself, first accept life as it is.

# 5<sup>th</sup> Habit of Transformation: Practicing Forgiveness

## The Self-Healing Function of Forgiveness of Oneself and Others

*There is no healing without forgiveness. ~ Caude DeShazom M.D.*

*Forgiveness means giving up all hope for a better past.~ Lily Tomlin*

*The weak can never forgive. Forgiveness is the attribute of the strong. ~ Mahatma Gandhi*

*Holding onto anger is like grasping a hot coal with the intention of throwing it at someone else; you are the one who gets burned. ~ Buddha*

As a schoolboy in England I was required to recite the Lord's Prayer each morning. I would mumble: "Forgive us our trespasses as we forgive those who trespass against us..."

And I was taught Jesus' instruction to *Love your enemies* (Matthew 5:44 KJV)

But I have to tell you that growing up in post World War 2 England I had the hardest time with the concept of forgiveness or loving my enemies. I found Christ's teaching to turn the other cheek when confronted by violence in his *Sermon on the Mount* to be completely unworkable in the times in which I was living:

*You have heard that it was said, "An eye for an eye and a tooth for a tooth". But I say to you, do not resist an evildoer. If anyone strikes you on the right cheek, turn to him the other also.* (Matthew 5:38-39 KJV)

My English father and grandfather had both gone to fight Germany in two world wars. My grandfather had been a prisoner of war in Germany and been doused with mustard gas. I walked past bomb sites in London every day as a small child and heard how my family members had slept in underground stations to avoid the hail of the nightly bombings of London during the blitz that went on for nine months.

I learned about the murderous tyranny and inhumanity of the Nazis and the struggle of the allies to survive at tremendous cost. I learned about the horrors of the Nazi death camps and their attempts to wipe out Jews, Gypsies, homosexuals and political enemies in Europe. As a young boy, far from forgiving my enemies, what made sense to me was: *kill thine enemies.*

The last thing that made sense to me was to love them. I played soldiers on the way home from school, and in the garden, and mowed down imaginary Nazis with the wooden machine gun that I had made.

WW2 seemed to me at that time to be a simple case of black and white, good versus evil—a "just war."

I mention this because I came to my understanding of the need and value of forgiveness, absolutely from a place of non-forgiveness.

I was in my mid thirties one day in my studio working

away on an illustration and thinking about this subject when something caused the light to finally go on:

*Oh! I'm not forgiving them for their sake.*

*I'm forgiving them for my sake!*

I suddenly saw that the act of forgiveness had *nothing* to do with condoning evil done by others.

This was what had been keeping me locked in a viewpoint of non-forgiveness, as I'm sure it does many people.

If you wish to progress spiritually, if you wish to gain peace of mind, if you wish to merely maintain good physical health as the years go by, you must learn to forgive.

That means to let go of all grievances, resentments, or grudges against those you believe have done you wrong. To let go of the desire for revenge, to cease carrying the intention for others to suffer and be brought down. Forgiveness has occurred when a harmful or painful event or person or group can pass though your mind and you no longer experience a negative reaction, or a desire to see them harmed.

When you can be in a state of love, and the thought of one who has harmed you does not disturb that, and you can wish those who have harmed you an awakening from their unconsciousness—then you have forgiven.

Why is this important? Because we are dealing with *your* energy, your creations, your consciousness. All the energy you create must be turned from negative to positive—all your thoughts, beliefs, emotions, intentions and actions must become positive—and we will investigate why this is important and how to achieve this. But the short answer is that you experience what you create.

Think of it as a boomerang—what you send out returns to you and you experience it. So if you are going to get anywhere—you *must* learn to forgive everyone and everything that has ever hurt you. Each of the principles that have been expressed as habits to practice in daily life is interconnected and interdependent with the others. They are all part of Consciousness. You cannot practice some and violate others and stay in balance. Acceptance makes forgiveness possible—forgiveness makes acceptance possible.

I'm going to list my realizations about this subject one by one, because it may help you take any of your objections to forgiveness apart as well:

**1) Forgiveness is for *your* benefit first**. The answer to your own recovery from past events is to face them fully, accept them, and forgive everyone involved, including yourself if that is part of the dynamic. If you forgive someone for something they did to you, then realize that you are doing that for *you*, not *them*. It may also help them, but that is not your primary reason for doing it. As with the airplane oxygen mask—first put the mask on your own self so you can breathe, then you are able to help someone else.

**That reframes the whole action does it not?**

2) Forgiveness does *not* mean you are condoning destructive, cruel or harmful behavior. **The misapprehension that is associated with forgiveness is that** *the act of forgiveness implies condoning the act that is being forgiven.*

It does not. Forgiveness has *nothing* to do with moral or ethical judgments of right and wrong. It has *nothing* to do with how harmful the act was that you are trying to forgive. It has only to do with undoing the very toxic harm *you are doing to yourself* by holding onto resentments and wanting revenge or a different outcome for what happened in the past, and failing to grasp that it is no longer happening in the present moment.

**3) Forgiveness does not mean you are abandoning protection.**

It does not mean you do not protect yourself or others from harm. Forgiveness does *not* mean you cannot or should not deal with someone who has wronged you in the real world in terms of lawsuits, assisting with police investigations, mediation, leaving an abusive relationship, or whatever process is needed to set things right in the world.

But even though you are following through with whatever you need to balance things in the physical world, do it without rancor, and with a calm mind and heart, and then forgive whoever harmed you.

And then take that world experience to protect you against the recurrence of similar harm.

**4) Forgiveness does not mean apathy.** We can still work to improve situations or help others. It does not mean we allow ourselves to be walked over or collapse or give up and do nothing!

**5) Forgiveness has nothing to do with allowing abuse or harm of any kind to be repeated.** If you are an abused wife, or an abused or incested child is involved, or any kind of abusive relationship or situation has occurred, your first priority is to ensure the abuse stops, and for good.

Forgiveness has nothing to do with allowing yourself or others to continue to be victims.

**6) If you cannot learn to forgive, you will remain stuck at this point and your progress will be blocked.**

Any energy that you direct into hatred and resentment about anything in the past is not free to you. It costs you.

It is costing you your attention, focus and the energy that you need to be running your present life.

Hatred and resentment is a low vibration emotion. If you continue to focus on these emotions, you are trapping yourself into resonating at a low vibration—and if you will observe how you feel inside when you do that—you will notice it feels awful.

This will also cause you to attract more low vibration people and events to you like a magnet because this is what you are broadcasting into the universe around you. You are in fact asking to experience more negative experiences in present time by refusing to let go of past suffering.

Is that how you wish to remain?

If you wish to experience love, joy and inner peace—levels of high vibration—then you must first let go of hate and resentment. You cannot reach and stay at a level of a high vibration if you are focused on a low vibration emotion. By forgiving all those who have wronged you, and forgiving yourself for all those whom you have also wronged, you allow yourself to move up in vibration.

You also cease to remain stuck in the role of victim.

**7) Forgiveness has to do with letting go of the past and ceasing to poison oneself with hatred and a desire for revenge.**

It has to do with the recognition that *the past no longer exists.*

*A past incident is no longer happening in the present moment.*

Look around right now and realize that this is true. To treat a horrific incident that happened in the past as if it is still happening in the present moment is to live with a delusional perception. That is why I am stressing over and over how important it is to come to that realization.

If you are carrying resentments about something in the past, you are still stuck in that delusion. You are not fully in the present moment.

Why? Because you cannot change or undo whatever happened in the past.

It is done. *Wishing it hadn't happened or believing it shouldn't have happened will not change it.* It will only cause you to suffer because of the energetic fight between what is and what you want it to be.

In the physical universe we have to take action to change things in the present moment.

If someone blew up your house you will have to rebuild it to have it again. Wishing won't achieve anything.

You may say: *Ok, I get that. But the person who did the bad thing to me is still alive—I'm not going to be their best friend now!* You don't have to be their best friend. You may not trust them and you may find them to be toxic, destructive, negative or even dangerous. You may choose not to interact with them.

That is your prerogative. Maintain your protective boundaries and physically separate yourself from the personality who is potentially harmful to you if you wish to. That is dealing with physical universe danger.

But in your heart, can you recognize that they are in a state of unconsciousness? Can you become peaceful and forgiving to them?

Which brings us to the next point:

**8) Forgiveness requires distinguishing between the destructive *action*, and the unconscious *person* who committed the action.**

Their destructive and selfish or cruel behavior came from unconsciousness. However, beneath that unconsciousness is an immortal spirit who may one day awaken and start to take responsibility for their actions and make amends and live with compassion. It may not be in this lifetime, and they may have to wade through an awful lot of Karma to atone for their actions before they are able to wake up, but some day this may occur.

And you have a connection to that spirit, because they are a fellow spirit, you come from the same source, which is God. So protect yourself from the unconsciousness, perceive the destructive action and its consequences, but don't condemn and disconnect yourself from their spirit completely, *because this will lower your consciousness and close down your heart.* In your own heart, acknowledge that fellow spirit's existence and potential for enlightenment, and let go of hatred.

Why should you bother?

Because you cannot love one person and hate another. You cannot hate and still maintain an open heart.

Hate is hate—it doesn't matter to whom it is directed, or how justified you are in your hate—do you see how this works? To hate *anyone* for *any* reason is to close down your own consciousness. If you intend to remain conscious, your only choice is to forgive everything and everyone. *That* is why Jesus taught to love one another, to love your enemies, and to forgive.

*Hatred does not cease by hatred, but only by love; this is the eternal rule.~ Buddha*

Does this mean, for example, you must even forgive

someone who murdered your child? I am using this as the most extreme and awful example I can imagine anyone having to face. My heart goes out to you if you have been in this situation; I once met a couple whose child had been murdered.

The answer is yes. If you wish to not be stuck at this point for eternity, at some point you must recognize this action came from unconsciousness, it is now in the past, and you must let go of all resentment if you wish the pain of the loss to cease. This is simply the nuts and bolts mechanics of the spiritual universe.

The Truth is that whoever you lost is not dead—their spirit is immortal, their body is dead and they have ceased to live in that temporary physical form, just as you also will one day. The more identified we are with the physical universe and all its temporary and ever changing forms, the more pain we cause ourselves.

If you wish to heal from your loss, cease protesting the reality of what is, and instead experience gratitude that you had the gift of your loved one in that physical form for as long as you did. It was time for them to leave that physical identity.

How do we know that? Because it happened. There are more forces at work in the universe than we are aware of. When it comes to the reality of what happens in life, what appears to be logical or just to you at a particular time may not include other factors of which you are unaware. Arguing with reality is always a losing proposition.

*All life is connected: we are all from the same source, so when you close your heart to one human being you close your heart to all.*

Mark this well because this is not a trivial detail: if you close your heart to those who do things you find reprehensible, then your heart will become closed.

Recognize when an action is the result of unconsciousness.

But do not be made unconscious yourself by failing to accept the reality it created. Recognize and acknowledge when someone is acting from great unawareness or from blind unconsciousness that we can classify as evil. But also recognize that underneath that weight of unconsciousness is an immortal spirit which has the potential to one day awaken and shine with beauty and compassion.

*And do not be so self-righteous and pious as to suppose that you may be completely free in all your history of committing similar acts of great cruelty and selfishness.*

Just because you may now be a person of sensitivity and ethical behavior, do not suppose you were always so. Just because you cannot remember having been otherwise does not necessarily make it so. You may have achieved your current awareness at a price of painful experiences—yours and others.

Regardless—the principal remains the same—if you close your heart to another human being for whatever reason, then you have closed your heart, and you will experience your disconnection from Spirit.

**9) Failure to Forgive will keep you from spiritual advancement.**

Failure to forgive is also a precursor to physical illness.

If you hate and resent strongly enough and long enough, the result will be experienced in your physical body through disease.

The Lord's prayer instructs us:

*Forgive us our trespasses, as we forgive those who trespass against us.*

Although you may think that is just morality or ethics, it goes much deeper than a religion giving us rules to live by. We are talking about a law woven into the fabric of our universe, just like gravity. Ignore them at your own risk because there are consequences, just as when you stick your hand in the fire.

It is, once again, pragmatically and purely a practical issue of your survival, growth, health and flourishing in your current life by aligning with the spiritual laws that govern us all.

The answer to your own recovery from past events is forgiveness.

If you refuse to forgive someone then the only person who is damaged by that refusal is yourself. Holding a grudge costs you energy, and does you harm. It is like paying someone to beat you up—not a good idea.

If someone else has harmed you in the past then they hurt you once, that one time. If you carry resentment and hatred about that event then you hurt yourself again every time you re-feel that event. Alcoholics Anonymous statistics tell us the number one reason for relapse is the re-feeling of old hurts.

Now it may be necessary to revisit that event fully with a therapist or trusted friend to examine the details and fully release the emotions held in that memory.

But unless you also forgive the perpetrator, then you will recreate the hurt in that event and continue to do damage to yourself. You have to also cease to be right and make the perpetrator wrong about what happened.

I used to have a huge button about justice and injustice. It could fire me up and get me passionately angry and self-righteous like nothing else. It also destroyed my inner peace and tranquility and got me into my ego by being self-righteous. By all means observe when something is unjust.

And if you wish to, do something positive to correct it. But first *forgive* the unconsciousness involved in it happening so you do not sink into anger and ego.

It is very important that you really grasp the mechanics of this and start to fully implement it in your life.

**10) The Law of Karma describes that the energy we send out to others, returns to us, positive or negative.**

So if we send out hate, anger and resentment to others, all that negative energy will return to us. We are therefore creating a future of negativity for ourselves!

Part of forgiveness is to cease sending out any negativity to others that will also impact you in the future.

We see again why Jesus taught to love your enemies. This is what he meant by turning the other cheek, and why. It means to respond to hate with love.

When you have thoughts or intentions to harm others, these return to you and create in your mind the fear that you can be harmed. Whereas in truth, as a spiritual being, you are quite invulnerable. So all your past intentions to do others harm now reside with you as fear of harm from others, and this fear attracts harm from others. This is why forgiveness and love is the ultimate path to protection. For when we rid ourselves of fear, and project no more evil to others, but instead project only love to others, that is what we will attract to ourselves. This is a law of cause and effect in the universe.

The law of Karma was described in Hinduism and Buddhism. Buddha said:

*All living beings have actions (Karma) as their own, their inheritance, their congenital cause, their kinsman, their refuge. It is Karma that differentiates beings into low and high states.*

We do not need to concern ourselves about getting revenge on those who have harmed us—their karma will return that injury to them. This is not a random or unjust universe, no matter how it may appear so karma may take until someone's future life to occur.

We are more than the sum of our parent's genes. We are also the product of our own Karma. Karma is the law of spiritual cause and effect. It is popularly described as: *What goes around comes around.* But it is more specifically accurate to say: *what you send to others, you will receive.*

Realize that you are even now creating your own future, moment by moment, by your own thoughts, intentions and beliefs. This is why you are completely responsible for your life, no one else. You are dreaming your own dream. You are the architect of your future life, just as you are now experiencing the result of your past thoughts and beliefs and intentions. This is why changing all that is negative within you to positive is of utmost importance. This is why learning to live in a state of positive Grace, Forgiveness and Love, no matter what, is essential to escaping the trap of suffering.

*All that we are is the result of what we have thought. If a man speaks or acts with an evil thought, pain follows him. If a man speaks or acts with a pure thought, happiness follows him, like a shadow that never leaves him.~ Buddha.*

This is the mechanism of escape from entrapment in the physical universe, and of continual incarnations, of being reunited with the universal Consciousness from which we came, and of which we are always a part, with only our identifications with the unconscious part of our minds and our identifications with the physical universe to isolate and separate us.

As the creations of our mind return to us, negative or

positive, we experience our Karma, negative or positive. Our past thoughts, beliefs, emotions and intentions created our present experience, and our Karmic debt. So we have to experience our negative karmic debt, and we are trapped here until this is fulfilled and we have learned our spiritual lessons, realized our true nature, and raised up the frequency of the vibration of our consciousness—so that we are living in love, forgiveness, acceptance, peace.

If however we experience our past Karma with negative emotions or other negative and unconscious reactions, such as harmful actions to others, we create further negative Karma for ourselves. We become caught in a never-ending cycle of entrapment.

Our only escape is to experience all our bad Karma with positive responses. And that is why the great spiritual teachers have all taught: love, acceptance, and forgiveness—regardless of the experiences the external world gives us.

That is the key that turns the lock to our final spiritual freedom.

This is the great spiritual lesson. If you adopt only one Truth into your life from this book—adopt this.

**11) Forgiveness of Oneself Does Not Equal Irresponsibility.**

One of the characteristics of sociopaths is that they do not regret the things they have done that harmed others. So how does this relate to the concept of forgiving oneself for the harm we have caused others? If we can forgive ourselves for this successfully, does that make us callous, insensitive, unfeeling, oblivious to others, or just completely irresponsible?

Well the defining points here are twofold: First that we

experience regret for the harm we have caused others, we wish it had not happened, and we are cognizant of the fact we made a mistake, and have the intention to never repeat the same mistake again. If we go through this process, then we are not in the oblivious condition of the sociopath. So is it ethically permissible that we forgive ourselves for harm done to others? Or should we just continue to punish ourselves with guilt as many people do? Such a response may be motivated by good intentions, but it is an impractical response to having caused harm.

Which brings us to defining point number 2: We have to look at *all* our experiences as a learning experience. *If* we learned a lesson from an action we took, even if it did cause others harm, then it goes from a negative to a positive experience. If we learn nothing however, it remains a negative experience for all concerned. The whole function of life is to provide experiences that present an opportunity to raise our consciousness. The idea or expectation that all our actions will be perfect and with no error is therefore clearly ludicrous. We are often attempting things of which we do not know the outcome. To make no errors means we attempted nothing, and also that we learned nothing. In order to learn, we have to risk making mistakes. The point is if we learned, if we gain in consciousness so that we no longer repeat that mistake, the whole incident was a success. The world experience exists to provide us with expanding consciousness.

We can only act and make choices with the consciousness we have right now. If making mistakes results in an increase in consciousness, so we no longer operate in that harmful way, then we have achieved what we are meant to, regardless of how messy it was. If we caused harm to others, we should make amends to them, until we have redressed the wrong, as best we can.

And then we forgive ourselves, let go of guilt and carry on in the present moment, doing the best we can now do.

This is the only sane, positive, constructive and conscious response.

The obsession about sin and punishment that some people have is simply a failure to grasp the actual mechanism that is at work. Once someone has had a complete shift in consciousness regarding a past harmful action, and then made amends as best they can, trying to punish them because of a desire for revenge on the part of society or the party who was harmed is counter productive to everyone concerned.

USA Today (Nov 25 2011) reported that according to a study of 200 Marines involved in severe combat, 3 months after coming home, 7% had post-traumatic stress disorder. Contributing to this was "moral injury"—guilt either that they had survived while others died, or that people such as women and children had also died, who had not been intended targets.

The issue of fairness comes into play here: because it is one thing to shoot someone who is shooting at you—it can be regarded as an equal contest. The soldier has agreed up front to engage in mortal combat with those he has defined as an enemy. But an unarmed civilian, especially a woman or child, is something else—an unintended victim. It offends the ethics of most people to hurt someone who was not trying to hurt them, or who was unable to defend themselves, or to hurt someone unintentionally.

The soldier is also skating on thin ice if they experience a revision of their personal ethical guidelines later on, such as all killing is wrong, and now decide their past behavior was morally reprehensible. This can bring about a collapse based on guilt.

In 2012 more US soldiers died from suicide than combat. These were people who were unable to forgive themselves for their actions, that they had come to perceive as unethical and indefensible.

All of these issues have the same solution:

A) To realize that what happened is in the past and cannot be undone by guilt or regret.

B) To clearly redefine the guidelines of one's personal integrity to what you are willing to live with, and what you are not, and what you will not compromise with in the future, under any circumstances.

C) Then make up the damage in some way, either to the person involved or if that is impossible, to a group that seems equitable to you. Until you feel the balance of harm has been made up by good.

D) Then realize that life is a learning experience—that is why you are here—to learn. You are not here to be perfect. If you are not getting into any difficulties or making mistakes you are unlikely to learn much. As long as you learn something positive from any life experience, it has served its purpose, and you have done your job. You can now move on.

E) Locate all the negative thoughts, feelings, beliefs and intentions connected to a painful, guilt-laden incident, or group of people, and change them to positive. Use positive affirmations and address them, with additional therapy that seems sympathetic to you.

F) Forgive, accept, become tolerant of, and learn to replace hatred with love.

In order to fully heal and feel at peace again you must undo all the negativism you are carrying concerning this subject. This requires serious work. But this is exactly why you are here.

**12) The final realization of forgiveness** is that we are always experiencing our own creation, the present moment that we have brought into being by our own past thoughts, beliefs, emotions and intentions. *So there is no one else to blame.*

Blame is pointless: what is, is. This is the truth of the physics of cause and effect in action—unconsciousness and the negativity it produces will result in only more negativity.

Sending out negativity will result in the same returning to you. Positivity of thought, belief, emotion and intention will result in a return of the same, and so that is the solution to changing our future experience. It is always our individual choice. You do not have to believe this or practice it. It will operate whether you care to believe and observe it or not.

In a specific situation you still may observe the unconscious behavior of another and decide to protect yourself from future damage from their unconsciousness by choosing not to associate with that person, while holding no resentment against them. Just because you forgave someone doesn't mean you want to be buddies with them. Just don't resent them.

### How Forgiven is Really Forgiven, Exactly?

*Forgiveness of others and of yourself is essential to your own healing and spiritual growth.*

So what do we mean exactly by forgiveness? How forgiven is *really forgiven?*

I am not speaking here of an insincere mouthing of some nice words that things are OK now: "I forgive you (you bastard!)" or just sending someone a Hallmark card.

I am talking of the *complete* letting go of all resentment and grievance and hurt of past events so that the recalling of the hurtful event or circumstance or the resented person no longer contains any painful or disturbing energy for you: so that you no longer need to dwell on those past events at all. So that you are no longer creating those past negative events to any degree with your own life energy and you are able instead to put all your energy into the positive creation of your life in the present moment.

When you have truly forgiven, you no longer feel the need for revenge or to see your enemies suffer for what they did to you; you no longer feel guilt for what you did to others.

*You know you have forgiven someone when he or she has harmless passage through your mind.~ Rev. Karyl Huntley*

True forgiveness means responding to hurt only with love, so that you create no more negative Karma for yourself, regardless of your current circumstances. Then, when you have worked out your Karmic debt by resolving your issues, only positive energy and circumstances will come to you.

You see that this is not a casual or simple matter at all; this will require some serious work and attention on your part.

This is part of truly coming into the present moment and being able to live your life in the present moment.

Regardless of what may have occurred in the past, if it is not happening to you now in the present, it no longer exists in reality. All that is left is your memory—electrons moving between neurons in your brain when you think about it. It is an illusion of reality. It is not reality.

*Failing to take this step will keep you trapped in the past until you do.*

### But What if the Thing to be Forgiven was REALLY Bad?

I hear someone saying: *"Wait until you have had something really devastating done to you—then tell me to forgive!"*

It is true I cannot counter with a story of a terrible wrong done to myself. I have, like everyone, experienced things that made me carry grudges and resentments for some years. But from my perspective I have not experienced anything that matches up to the horrors of so many people.

However one person who did experience such a great wrong done him and survived the experience with incredible insight and humanity was Viktor E. Frankl.

Viktor Frankl was a Jewish psychiatrist in Germany when the Nazis came to power and he was imprisoned in four concentration camps, including Auschwitz. At the hands of the Nazis he lost his parents, his brother and his pregnant wife. He endured three years of unspeakably cruel mistreatment and degradation and witnessed fellow Jews killed at the hands of his captors in the camps. It is hard to imagine a more devastating experience that a human being could experience. And if any man had a reason to hate it was Viktor Frankl, and I imagine his suffering can match just about anyone's.

So let me answer the challenge of: *"Wait until you have had something really devastating done to you—then tell me to forgive!"* with Viktor E. Frankl's experiences and his responses, for they are profound enough to speak to anyone, regardless of how devastating their experiences may be.

After World War 2, Viktor Frankl wrote a book called *Man's Search For Meaning*. The book, published in 1959, has since sold

12 million copies. A 1991 Library of Congress survey listed it as one of the 10 most influential books in America.

The deepest realization that Frankl gained from his experience was that although you cannot control all the experiences that will impact you in your life—you *can* control your reactions to those circumstances. He realized that a certain experience does *not* have to be followed by an inevitable reaction within the person who is having the experience.

How we choose to experience even the worst kind of circumstances in life is a freedom that can never be taken away from us—even though all other freedoms may have been taken away and we find ourselves in a situation of utter powerlessness to control our situation in life for a while.

Viktor Frankl realized that to believe that strong negative emotions were automatic and unavoidable human responses to suffering, was to surrender one's true power over one's own internal experience.

He said, *"Freedom is that point in time just after they do something to me and just before I choose my response to it."*

He realized that he could *choose* how he experienced the suffering he was enduring. In the midst of extreme suffering he was able to identify his ultimate freedom.

He emerged from his nightmare experience, not crushed, but in possession of a great wisdom. I am truly humbled by the depth of his insight in the midst of such suffering.

We will examine this further in the *16th Habit of Transformation: Controlling the External/Internal World Connection.*

### Ending the Cycle of Revenge and Violence

Various groups of people have got themselves into endless cycles of violence and revenge at different times.

Someone on one side kills someone of the other side. The other side feels pain and loss and so they respond with revenge and violence—killing someone on the other side. The new victims feel pain and loss so they respond with revenge and more killing. It goes on and on, back and forth, with no end in sight.

The pain and loss and outrage felt by each side is so extreme that the only solution they can come up with is to repeat the same actions that brought pain and suffering to them to begin with. This has happened in gang wars over territory in many places: in Ireland between Catholics and Protestants; it is currently happening in the Middle East between Israel and Palestine.

It is a pointless and unintelligent exercise because revenge and violence only produces further suffering and a continuation of the cycle of pain. Governments from time to time try to sell their people the solution of war, very profitable for a few, very damaging for the majority.

So what is the solution? Forgiveness. Eventually one side needs to say: *"Enough! No more killing! Let us negotiate a peaceful agreement we can both live with."*

This is how social evolution occurs, when people have experienced enough suffering to want to change their approach away from violence and revenge.

### Making Amends

Even if you tell someone that you forgive them, they still have to forgive themselves—after they have raised their awareness to the point that they can feel and be aware of the damage they have caused others by their actions. They may and should make reparations to those they have harmed if it is their desire to do so. Simply shaming someone into making reparation may work for others but it will do nothing for the person making good on the damage they've done unless they become a willing part of the process at a conscious level.

If you are aware of having caused others hurt, you should make up the damage to them. It will bring about a balance that will be healing for you and them. There is an appropriate English expression: *putting your money where your mouth is*. In other words don't just say the words *I'm sorry*, although that is a major step. But also do something constructive about it as well.

The act of forgiveness is an act of letting go, of reclaiming your attention and your energy; of your dignity, your power and your soul.

It is also recognition, as I mentioned, that the act you are concerned with is now in the past. As with all things, to treat the past as if it is still in the present moment is to squander one's precious life energy to no purpose. It is a delusional perception and action. A memory is no longer real life. It is important to make this distinction and treat each—the past and the present—appropriately.

**Thus it is time to let go of the past—so that you may fully experience and create your life in the present.**

### A Forgiveness Book

A friend of mine, Jim Dincalci, has written a wonderful book on the subject of forgiveness entitled *How To Forgive When you Can't.*

He also has a website and a healing practice devoted to the practice of forgiveness: http://www.forgivenessfoundation.org

I strongly recommend this book to anyone who is still

having difficulty forgiving a person or event as the book contains many practical techniques to achieve forgiveness.

### Forgiveness Teachings

Two teachings from completely different sources, tell us a similar thing regarding forgiveness, because this is a universal truth:

*Do not judge, and you will not be judged; do not condemn, and you will not be condemned; Forgive, and you will be forgiven.* ~ *Jesus* (Luke 6:37 KJV)

*Forgiveness is unlocking the door to set someone free and realizing you were the prisoner.* ~ *Max Lucado.*

To fail to forgive anything and everything is to still be caught in the Grand Illusion. It is to believe the Illusion is real—and it is our belief in the Illusion that keeps it in place for us and keeps us imprisoned by it.

To hold on to grudges and resentments is to be trapped in a mental delusion, it is to be living out of the present moment, believing in things that no longer exist, that are no longer happening.

All negative emotions and beliefs have their foundation in illusions, in identifications and attachments to the temporary and always changing physical world, which in our essence we are not part of.

We try to desperately hold onto scraps of illusion, when the banquet of heaven we crave is in front of us, hidden from us only by our own fears, identifications and attachments.

# 6th Habit of Transformation: Practicing Gratitude

*When it comes to life the critical thing is whether you take things for granted or take them with gratitude.* ~ G. K. Chesterton

Our appreciation and enjoyment of life in its myriad forms is an expression of our love. I realized one day how blessed I was to be able to deeply enjoy and love so much in my life: people, music, art, movies, nature, and all the many aspects of life that have touched me. Because without this ability to love that exists within us, life is a grey and colorless thing, no matter our surroundings or wealth.

Realize this: your life will be as vivid and joyful and exciting and amazing and moving and rich and beautiful as you decide it will be, as you *allow* it to be. It is *you* who brings the magic of your experience to this moment, or who fails to do so.

We have to stop expecting something *out there* to enrich our life. Our life can be utterly transformed in a second by making a shift in attitude and focus. You can be in the most incredibly luxurious and beautiful surroundings and you can still feel empty and dull and unengaged if you take it all for granted, or if your attention is stuck in your mind somewhere, and out of the present moment.

But, if you deliberately bring all of your attention out

from your thoughts and judgments about the world fully into the present moment, right now, the amazing beauty of the world can become so rich and overwhelming it can drop you to your knees in gratitude and love for all that is available to you in this fabulous universe.

If you develop the practice of gratitude, each flower, each tree, the sky above you, each breath, can become delicious and magical. If you take everything for granted however, and stay locked in your mind with negative thoughts about what you do not have, or what you need the future to bring you, then no matter what you are given, you will not be able to find joy that does not fizzle out in a short while. Every positive thing around you is there deliberately, nothing is an accident. Become aware of the amazing dance of co-creation in which you are involved, this daily miracle that we call life.

Don't take *anything* for granted.

Imagine you have one day left to live: *this day*. How much are you then going to take each step you take, every single thing that you get to do, for granted? How unimportant would each ordinary thing that you do be then? Well what makes you assume you have more than today left? What makes you assume you have 10 or 50 years of life left, so that you can afford to squander this one by being bored and dissatisfied with everything that is around you?

So you think you do not have enough? Can you walk down the street without pain? Tell someone who is bed-ridden or paralyzed that that means nothing, and that it is insignificant and boring. Can you speak sentences that can be understood? Tell someone who has had a stroke that the gift of speech to another human being means nothing. All that we need to do to be consumed with joy is to wake up to *all that we have right now at this moment, with gratitude.*

I make that statement because the most overwhelming joy I experienced, happened at the moment I was emotionally devastated, alone, hungry, and both my parents were dying, as I have described. So I know from personal experience that at any moment we can transform our life experience by simply bringing our attention completely and utterly out of our minds and into the present moment around us. When this happened to me I experienced becoming consumed with gratitude for the gift of simple existence, moment by moment.

The ability to experience real magic lies within yourself, in your power to shift the focus of your attention, and your decision of what you wish to experience: positive or negative, creative or destructive, to succumb or survive, to feel joy or to suffer.

In the movie *White Christmas*, Bing Crosby and Rosemary Clooney sing the Irving Berlin song *Count Your Blessings*, in which the lyric suggests you do can just that when you are worried and you can't sleep.

Dear friends of mine who live in England—an English wife with an American husband, have celebrated Thanksgiving for many years. She prepares a full Thanksgiving dinner for him and their family and friends. I think there were around twenty-four at the one I attended—one American and twenty-three English.

She requires everyone at the table to recount what they are most thankful for that year. I must admit that I used to regard all this sort of thing as harmless sentimental nonsense, but I came to realize what a valuable practice deliberately focusing on gratitude is.

It is an unfortunate trait of human beings that we tend to ignore and take for granted all the things we *already have* in our lives, and fixate instead on the things we want and *don't yet have*; so that we fail to realize all the positive things we do have in our lives, or believe we must first have more in order to feel happy, or fulfilled, or be able to start to create and achieve what we wish to.

It is a symptom of the falsehood we believe, that only the future holds what will complete us. That only the future can provide what our ego-based concept of ourselves sees as necessary to make us finally special enough to feel satisfied and fill the emptiness in our lives.

I finally realized, once my body was finally free of chronic pain at one point in my life, that having a healthy body that is pain-free and enabled me to do what I want in life, is in itself a tremendous gift. We never seem to grasp this at all until we have experienced chronic pain or can't walk down the street. Many of us who do have healthy bodies are fixated that they don't look exactly like the perfect vision we have in our heads, and especially in younger people this can lead to all kinds of anguish.

When I think of all the insults I gave my perfectly functioning teenage body—I'm kind of surprised it didn't just quit on me out of disgust at my gross ingratitude! We probably have all done this—and it's a mistake.

Again, this is the wrong focus—the point is—how perfect of a body do you need to achieve what you want to do in life?

So you don't look like a movie star or model—so what, get over it. As long as people don't run screaming from your appearance in the streets, you have a vehicle by which to achieve something wonderful in life if you work at it. That is the point! Instead of being upset with your body, try being grateful to it for all the things it does do well.

You may start to feel much better about it as a result. Then focus on what you want to achieve, and how you can bring that about.

And by the way, most movie stars, singers and models don't look like that either, before make up and retouching on their photographs. I know because I retouched a lot of them in days past, on record albums, magazine covers and movie posters, to make stars look fabulous. Today some movies have digital retouching in them that travels with the actor through a scene to make stars look perfect. So don't believe everything you see in the media!

Cultivate gratitude for your body! Believe me, whatever age you are now, you will someday look back and wish you were still that age physically—if not emotionally or spiritually!

If you had something you liked greatly in your life but that you no longer have, whether it was looking and feeling young and fabulous, or having a loved one who died, or losing a great deal of money, or whatever it may be, try to experience gratitude that you once had that in your life rather than fixating on its loss. The idea that you are entitled to *anything* is a lie. Everything positive is a gift to be treasured.

Remember that everything in the physical universe is changing constantly and if you are still holding on to the idea that anything is permanent in your life that is another myth you need to let go of if you are to achieve peace of mind.

Everything in life is transient. The concept that anything should be here forever is not true. So is the idea about everything you believe you s*hould* have, that you are *entitled* to. By all means work towards all you wish to achieve, but do not fixate on this so much that you miss everything in your life *right now*. Some of the most magical and richest times of my life happened when I literally owned only the clothes I wore. Meanwhile I had friendships and experiences that were utterly priceless and I relished them. I have never once felt poor in my life, even though looking back I see at times I was, monetarily.

*I've never been poor, only broke. Being poor is a frame of mind. Being broke is only a temporary situation ~ Michael Todd, American film and theater producer, and Elizabeth Taylor's 3rd husband.*

Let go of the myths and start practicing gratitude for the magnificence of all you *do* have in your life and your life will become rich and joyous in your experience of it.

Feeling frazzled with looking after and providing for your children? Do you see your offspring as a burden? Well by all means figure out ways to feel less stressed about it, but talk to someone who has had a child die, and you will realize how all the work and stress of child rearing would vanish into insignificance for them were there any possibility that their child could be miraculously given back to them.

Dissatisfied that you don't have enough money? By all means plan and work towards a life you wish to have. But also consider that if you have a roof over your head and you are able to feed yourself and your family, exactly how much money do you need to experience comfort, happiness and contentment? Statistically if you even have a bank account with *any* money in it, you are among the top percentage of wealthiest people on the planet.

There are many, many people alive in different places in the world who would swap with you in a heartbeat and consider themselves blessed beyond belief. Don't believe me? I invite you to travel to places where people live in shanty towns made of corrugated tin and packing cases and left-over junk. The first time I saw such places in Jamaica and Morocco it changed my perspective of wealth. Just as I had another change in perspective of wealth at the other end of the scale, after I walked around the marina in San Tropez and saw all the incredible yachts moored there—an amazing concentration of wealth.

I am not saying that we shouldn't try to improve things in our lives, or that we should give up and just get used to deprivation or poverty. What I am saying is that we need to be able to experience internal joy in whatever situation we find ourselves by establishing and maintaining our connection to our spirit through all the methods we are discussing in this book. One of which is practicing gratitude for everyday miracles of creation in the world around us.

If however we focus completely on the physical world, and only our desires and what we are lacking, and we expect the physical world to provide us with happiness, then we are setting ourselves up for suffering.

When it comes to possessions *it is not how much you have but how you experience what you do have.* If you take everything you have for granted because you feel you are entitled to it, you are negating the joy you could be experiencing if you truly appreciated what you have. Practicing conscious gratitude will enhance your experience of all the positive aspects of your life.

Change your perception and your orientation away from an ego based outlook and you will be released from the endless craving to obtain ever more and actually be able to enjoy what you do have in peace. Otherwise, no matter how much you accumulate, you will never be satisfied or experience contentment.

Warren Buffet is one of the richest men on the planet. Yet

his orientation towards possessions is surprisingly normal judging by where he lives and his house and car. He doesn't live a life dominated by consumption of material goods and ownership of fantastic things, although he certainly could. And he clearly doesn't base his value on how much he has or the things he owns.

### Health Benefits of Gratitude

My local New Mexico news station recently carried a piece by cardiologist Dr. Barry Ramo on a study of 3 groups who were asked to keep journals for about 10 weeks: the first group on general events, the next on those things that bothered and irritated them, the last group on everything they felt grateful for. The last group who focused on gratitude experienced significant health benefits compared to the other 2 groups. He is also involved in promoting meditation for health benefits with the New Mexico Heart Institute.

It is interesting that the motivation towards spirituality and mindfulness here is because of its health benefits for the physical body, but whatever introduces someone to spirituality is worthwhile, and the fact that the Western medical profession is encouraging meditation based on verified physical benefits, brings credibility to those who might otherwise dismiss it.

Here is an important thing to realize: *if you are ungrateful or unaware of all the gifts you have been given, you are pushing those things away from you.*

*If you practice the joyful recognition and appreciation of all that is in your life, you are attracting more of the same into your life.*

**Exercise:** Here is a simple exercise in gratitude to practice regularly:

Look around you and feel gratitude for all you have

that is positive in your life. Get in the habit of practicing gratitude on a daily basis; be consciously aware of each good thing that shows up in your life. If you like what you have, be grateful for it or you are encouraging it to disappear.

Try deliberately admiring other people—noticing things you like about others—what are all their good points? The more you get in the habit of freely appreciating the positive aspects of others, instead of focusing on what may irk you about them, the less you will be affected by envy, and the more you will feel enjoyment in their company, the more love you will feel for others. They will appreciate it, but who will benefit most from this practice will be you.

List all the good things you have and have had in your life since you can remember, if necessary write them down. Reflect on feeling grateful that these things, conditions or people who are or were in your life. This can be a transformative and very moving experience, as you begin to see just how blessed you have been in your life.

This is a useful thing to do when you are feeling hopeless or depressed or feel that you will never achieve something.

This reflection will tend to bring you into the present moment to experience the joy of your existence and out of fixation on the future or the past and what you may think you need to be happy.

Imagine all the good things in your life being taken away and how you would feel. Now realize that all those things are still with you, and experience your gratitude for them.

Say a prayer of gratitude and appreciation for all the positive people and things, talents, successes and blessings in your life, for everything that brings you joy in life. Feel this resonate within you, this is a good thing to do at the beginning of each day.

Gratitude is a form of love. Resonating with gratitude, love and joy for every good thing in your life and thanking the universe, or God for those things, will tend to attract more of the same into your life. So make this a part of your regular spiritual practice. Cultivate an attitude of gratitude!

# 7th Habit of Transformation: Non-Judgment, Tolerance, and Love

## The Definition of Judgment—Tolerance—The Relationship to Love

*Love is the absence of judgment. ~ Dalai Lama XIV*

*My religion is kindness. ~ Dalai Lama*

Let us first define what we mean by the word *judgment*, because when I first encountered this concept that we "shouldn't judge" I thought it was ridiculous, because the word meant something quite different to me than the sense in which it was being used.

The dictionary gives us one meaning for judgment as: *the ability to make considered decisions or come to sensible conclusions.* Nothing wrong with that I thought.

This is *the* basic survival skill. And had not the subjects I had pursued for years of art and music demanded minute and specific judgments about color, form, composition, time, rhythm, pitch and harmony? Yes—but this was not the meaning of the word being addressed in spiritual teachings.

There is another sense in which the word is defined: *to pass judgment on: criticize or condemn someone from a position of assumed moral superiority.* This is the sense of the word that is warned against in the teachings of Jesus, Buddha and others.

So let us examine exactly why this should be such an issue for each of us:

There are 3 categories into which you can place every event in life.

Imagine it as 3 boxes marked 1) *Yours* 2) *Other People's*, and 3) *The Natural World*. As long as you categorize things correctly into these 3 boxes, and you attend to what is in *your* box and have an awareness of what is happening in the third Natural World box, you will run into a lot less problems.

The trouble starts when you categorize things incorrectly, for instance when you place what belongs in the Other People's box into your box of things with which to concern yourself.

This subject of non-judgment and tolerance largely comes down to just focusing on our own life, which is our own business—and letting others worry about their own lives—which is none of our business.

OK, what if the things others are doing impacts you or others negatively? Then you need to get involved and sort things out so that ceases and everyone can get along peacefully. But if someone else is doing no harm, but just has a different idea than you do of how to live their life—what on earth does that have to do with you?

The idea that everyone has to look, think and behave exactly as we do is clearly false. This is revealed to us if we start to travel and pay attention to other cultures, because some of them are nothing like us—they look different, have different customs, religions and sometimes quite different values.

It is the height of arrogance to believe only our culture

knows how to live and everyone else is just ignorant. It is stupid and arrogant to believe that we must enforce our way of looking at things on them. Different is not the same as wrong!

Once we grasp this, we have tolerance, respect and a foundation for peaceful co-existence.

The truth is that no one culture has a monopoly on wisdom—or stupidity. There are different wisdoms to be found almost everywhere if we are willing to look and learn.

And there is a connection between non-judgment, tolerance and our experience of love.

The greatest gift we can have is our ability to love.

The less we judge, the more we are free to love.

When we judge and categorize and evaluate, rather than simply *experience* the world around us, we turn off our enjoyment of the world like a faucet.

Each judgment we make about another person is a brick in a wall between us and our ability to love that person and life in general. Until, in the end, we have built a wall of judgment between us and everyone and everything else, with a tiny door left through which only those people and things that meet every one of our criteria of judgments can squeeze through.

The result is we cannot feel love or even approval for most people, or for most of life itself.

We have all met people like this: they are morally or otherwise superior to almost everyone and everything because they judge everything and everyone and find them lacking, and of course this is all tied into their ego as well. And of course they are rarely ever happy, or if they are it doesn't last for long before someone or something that they judge to be *wrong* upsets them. This is a very uncomfortable way to live!

But if we reverse our process of *judgments,* and replace it with *tolerance,* then we see that other people's lives are none of our business, that we are here to work on our life, and we do not assume that we know what is best for other people. What works for us may not work for them. We see that other people are just here in Life School working on their own curriculum of life experiences trying to learn their lessons.

Some are doing better than others, as is always true in school. But we wish them all well, knowing they are our spiritual brothers and sisters.

Suddenly we have broken down our wall of judgments, and we are free to love other people, and experience our spirit connection to them; we are free to love life.

I like how John Lennon expressed this: *It matters not who you love, where you love, why you love, when you love, or how you love, it only matters that you love.*

We may not love things that others do, because it may not be our personal taste, but if it passes the criteria of not hurting anyone else), and we can develop tolerance of it, then we are avoiding closing down our ability to feel love by criticizing and condemning others because they are not like us.

### What Creates Love?

If we examine what is happening—what are the mechanics at work—when we love someone or something deeply, we find these elements are always present: *We are not being critical of them. We are not condemning them. We are tolerant of them. We forgive them. We are grateful for them. We treat them with integrity. We communicate positively to them.*

And what is the result? We are able to experience strong love for them!

All of these habits just listed, when we practice them, enable us to experience deep love for others. They open our hearts and create connection with others, and suddenly we experience love.

We are actually experiencing our own natural state—which is love, because we are not violating any of the spiritual laws. When we align with the universal spiritual laws, we become our natural selves—we become love. This is the highest vibration we can inhabit.

We may justify our lack of judgment of someone or something we love by saying:

"Well of course I love this person or thing—they are wonderful!"

But what someone considers wonderful or thrilling or awful or boring is mostly a matter of personal taste, isn't it? People who marry each other may have found something wonderful about each other that others don't—but they are a perfect fit to enable each other to discover consciousness through making a life together.

You can probably find plenty of people who find the same person or thing you adore as mediocre, boring, unattractive or even obnoxious. The saying that describes this is: *Love is blind.* Or as I like to say: *One man's "cheese" is another man's filet mignon*—it all comes down to personal likes and dislikes and judgments.

So what is really going on here is that when two people love each other deeply—although it is highly unlikely that both of them are perfect in all respects—the two people have managed to appreciate the other instead of judging, condemning and being intolerant of their faults or short comings.

We can even describe a principle that accurately says: **if**

**you wish to experience love you must suspend judgment, condemnation and intolerance.**

And so practicing these is our 7th habit. This is what will enable us to start to love our friends, neighbors, and even enemies, and as a result God. This is the teaching of the enlightened ones that shows up again and again, that says we must love, and this is why.

By learning to love others, we are practicing learning to love God.

Love is the highest vibration we can achieve, and we cannot merge with God unless we can match his/ her vibration.

The path to enlightenment is the path to love. Because God is love. God suffers from no illusions, attachments, or identifications. God consciousness can accept and comprehend *all* things, all expressions of life, because every expression of life *is* God.

God accepts and comprehends each side of every dichotomy in life, but is identified with none.

If you wish to achieve enlightenment, then that is your task also. Your path is through non-judgment and tolerance and love.

And consider this—when we find someone we can love deeply in this life it is not a requirement that they are perfect—it is only important that they are perfect *for us*.

The point of relationships is not to make each other happy, despite everything the novels and movies tell us—it is to make each other *conscious*. And this may include a partner who does things that drive you nuts until you learn not to respond negatively to them. The most annoying person in our life may be our greatest teacher.

It is unlikely you are going to run into a fully enlightened being, and unless you are one yourself, would they wish to be with you? So don't fall for the myth that there is someone out there with no issues, who will not annoy you—if they had no issues it is unlikely they would still be here.

Anyway, you can't fix other people's issues for them, that is their responsibility, not yours. You are here to fix *your* issues.

As we experience more love for the world around us, we experience less fear.

As we experience more connectedness to others and the universe around us, we experience more faith that we will be OK regardless of what life is bringing to us.

As we surrender to life and experiencing whatever is coming towards us, which is beyond our control anyway, regardless of money or power, we experience more internal peace.

Remember, our life is *predetermination* meeting *free will* in an interactive universe. So align yourself with the laws of the universe, do your best, and surrender to what life is bringing you, trusting that God knows what he is doing. Because you can only control so much, beyond that you have to let go and trust that what happens to you is bringing you the life lesson that will best help you to gain consciousness.

And keep in mind this is not the same thing as being the most comfortable you can be. We usually have comfort and ease as our goal, which is not the goal of universal Consciousness for us. It wants us to wake up and become Conscious and join it. Not the same goal at all!

If we just stay a little bit conscious and still very comfortable, we will just have a really nice ride on the merry go round, but will never get off.

That is why we cannot judge life events from our human

sense of logic and desirability. What appears to us to be our biggest disaster may in fact be the best thing that could have happened to us to push us towards consciousness.

Despite all appearances sometimes, life is not unfair, random, unjust or cruel.

To increase our awareness, we can try to shift our experience of life from a purely left-brained one—which is the side that does all the logical categorization—to a more right brained one, so we can experience the beauty and energetic presence of everything around us. So we are going from our inner accountant to our inner artist. Aesthetics is a very high vibration—right next to love.

This is a very Zen-like approach to life: to practice pure experience, without automatically involving our mental compulsion to label, categorize, and compare—asking ourselves: 'Is it better than, or worse than?' "What is its name?"

This is another form of judging that gets us in trouble—the left brain accounting of what is around us, instead of the right brain's pure experiencing of it. When the left brain is allowed to run the show, life can get very dull and boring. We know where everything is and how much it costs, but we aren't having much fun.

I had first had experiences of this when I was drawing and painting full time as a student at art school. Focusing on something you are painting or drawing for weeks on end is a form of meditation if you can calm your mind down and just focus on doing that without too much obsessive thought.

I had read about this Zen approach to painting, to grasp the essence of what one was painting, and I was trying to do just this. The mantra I was told by teachers was: *Don't just see, learn to perceive.*

One day in an art studio many years ago while working on a painting, I suddenly experienced an altered state where I realized I was no longer just occupying the space of my body but I was occupying the entire studio. I felt expansive and joyful and connected to the universe around me—I felt absolutely wonderful, content, happy—and I felt love for everyone around me. I remember going home on the train that night grinning like an idiot at everyone I saw. And this blissed-out state lasted until I fell asleep that night.

I woke up the next morning squished back into the usual amount of space I occupied and feeling like I had been kicked out of heaven. I was back in the habit of thinking and judging everything instead of just experiencing everything in a state of no-mind, without realizing that was what I was doing again.

This altered state in the studio was triggered because unknowingly, I had stopped judging the subject matter I was painting—it was a life study of a girl—and I was just experiencing what I was painting without thinking or judging her. As the days went by, looking at the same thing and focusing on comprehending and rendering the forms in front of me, I had simply exhausted all my thoughts about it and come into a Zen-like state of simply being there in no-mind.

Freed of my mind and its endless judgments, I was temporarily able to have a nirvana experience of bliss. I didn't understand the mechanics of what had happened to me until much later, but this experience was so profound that it, and along with others like it, kept me on this path of comprehending what I had experienced and learning to access it.

This shows, incidentally, the spiritual benefits of creative and aesthetic pursuits—these can be another very powerful, spiritual path, although financially it can be very trying, and it is a path of great integrity. The vibration of aesthetics is very close to love, our highest vibration and our natural state.

So we have looked at two kinds of judgments: **condemning** and compulsively **categorizing** and **labeling**, that limit and confine us.

Avoiding these, and instead practicing tolerance and experiencing the world around us without compulsively labeling everything, are our 7th habit of spiritual transformation.

# 8ᵗʰ Habit of Transformation: Integrity—The Hero's Journey

Developing And Living By Your Own Ethical Code—The Dangers Of Compromise—Being Tested By Life—Overcoming Your Fears—Keeping Your Word—Your Internal Compass—Thinking Rationally—Exchange—Developing Competence

*To thine own self be true,*
*and it must follow, as the night the day,*
*thou canst not then be false to any man.*
*Polonius in Hamlet. ~ William Shakespeare*

*A man cannot be comfortable without his own approval. ~ Mark Twain*

*Be yourself, everyone else is taken. ~ Oscar Wilde*

### A) Developing And Living By Your Own Ethical Code

When I was a schoolboy I had a physical education teacher—in England they were called Games Masters—who would tell us: *"It is more important for you to play the game well, than whether you win or lose."* It was many years before I understood what he meant.

At the time I considered this to be just more useless advice from adults. But this was actually a lesson in integrity: meaning that *the precise manner in which we move through life, and the choices we make along the way, are the most important thing.*

My wife told me a wonderful story about her grandfather. It illustrates how the direction of each of our lives is shaped by our own natures and consequent choices.

He was a Londoner, who coincidentally lived a few miles from my own grandfather, although he later emigrated to America. Both our grandfathers also served in the British Army during World War One.

When my wife's grandfather was in France during the war he was marching down a road with his unit one day. He saw an injured bird by the side of the road and being a kind man, he stopped to kneel down to see if he could help the bird.

At that precise moment the line of men was sprayed with German machine gunfire. Every man in the line was killed except for her grandfather, who was missed by the fire as he knelt to examine the bird. One bullet did strike him, but his metal water can stopped it. When he died, many years later, it was from an aneurism in this same place.

His life was spared because he showed concern over an injured bird. I am grateful for that, because without this action of kindness, my wife and my children would not have been born.

When we are connected to our own hearts and act from our own sense of integrity, the impact on our own life and the lives of others can be profound, and in ways far beyond our understanding.

You have no idea of the value of your kindness and honesty to others. Or how your disregard or dishonorable actions may hurt them. You have no idea how interacting with you, and your behavior, positive or negative, may impact another's life deeply. The people who stay in your life for a while are there for a reason for both of you.

It became very clear to me that if I wished to maintain the state of peacefulness and open-heartedness that was now so precious to me, I needed to be very clear with myself about how I was going to live my life.

Because I found that the moment I stepped off the path of what I considered right living, I experienced the loss of my inner peace, my heart closed down and I lost my connection with Consciousness in the world around me.

Once you experience the joy of contacting your own spiritual consciousness, and experience the bliss of your heart flooding with love for all of creation, the loss of it and returning to the mind-based consciousness that you were in before, is a little like watching a high definition full color film and seeing it shift to fuzzy black and white.

Your consciousness, or loss of it, becomes your greatest motivation.

At this point there is no need for you to be policed or regulated into a code of moral or ethical behavior by an external source, because your own consciousness is a far more stringent judge of your own behavior and motives.

The concept of right and wrong conduct is something that we use to organize societal behavior and agreements and which we then attempt to enforce through policing and legal systems. As we have all witnessed, this is a far from perfect system but is certainly preferable to a feudal or a totalitarian system.

There have been many expressions of the truth of the relationship between right *conduct, ethical behavior* or *living with integrity,* and personal spiritual evolution.

The Ten Commandments in the Old Testament were an early attempt to establish rules by which society could function more easily and they have been very influential.

Many other teachings throughout history have talked about right conduct:

*"Whatever is disagreeable to yourself, do not do unto others."*~ Zoroastrianism: 600 BCE, from the Shast-na-shayast 13:29

The Legends of King Arthur, Camelot, Merlin, The Knights of the Round Table and the their code of chivalry: acting with integrity, courage, duty, protecting the weak and less fortunate, and of men protecting women, and the search for the Holy Grail (the chalice used by Jesus at the last supper, then used by Joseph of Arimathea to catch drops of Jesus' blood while on the cross), was hugely influential throughout the Celtic cultures of England, Scotland, Wales, Ireland and Europe.

The Arthurian legends were retold first verbally for long years, and then in written form, and more recently in plays and films, being retold over and over again.

These very powerful myths were very influential in shaping the sense of ethical values and strength of character in these regions.

*Love all, trust a few. Do wrong to none.* ~ William Shakespeare, from *All's Well That Ends Well.*

A quotation of Confucius from the Analects, translated by David Hinton, XV.24, Adept Kung asked: "Is there any one word that could guide a person throughout life?" The Master replied: "How about 'shu.'(meaning reciprocity) *Never impose on others what you would not choose for yourself.*"

In other words, **treat others as you wish to be treated**. Within this simple concept are included all the other rules and commandments of right conduct.

**The only test of the rightness of your course of action in the final analysis is whether it leads to an increase, or decrease, in your consciousness, and whether it causes harm to others.**

There is a reason for this that is beyond mere ethics or attempts to assert moralistic restraints on others: it is beyond all these man made judgments and opinions. It is about a law of the universe, because all energy that you put out into the universe, whether thought, belief, emotion, intention, desire or action, returns to you like a boomerang.

**You experience in the future all that you create in the present moment.**

And this is why it is essential that you start to only create that which is positive, in all things.

This is the route to ending negative karma, suffering, and escaping endless reincarnations. This is the principle behind the subject of ethics.

This is the route to enlightenment. This is the practice of integrity in your life.

So we see how important it is that *you* decide upon your own, *personal* code of ethics, and follow that as you make your way through life. So your actions are coming from inside of you, not being imposed from outside of you by another.

You need to be very clear about how you should behave, *before* you are thrust into future situations that will test you, otherwise you may commit acts with dire consequences which may take you years to resolve.

The young man who loses his temper and kills another in a moment of rage has put his life on a very hard path. The soldier who does things in war that he later cannot later ethically encompass has also put himself on a hard path to resolve.

If we wish to progress on our spiritual journey we each need to define what *we* consider to be right conduct, and we need to start living by our own code.

This code is constructed with our intellect, ratified by our heart and implemented by our will. We will then be operating with those three centers of mind, will and heart in accord (Chakras 4, 5 & 6).

Right or wrong action as it applies *to you* then becomes not a legal definition or a societal decision. It is not a subject to be decided by debate or moral jury, by religious or cultural tradition. It becomes based simply on these simple criteria:

*Does it hurt another?*

*Does it result in greater awareness and consciousness or less?*

We are thus moving away from the concept of punishment and reward from an outside source to keep us on the straight and narrow, which has been the stock in trade of religion and social organization and control. This is a parent and child relationship where government in this life, or God in the afterlife, will punish or reward us for following the rules.

Living a life of deliberate personal integrity becomes something that the individual is taking control of and responsibility for, and it may or may not agree with society's current idea or what is right or 'normal' or various people's interpretation of religious scripts.

### B) The Dangers of Compromise

A nurse, who cared for many dying patients in the last 3 to 12 weeks of their lives, described her conversations with the people in her care. The number one regret that people expressed was this: *"I wish I'd had the courage to live a life true to myself, not the life others expected of me."* They were describing regret over a lack of personal integrity and authenticity throughout their lives.

Some examples of individuals who followed their own integrity and refused to compromise include: Gandhi's peaceful protest of British occupation of India; those Germans who denounced and resisted the rise of Fascism in the thirties, and all those who fought against the Nazis during the succeeding Second World War; those who defied laws on segregation in America during the struggle for legal racial equality for African Americans; the Americans who refused the law of taxation without representation in the American War of Independence; those Americans who opposed slavery; those who refused to bend to pressure during the communist witch hunt of the Hollywood entertainment community during the forties and fifties by the House Committee On Un-American Activities; America's Equal Rights movement during the 1960's lead by Dr. Martin Luther King; Nelson Mandela's refusal to accept the laws regarding racial segregation and inequality in South Africa; and let's not forget that well known activist and social reformist, Jesus Christ.

These are all people who paid a heavy price for their ethical convictions, many with their lives. They changed the world with their actions and social evolution occurred because of them and people like them. Their consciousness was in advance of the majority, but the majority eventually adopted some of their concepts and they became society's heroes.

I have observed that in a state of extreme open-heartedness the following are *natural* behaviors and states of being:

Kindness, patience, respect, consideration, fairness, love, compassion, forgiveness, gratitude, joyfulness, humor, aesthetics, honesty, courage, enthusiasm, energy, responsibility, generosity, integrity, and doing whatever we do to the best of our ability, and for a positive outcome for all concerned.

To these we could add being accurately informed about our life, although this is an aspect of mind, not spirit. Accurate knowledge helps us to dispel superstitions, false beliefs and ignorant behavior that can lead us to do destructive things against our intentions, and thus compromise our integrity.

Therefore consciously practicing these behaviors in our daily lives is in harmony with raising the level of our vibration and consciousness.

There is a Sanskrit word for right action—it is called *dharma*. Dharma means doing the right action for that moment, place, and time, that doesn't lower our consciousness.

It would follow that avoiding their opposite—adharmic behaviors, would also assist us in this aim.

They would be: Anger, hatred, impatience, arrogance, rudeness, manipulation, dishonesty, selfishness, inconsiderateness, crassness, laziness, irresponsibility, cowardice, deception, cynicism, rigidity, meanness, jealousy and ignorance.

### C) *Being Tested By Life*

Part of your spiritual journey will be temptations to abandon your own code of ethics. The question will be— how serious are you about your resolve to achieve and live in truth? What is your temptation? Is it money? Power? Sex? Comfort and security? Success? Fame? Beauty? How much pressure will life have to exert on you to get you to compromise?

At the point that you sell out, abandon your dreams,

abandon your aspirations, betray your friends, or compromise to get something you want, is the point you have failed life's test. If you are to get past it, you will have to regroup and try again, because the test will be coming around again and again until you pass it. This is how the school of life works: We are given the same life lesson over and over again until we learn it.

This is the meaning of the story of Jesus being tempted in the desert—the lesson is that to be enlightened your personal integrity must be able to withstand any temptation.

There are few consequences that can be imposed on you from external sources that are as difficult to endure as self-condemnation. At the end of life you may have to consider... at what cost was my wish to win? And how much is a win worth if it costs you your own integrity?

*For what is a man profited, if he shall gain the whole world, and lose his own soul?* Matthew 16: 26.

Your test will occur when circumstances or authority bring pressure to bear on you to compromise your integrity. Your strength will be forged by surviving these life tests with your integrity intact, despite the apparent cost.

One confusion in our life comes about when others have done or intend harm to us: how do we respond in a way that protects ourselves and those who are dependent on us, but without violating our own code of ethics? As I am writing this, the media is filled with the topic of the United States using torture on suspected terrorists to obtain information.

This is the age-old conundrum: how does one respond to aggression and evil in a way that does not compromise one's own integrity and sense of ethics? Because in violating it in the name of achieving the greater good, one finds oneself on the slippery slope of becoming that very thing which was abhorred and opposed in the first place.

For many, the answer lies in a simplistic loyalty to a nation or tribal institution—

"My country, my team, right or wrong."

However, once you have taken the step into your own awakened consciousness you can no longer play the child and let others make your decisions for you. You must make your own decisions, and life can be a very dangerous place ethically when you live it without having clearly defined for yourself what you are, and are not, willing to do. For then you can commit acts in the heat of the moment, or by trusting in others to make your decisions that, later on, you have a hard time living with.

"I was just following orders" was not an accepted defense at the Nuremburg Nazi trials, and it will not be an acceptable defense for our own conscience when the dust has settled on our own actions.

We need to live a human existence in order to learn our spiritual lessons. And there have always been unconscious forces around who would hurt or enslave others, who would seek to destroy the wisdoms that are the only beacons of light to help us evolve out of suffering. An example of this was the rise of the Nazis before WW2 .

It was one of the darkest chapters of human history that sought to extinguish the lights of the world.

And so it is clear from one perspective, that we must defend ourselves when needs be against those who would enslave us, who would kill us or our loved ones. If we are not alive we cannot learn the lessons we need to.

There have been past organizations of defense with strong spiritual convictions, such as the Knights Templar involved with the Crusades, protection of Christian pilgrims and charity; and the Shaolin monks in China in the 5th century who combined a study of martial arts with Buddhism.

But this approach must always be done carefully with the minimum of violence and without giving into hatred or other negative emotions and it must include forgiveness if defense is not to result in unconsciousness.

As with everything, the decision of what is right conduct lies with the individual. Some people choose complete non-violence, non-defense and pacifism. Others find that to fail to defend others from harm, when it is within their power to do so, to be unconscionable and without honor.

For example, in a situation where we could shoot one individual who is about to kill one hundred people, many would say that to fail to do this is cowardly and would cause much greater harm to others.

Some could say that Jesus' casting out of the money-lenders from the Temple was a violent act. Others would say it was right on target given recent world events. Others would point to Jesus knowing he was about to be arrested and crucified and doing nothing to prevent it.

We all have individual paths. That is why integrity must be the choice of the individual.

### D) Overcoming Your Fears

You cannot ever allow yourself to live a life motivated by fear. This would compromise your integrity. If you will compromise your integrity because of fear, just as with addiction, your will is never fully intact.

What you seek to avoid out of fear will be attracted to you by your own energetic field. When you *cease* to fear it you will no longer attract it as it will be of no consequence to you. You must face your fears in life until they can no longer compromise your integrity.

At a certain point one's integrity becomes more important than one's life.

This is a crucial test for the heroes and heroines of many mythic stories for good reason. The conquest of fear by the courage of one's conviction and integrity is a baptism of fire.

The character of Evey Hammond passes this test in the story *V For Vendetta*.

One of my boyhood heroes was Wing Commander Yeo Thomas, a courageous British spy in Germany during World War 2, who was finally captured but survived Nazi torture with his integrity intact.

This is the spiritual warrior's path, walking towards possible death and destruction because it is the course of action that you have decided is the right thing to do. It is the willingness to choose an ideal over one's life, or the willingness to live your life entirely on your own terms, regardless of the consequences.

Because this is the achieving of the death of your fears. When fears have no authority over you, you are free. You cannot be intimidated, you cannot be controlled.

And that is your criteria: that you are not motivated by fear, you are not caving into fear. You are no longer identified with false concepts that you can be harmed, or that parts of the physical universe which were never you and never could be you, can be taken away from you. At this point you have awoken from the *Grand Illusion*.

### E) Keep your word

Do what you say you will, don't agree to anything you

cannot or don't intend to do. Honor your contracts and agreements. If you can no longer agree to something then let the other party know. Do not say anything untrue just to appease someone or gain their favor.

You will become known as someone of integrity who others wish to work with, and you will have the peace of mind that living with integrity will bring to you.

Don't be deceptive or manipulative. Any gains that you may think you can achieve through dishonesty will be short lived and will play hell with your peace of mind and spirituality. For you, spiritual seeker, honesty is the *only* policy.

But do not confuse this with indiscretion or fool-hardiness. Judge your audience's reality level before you speak. Remember Jesus' teaching:

*Cast not your pearls before swine.* Matthew 7:6.

"Practicing integrity" is not the same thing as just being an egotistical and unaccommodating show-off.

### F) Developing Your Internal Compass For Guidance

There are consequences to our actions. As we evolve in awareness we experience energetic repercussions immediately if we act in ways that are harmful to others or ourselves. I refer to this as developing our own **internal compass** to guide our actions.

This becomes our personal bio-feedback machine: does this activity fill me with love, or close down my heart? Does this fill me with energy and enthusiasm or does it fill me with exhaustion, anxiety or repulsion?

In all things we should go towards that which fills us with joy, love, peace, calm, connection, enthusiasm, energy, and avoid that which closes these things down.

If someone is firmly entrenched in a strong ego-based

unconsciousness and uses energetic means to manipulate and profit from others, the one who operates in this un-ethical way will eventually collapse and experience the consequences of their harmful actions.

The stories of the powerful black magician who is eventually overthrown by a hero who is pure of heart are archetypal accounts of this Truth. Darth Vader is one of these characters.

The chapter on *Non-Judgment* talks about attempting to cease judging and labeling that which you encounter, so that you can experience things directly and at first hand, rather than just experiencing your mental construction of life in front of you. But this does not mean you should deny your *perception* of what and who you encounter along your way. Or that you should cease to defend yourself when necessary by removing yourself from associating with people who are in an unconscious and toxic state.

Many are so thoroughly identified with a violent, fearful, mind-bound view of the world that they cannot perceive their connection to others and will gladly do them harm if they consider it advantageous. You can still acknowledge the un-awakened divine spirit within them, but do not assume that your own perception or awareness alone will make you immune to their destructiveness.

Our own minds are not always reliable judges of our own integrity. Our minds are capable of multiple shifts of perception of reality to make ourselves seem right, justified, honorable and to avoid confronting our own culpability and short comings.

The film by made by Japanese director Akira Kurosawa entitled *Rashomon* in 1950, cleverly examines this subject of how we can change our version of events to make ourselves in the right or serve our own interests.

The lesson of the film is that we all live in our own realities, and our mind can distort things to what is convenient for us. Your mind (6th chakra) can deceive you, but your heart (4th chakra) never will. When people make unethical decisions with their intellect because they were able to rationalize doing something that was convenient but that hurt others, it is their heart that gives them trouble. We may be able to manipulate our mind but not or heart—our feelings tell us what is right or wrong according to our own code of ethics.

Our gut feeling (3rd chakra) is a reliable guide to what is right when it comes to us operating in the world. If you have reasoned out the path to take in a particular situation but you still have an uneasy feeling in your gut, then your conclusion probably isn't the best one. When you can reconcile your mind with your heart, your gut will tell you have made the best of choices and this is an invaluable way to maintain your own integrity and to steer a true course.

You are trying in this process of awakening to access your intuition instead of your logical mind, your inner artist instead of your inner accountant. You are in the process of quieting down your mind, so that in the stillness you start to experience your own energetic responses to things, such as concepts or life situations, and you can notice the subtle inner energy within you.

This is the *internal compass* that tells you what is true or false, by giving you surges of energy and certainty and floods your heart with love when you hit truth, or turns off and closes your heart when you wander off the path into falsehoods. You must cultivate this knowingness within you. You must cultivate access to your own internal wisdom. This is what was used in the writing of this book.

Only your internal spiritual wisdom can comprehend spiritual matters. Your logical, rational mind cannot. It will argue, be skeptical, raise objections, think it is cleverer than, say *"yes but…"* and eventually get you absolutely nowhere.

### G) *Thinking Rationally*

It is important to educate your mind and teach it to think logically, using the scientific method and using correct language. You need all this to navigate life and be able to think clearly, so your mind is not a liability, and does not get in your way, or deceive you and so compromise your integrity.

Education in what is established fact (although this can be a changing landscape as new information and science develops) removes false belief and superstition from our minds, and so is therapeutic for our intellect, or 6th chakra.

Becoming familiar with the subjects of Logic, Semantics, Scientific method, and being aware that correlation does not equal causation, are vital to thinking rationally.

Routinely challenging all you believe to see if it is really factual, or just supposition, or superstition, and being willing to change your belief if you find it to be unsubstantiated, will bring you integrity of thought.

We need all our chakras to be aligned, including our intellect. This is a necessary step on the path.

But do not think for a moment your logical mind can think you all the way into wisdom and spiritual freedom. It cannot.

The mind will only have you wander forever in circles in the domain of the mind, meanwhile thinking: "look how clever and accomplished I am!"

The spirit resides outside of the mind, where the mind cannot go. And we reach it through *life experience*.

Behaving in a way that causes harm to others, always causes harm to ourselves. The very unconscious person may be able to function while causing harm to others for quite a while, until the day that a shift in consciousness brings the sudden realization of the full import of their actions. At that point a strong man will be brought to his knees in anguish from the recognition of the harm he has caused.

Another version of this occurs when an honorable man follows a course of action he believes to be right, but events transpire to cause harm he never intended. Then he is stuck with the enormous weight of the guilt of the harm he has caused. This is sometimes the plight of the soldier who goes to war, following orders.

The solution is always self-forgiveness, and this may only be achieved after one has made considerable amends to others. A whole life may become dedicated to helping those similar to those one has harmed. And there will come about a strengthening of one's personal integrity, such that we never again allow ourselves to follow another's instructions where it may cause others unintended harm. Sometimes ex-soldiers are the greatest proponents of peace. The experience of war has taught them the lesson of connection to other human beings, and the sanctity of all human life.

We are trying in our lives as we become conscious to align all our chakras, so that we are doing what we *think* is right, and what we also *feel* is right, on all levels. When *all* our chakras are in agreement in our lives, we are living with *full* integrity.

### H) The Law of Exchange

Exchange could be defined as *giving back the same value as we receive*. It is important that we exchange with those who give to us and it is equally important that we return equal value. Think of this in terms of energy that is moving back and forth; if one side is always giving more than it is receiving eventually the energy flow becomes blocked; the system becomes unbalanced and will collapse.

At the basis of much wrong action that harms someone's integrity is a violation of the Law of Exchange. This law is simply that *we must exchange equally with each other in our encounters in life.* In terms of one's parents and some others there may sometimes be no way we can equally repay them; in that case we pay it forward to our own children or others in life.

**Criminality is, at its root, an unwillingness or inability to exchange.**

Criminality is not therefore a problem of just ethics, but more basically it is a problem created by energy exchange.

If I steal food from you, I am taking something from you without exchanging. The appropriate exchange would be money or work equal to the value of the food. And this should be based on agreement that you are willing to part with this food and don't need it to feed yourself. But if I have no skills with which to work or make money, I may be willing to exchange but unable to do so. But I still need to eat, so I may steal your food.

Or I may be unwilling to exchange and have the mistaken idea that I am entitled to take from others without needing to exchange, through some false logic of convenient entitlement that I will work hard to keep in place.

Same action—quite a different motive. In either case the law of the land of course takes the view that a crime has occurred. Although, at least in Western countries, we no longer hang people or, as in the past, ship them off to Australia or chop off their hand as punishment for stealing food—even if they were starving at the time.

In the case of *unwillingness* to exchange, the criminal always has a strong mental mechanism held in place to justify why it is ok to steal. As an example, I read an account of how Bernie Madoff, currently the biggest financial swindler in history, had told someone in prison that those from whom he stole billions: "Deserved what happened because they were greedy."

So apparently in his mind, if this quote is indeed true—he apparently believes he is morally justified and off the hook for stealing billions of dollars, as long as he keeps this piece of false logic in place.

The logic of the employee who steals from or short changes his or her employer, becomes that the company makes too much profit and they get paid too little, so they deserve whatever perks they can rip off. Of course at the point in time when they were out of a job and agreed to their current situation and exchange rate, it was a different story.

In group situations the same thing applies: For example those who profited from slavery had to nullify the worth of those whom they enslaved. The basis of racism between groups of people who had an oppressed and oppressor history is this same principle: "I have to make less of your worth if I have oppressed you or else I will have to confront my own misdeeds, or those of my ancestors and change, and desist from my criminal behavior, and make reparations."

It is much easier to adopt racist viewpoints that blacks or Indians or Jews or whatever group had been oppressed, are primitive or inferior. Therefore what was done to them "was not really morally reprehensible."

See how that false logic protects a person's sense of self-worth? And so we see racism continue to persist in parts of the world to justify history—it is easier than confronting: "I guess great-grandpappy was actually a selfish, racist, heartless man."

The Catholic Church got over the problem of guilt over enslaving the South American Indians by saying they didn't have souls!

All this "logic" of denying worth to others is of course complete nonsense, so it will never lead to anything workable for either side. For anyone who finds that he has generalized group attitudes or beliefs about other races or groups of people that are not based on very specific, verifiable information and fact, it is time to awaken and confront the lies and let go of them.

Remember, there is no such thing as a generality that defines all members of a group, so approach each new person with an open heart, even if you always also have a ready sword-arm in self-protection.

Remember also that you are not here to judge others and so close your own heart—you are here to learn your own spiritual lessons.

In any relationship there is exchange and the things being exchanged may be quite different, but each is of value to the other and at some point there is an understanding or agreement reached between both sides as to what each side expects and feels is fair to receive from the other.

However, when one of the sides in this agreement starts a pattern of providing the other with *less* than has been agreed upon or that each feels is fair, then the relationship is impacted negatively.

Moreover, the one who is giving *less* than the other will

start to view the relationship negatively. They will start to devalue the other and their contribution, and what they saw before as desirable and were satisfied with, now becomes viewed in a critical light.

Note that this isn't usually on the part of the one who is doing the most work, initially that is. Though it seems illogical, the dissatisfaction often starts with the one who is contributing the *least*.

This is because at some level the slacker side of the partnership knows that it is wrong action and brings some insidious mental gymnastics into play to justify the imbalance.

If the one doing the greater contribution becomes downgraded mentally by the slacker, then it makes things ok for them to continue to slack off!

In a relationship this attitude causes the core trust, camaraderie and love to begin to break down. As the slacker starts to vocalize their criticism and devaluation, the other person, (who is really contributing more) becomes hurt and resentful that all their contribution and hard work is not appreciated.

Therefore the convenient "logic" of the man or woman who is getting a free ride from their partner is that it was OK because the other person was a loser, a nag, a bitch or bastard and so of course they deserved whatever bad things were done to them.

This mechanism occurs in work and emotional relationships. They might not lead to divorce or break up or quitting a job, but like the slow oxidization of once perfect chrome work on an old car, it takes the shine off the relationship. People wonder how they went from being madly in love with someone to experiencing a low level of resentment in a relationship that is no longer any fun. Every time someone did less than they felt they should have to have helped the relationship, they are chipping away at the affection they previously felt.

We must first make sure our own house is completely in order before complaining to the other person or side of a relationship. If we are doing all we agreed to and feel we should do in any relationship and still feel it isn't working, then at least we have an honest place from which to negotiate.

So anyone who wishes to stay in any relationship must honor that relationship and maintain his or her exchange with it and do nothing to harm it. Not so that they won't be left, but rather that they won't be the one doing the leaving.

So if you want to enjoy relationships and have them flourish, contribute to them, take care of them and do the best you can in all things, so that you don't sabotage them because of your guilt over lack of exchange.

The book *Leadership And Self Deception* by the *Arbinger Institute*, examines in detail the phenomenon of failure to exchange in business and personal relationships, along with the resulting negative impacts on the one who is failing to contribute what they have previously agreed to, and the solutions to this situation. It is recommended reading to anyone wanting to investigate this more.

### I) Altering Sequences

If consequences ensue from our failure to exchange then we may possibly take this as a justification—and mentally alter the sequence of events in our favor, and place the cart before the horse. For instance if someone steals from your place of business and gets caught and fired—the firing can become the reason why it was ok to steal in the first place: "Those bastards deserved it! See what they did to me!"

If someone received a reprisal after doing some destructive action, they may put the reprisal *earlier* in time than their destructive action in their version of things, so their victim *deserved* what they did to them. It is an adult version of the *"he hit me first"* defense of the schoolyard bully.

The amount of mental gymnastics required to keep all this in place is considerable—and anyone who thinks they can maintain such a mind warp of "logic" in place, and still gain inner peace and experience the joy of connectedness with the world, is sadly mistaken.

## J ) Developing Competence

*"The most important thing I have learned over the years is the difference between taking one's work seriously and taking one's self seriously. The first is imperative, and the second disastrous."* ~ Margot Fonteyn, ballet dancer.

It is important that you decide what you like to do in life and then work to obtain training in those areas and practice them so that you develop *great* competence and excellence at them.

**Competence is integrity in action**.

By mastering competence you will be able to exchange with others in ways that bring you joy and pride in the value of what you can give others, and you will be able to receive appreciation from others for your valued gifts to them.

The excellence of your work in whatever field you choose will give you stability, self-respect, and more power to live as you wish because society will be willing to exchange with you for your valuable services.

Tend to your skills regularly and update them because technology is constantly changing and can make entire job skills out of date very quickly. You may have to learn several quite different skills to be employed and earn a living in a lifetime due to developing technology. But the disciplines you develop in one area will transfer to learning new skills in another.

Competence allows integrity to be expressed through one's actions.

Competence and responsibility walk hand in hand.

Just as do incompetence and irresponsibility, and ignorance and arrogance.

When you become competent, your good intentions are not betrayed by your lack of skill or knowledge.

As a parent, one of your duties is to enable your children to attain competence at a life skill of their choosing. This will be the basis for their success in life. What they do with that competence, positive or negative, is their responsibility, but you will have discharged one of your responsibilities to them in so doing.

Great musicians, artists and artisans exhibit enormous integrity in their work: they devote a lifetime to developing and improving their skill. And what you see or hear is their contribution to the world with everything available for examination.

Not all of them are able to apply the same degree integrity to other parts of their lives but we are instinctively drawn to and admire the integrity of their art.

And many people cannot profess anywhere near the level of integrity of the artist in their own line of work.

## K) Nature as Example

We only have to look at Nature for a guide as to what living with integrity really means. An apple tree that is given enough water and is kept free of disease will grow to be a perfect tree, which produces perfect apples. *Each* apple is perfect. The tree never tries to get by with substandard or shoddy apples that merely look good on the outside but contain inedible fruit inside. An apple tree has complete integrity and is completely trust worthy to be the best apple tree it can, as long as it is alive. That is simply what it does.

Similarly a rose bush produces perfect roses. Some may even seem to be more perfect than others, but as long as it has the right soil and enough water and it doesn't get mildew or become overrun with aphids or other destructive insects, a rose bush produces exquisite blooms time after time until it dies. It lives in complete harmony with the natural world around it and the bees, insects and hummingbirds that collect its nectar and distribute its pollen.

Animals also follow survival tactics according to their species. They play by their species' rules with integrity. The leader of a herd of horses doesn't suddenly decide to act insanely to betray its own kind and stampede them off a cliff to destroy the herd.

*A horse is a horse, of course, of course.*

Man seems to be the only creature who sometimes lives without integrity, who betrays his own species, and who then wonders why he suffers as a result.

And this is due to having a mind that is capable of incredible feats of abstract thought and creativity, and which can also lose its integrity by becoming riddled with false beliefs and hypnotizing its owner into performing acts of unconsciousness and cruelty based on fear.

The evolution of humankind is therefore about *our ability to use a human mind but still remain conscious and live with integrity.*

### L) *Your Integrity Is Between You And God*

This last quote always moves me when I read it, it speaks to the subject of personal integrity so profoundly:

*People are often unreasonable, illogical and self-centered. Forgive them, anyway. If you are kind, people may accuse you of selfish ulterior motives. Be kind, anyway. If you are successful, you will win some false friends and some true enemies. Succeed, anyway.*

*If you are honest and frank, people may cheat you. Be honest, anyway. What you spend years building someone could destroy it overnight. Build, anyway. If you find serenity and happiness, they may be jealous. Do good, anyway. Give the world the best you have, and it may never be enough. Give the world the best you have, anyway. You see, in the final analysis, it is between you and God. It was never between you and them, anyway.* ~ Mother Teresa

***Exercise:*** Compile your own code of right conduct. Write it down in a journal or notebook. Update it as life teaches you lessons of things you should not have done and of more elegant ways to have handled situations. Then live your life according to your own code. If you stray from it, forgive yourself, make note of what led you off your path so that you can avoid it in future. Make amends to others if you caused harm. Then resume living your life with integrity on your own terms.

# 9th Habit of Transformation: Practicing Positive Communication

Speaking Truth and Love—The Power of True Listening—Successful Communication Principles

*The words of the tongue should have three gatekeepers: Is it true? Is it kind? Is it necessary? ~ Arabic proverb*

It is important that like everything else, our communication remains positive. We should only say that which is true, kind and helpful.

Let your communication be an extension of your spirit: treat your communications to others with the respect that they deserve, because your words can have a powerful impact on others to empower them, or to injure them, and can last a lifetime in some cases.

Use the power of your communication in a positive way to communicate truth and love and empowerment to others.

Think back to when you were small and remember a time when someone praised you or recognized your actions or abilities and how that made you feel or affected your estimation of your abilities and the effort you subsequently made in a particular direction.

When I was about nine I had a teacher who got very excited about something I had drawn in art class. It was a crayon drawing of a monkey wearing a red suit and hat. He made a simple paper frame for it, stuck it on the wall where it remained for a few weeks and told everyone in the class to study it.

He said the most important words anyone had said to me up to that date: *"Look at Christopher's drawing—this is the sort of work you should all be doing."* I don't know how that affected everyone else, but for me at that moment, I decided I was an artist, and that was the beginning of a career for me as a graphic artist, illustrator and painter.

Now recall a time someone called you stupid or told you that you were no good. Perhaps you still believe you cannot do math, or play sports or that you are ugly or stupid, or that you cannot draw or play an instrument. As children we are particularly vulnerable to these kinds of pronouncements because we give weight to the words of those who we believe know much more than us—and to a child that is most adults.

Speak truth, speak kindness, speak love, speak encouragement, speak respect and you will be listened to and respected in return.

Do what you have said you will do, so that your words are not empty.

Let your word be your bond. You will become known as someone who can be depended upon when you speak.

Then your voice will be a force for good in the world and you will become trusted and respected by others.

Tell people that you appreciate what they have done for you, when this is true.

Thank everyone for what they do for you. Realize that everyone is a human being who is just as important as you regardless of their job or station in life—don't reduce anyone to a faceless robot or servant. Give everyone you meet your respect.

You have no idea how much your kind words of appreciation, encouragement or affection can impact and empower another person.

Tell the people you love that you love them. You do not know when you will get another chance to tell them this. Never assume you will have more time with someone to say what is important and heartfelt.

*"Sticks and stones will break my bones but words will never hurt me"* ~ *English saying.*

Do you remember that schoolyard chant? It is actually sometimes far from the truth. Negative words from another can do great harm—but as with all things—*only if you let them in and believe them.*

It is your own belief that gives negative words their power over you. You have let them into your system and given them strength and reality. Until you do that, they have no power over you.

But if you do let them in and they become a negative belief in your conscious or unconscious mind, then they become Law for you and have power over what you create in your life.

For example, if you were told often when you were a child that you were stupid, or that you were no good, or that you would never amount to anything, and you started to believe it, then that can have had a big negative influence on what you could achieve in your life.

On the other side, if you were raised by very positive parents who told you that you would succeed in life and this became a strong part of your belief system, then it is more likely that you would achieve success.

The childhood playground chant was an attempt to keep the cruelty of another's words from entering into our consciousness and causing harm. A way of saying to ourselves: *I do not accept your words or their harmful intent.*

This intent to not let negatives into our belief system, but to reject them, is a valuable lifelong practice, because if we are not centered, then we can determine our value on other's opinions, and we can let other's negative words into us to form beliefs in our subconscious that affect what we manifest in the world around us.

We need to be wary of other's negative statements, to identify them as products of other's fears and feelings of inadequacy, and not accept them as real in our universe. We need to locate the one's we have already let in that are now negative beliefs and deliberately replace them with positive beliefs through affirmations or other methods.

It is also important then that we become very aware of what we say and how we say it, because our words can have power over others, and we do not want to create negative effects on them just because of our own frustrations or fears. We need to be aware of that power with respect to children and juniors at work and others that we are in a position to influence so that when we speak we are responsible and accurate.

Our positive and wise words can have a great empowering and motivating effect on others. I can still remember the kind and encouraging words of certain teachers who were in my life. The encouragements of some altered the course of my life. Two of my art teachers encouraged me and as a result *I began to think of myself as an artist.* I believed from that point on that I could be successful in that area.

That gave me the courage to apply to art school and later

have a career as a graphic artist and exhibit as a painter in galleries.

Another of my school teachers became the catalyst for my lifelong spiritual search which resulted in this book through his wise words.

I can also remember answering back with a great deal of anger and hurt to other teachers and adults who sought to belittle me when I was young, and the heavy impact that someone who I looked up to as having experience and knowledge had on me as a child. I can remember how much their harsh words burned at the time.

Always observe the rule not to gossip. What has been told to you in confidence should stay a confidence and never used for entertainment value.

Our culture tends to be very flippant about phrases that are actually very strong in meaning. For example, if we disagree with someone we might say: *they are crazy, he is delusional, you are out of your mind,* and so on.

In fairly recent history a statement like that made by someone in authority might have been enough to condemn someone to the hell of an insane asylum. You do not know the history of the person to whom you may be speaking. Your words may have a far greater impact than you intended.

If you were raised in an environment where verbal violence was common-place and you have a habit of using similar speech patterns, this is something you need to consciously disassemble.

There is an excellent book: *Nonviolent Communication, A Language of Compassion,* by Marshall B. Rosenburg Phd. that I recommend reading and applying to help achieve this. It is very helpful in repairing relationships by taking all the negativism from the communication. Otherwise bad communication habits can create an environment that is very corrosive to love and trust and feeling nurtured.

In his wonderful book *The Four Agreements,* Don Miguel Ruiz talks of being "Impeccable With Your Word." This is about the importance of cultivating integrity in what you say, saying nothing you do not mean, not speaking against others or yourself, and not gossiping against others. Using the power of your word in the direction of truth and love.

The two most important things I have learned about communication are these:

**1) We should only ever use our words for forwarding truth, compassion and love**. If we have internal negativism, do not allow our frustrations to vent on others and cause them harm by saying destructive things. We should remove the reactive, negative phrases we say to others in moments of frustration from our language completely. We should instead express the love, appreciation and gratitude we feel for others. Don't use your communication to put others down.

And don't use it to put yourself down either. Saying negative things like: *Oh I'm not very good at that, I'll never be able to do that, I have no talent at that, I'm fat, I'm stupid,* etc. etc. etc. is self defeating, negative, and violates your integrity.

Just because you cannot do something *now* does *not* mean you won't be able to do it or achieve it in the future, or that you were not able to do it in the past. All you need is a decision to do something, persistence, hard work and a maintained positive belief and you will be able to achieve more than you may have ever believed possible, within the physical limitations of the body you have. Don't make any false assumptions about that either.

Just because you may not be able to compete at a world level at something doesn't mean that you cannot achieve things that will be completely satisfying to you.

Life isn't about competing with others, despite all you may have been told to the contrary. It is about your experiences and the lessons you are able to learn, regardless of other people's achievements.

**2) The ability to listen to another person with attention, compassion and non- judgment, so that they feel safe enough to verbalize their inner issues, can be one of the most healing things you can do for someone.**

Listening to someone does *not* include then giving your unsolicited advice, opinions or judgments—*just listen to them.* If you are a parent and you want happy children, you must develop the skill to listen to them.

The first time someone really listens to you with their full attention, and without any judgment, or unsolicited advice, can be an amazing and healing experience.

How many times have women talked to the men in their relationships about something upsetting that just happened, and when the men started to tell them how to fix it, had to say: " I don't want advice—I just want you to listen!"

Listening also does not mean thinking about what the other person is saying in a judgmental and dismissive way while they are talking.

First, *understand* what they have to say. Understand their point of view. This is not the same thing as *agreeing* with their point of view. You have to be able to receive and understand what is being said, regardless of whether you agree with it. Listening involves non-judgmental attention and comprehension, giving them your full attention.

Even if you are only thinking negative thoughts, a sensitive person may be aware of this on some level and will not wish to talk to you.

### Successful Communication Rules

Communication is an invaluable tool in the resolution of just about every kind of problem. But like everything else there are rules to successful communication, and ignorance of these can undermine the resolution of the problem at hand.

Poor communication skills in the presence of strong negative emotion on the part of one or both of the parties can easily result in an upset or argument as the emotion acts like lightning looking for the easiest route to ground. Now, the initial problem is compounded by the new upset on top of the original one.

Learning and practicing good communication skills is essential to the health of any kind of relationship, yet it is amazing how little understood the matter is.

Simply learning how to communicate well is the basis of all strong relationships; it allows any information being discussed to receive a fair hearing on its own merits, without being dismissed because it is being communicated by someone whose poor communication skills have antagonized the recipient.

Practice respect and politeness to everyone, regardless of their social status.

Be kind, generous and gracious to others.

Be agreeable while you disagree. Don't allow your impatience or frustration to show in your face or body language and sabotage any chance of reaching an understanding with someone. You will never regret this as a practice.

And go back and apologize to people you have called names in anger and in whom you may have implanted a negative belief about themselves.

### The Vital Skill of Listening

A simple, one way communication in essence is the transference of information from one person to another, with the essential ingredient that what was intended by the one speaking was received and understood by the one listening.

A two-way communication, such as a normal conversation, reverses the roles with the listener becoming the speaker and the speaker becoming the listener. When this process switches back and forth, an exchange of information is occurring and communication is taking place.

In order for this to happen easily, be precise whenever you say something. Don't be ambiguous or unclear. Don't speak until you have made up your mind what you want to say. Some people simply verbalize their stream of thoughts and spray out random nonsense over everyone around. The result is people tend to tune them out.

While one person is talking, or sending the communication, the second person's job is to *listen*: this means actually paying full attention to what is being said in an effort to completely understand what is being said.

So many people fail to actually do this, and all kinds of problems result.

Listening is *not* the same thing as simply waiting for a gap in the conversation so that you can start talking! It does *not* mean thinking about what you are going to say next, the moment the other person stops talking. Listening also does not mean thinking about what the other person is saying in a judgmental and dismissive way while they are talking.

Listening includes *understanding* what someone has to say. Understand their point of view. This is not the same thing as *agreeing* with their point of view. You have to be able to receive and understand what is being said, regardless of whether you agree with it or not.

### 6 Easy Ways to sabotage Your Communication

In any communication, and especially if you are discussing something that has emotional upset attached to it, you need to avoid the following, or you will quickly sabotage your chances of achieving any resolution. Your communication errors will act as a lightning rod for the other person's negative emotion, which will probably be directed at you.

**1. Negative Body Language**: One researcher has suggested that in-person communication consists of: 7% actual content (ie. what is said), 38 % is tone of voice, 55% is non-verbal communication (ie. body language, gestures, appearance and so on). So you can be saying all the right things but communicating with poor body language and poor tone of voice and it may still be received negatively.

For example, rolling your eyes or looking disgusted because you disagree with what the other person is saying. Looking disinterested, bored, frustrated, looking at your hands, looking out the window or around the room, being slumped in your chair, speaking angrily, sarcastically. These kinds of gestures are by themselves clear negative communications and will sabotage any attempt at resolution of a problem because, in so doing, you have just communicated *I totally disagree with you* with body language.

Instead, be polite, speak in an even tone even if you are

angry, pay attention to the other person while they are talking, and don't make any negative gestures.

**2. Interruptions:** Interrupting someone before they have finished speaking and doing it repeatedly will either end the conversation or very often have it escalate into a shouting match and increase antagonism. You will, at the very least, offend and irritate the person to whom you are speaking by doing this.

With someone who habitually does this while you are talking to them, you can attempt to get their agreement to establish ground rules where one person speaks and the other listens and is silent until the first is finished, then the second person has their turn and the procedure is reversed.

Some people who are aware of this problem in each other agree to the Native American talking stick system. The one holding the stick talks until he is done and then hands it to the other, in continuous turns holding of the stick to clearly designate the rôles of speaker and listener

**3. Negations**: Telling someone they are flat out wrong is a good way to end a conversation or igniting a conflict. Telling someone you disagree with them or that you have a different viewpoint on a situation is less likely to inflame a right/ wrong ego confrontation and often a more accurate way of describing something. Unless you are discussing a verifiable issue of fact such as the average rainfall in southern California in 1980 or the temperature at which mercury becomes a solid, then you are in the arena of opinion and subjective reality and this should be acknowledged.

*I disagree with you* and *you are wrong* are not synonyms.

"That is inaccurate." Or "I can't agree with you on that for this reason…" is quite different from "You are wrong."

The phrase: *let us agree to disagree*—can prevent escalation to argument because you are respecting the other person's viewpoint. You are not agreeing but you are not negating it.

**4. Making Assumptions**: It is the responsibility of the listener not to make assumptions if they do not comprehend precisely what is being said. Assumptions are always potentially deadly in any situation. *Do not make assumptions about anything!*

If there is a blank in your comprehension of what was said to you, say so. Get clarification immediately. Always.

**5. Speaking in Generalities:** "*Everyone knows that… all you people do that… this always happens…. you are always doing things like this! You are just like your father…*"

These kinds of statements are upsetting because they are untruthful or impossible to verify. Life happens in specifics, not generalities. Nobody can reply to a generality, except perhaps to disagree! Talk only in specifics or there goes any chance of a resolution in a conflict and you are asking for a full-blown fight. Stay on the subject at hand—don't wander off onto other hot topics or you are asking for a fight! Instead of emotional upset being dissipated too much is stirred up and the person becomes overwhelmed by it.

**6. Poor Acknowledgements:** An acknowledgment is anything that lets the other person know you have heard them. This can be anything from a simple "OK" to a nod of the head, to a phrase like:" I get what you are saying," to a repeat-back, where the listener rephrases what has been said to them, and says something like: "Ok, if I understand you correctly you are telling me........." and paraphrases what was just said.

A repeat-back would be used during a negotiation of some kind where the communication being received is of significant importance to the one talking.

The acknowledgment simply lets the person talking know that they have been heard and understood.

If they have not been understood, then to acknowledge them as if they have been understood is a lie and the communication is destined to fail or at least come off the rails sooner or later.

Say something like: "I'm sorry, I am not following what you said there. Would you explain that to me again please."

There are 2 ways to mess up acknowledgements:

The 1st is to not acknowledge the other person at all. This leaves them uncomfortable, because there is no rapport being established. The person speaking doesn't know if the one listening is actually listening or is just lost in thought, angry, sulking, stupid, completely uncooperative, or being passive- aggressive. Children will sometimes resort to this as a response to adults when they are in strong disagreement with adults but feel powerless to say so.

So the one talking starts saying things like: *Are you with me? Does that make sense to you? Are we on the same page?* And so on to see if they are being tracked with.

They will probably go away irritated and with the desire not to communicate to with that person again if it can be avoided.

That is why in the military there is a precise drilled

response to orders given: *Sir, yes sir!* is required for the practical purpose of letting the one issuing the order know the message has been received, or at least heard.

If you are dealing with someone who is already angry with you and you fail to acknowledge them, you will quickly have a fight on your hands. The person talking wants to have their communication received and understood. When people feel they are not being listened to they can become irritated and talk louder and approach closer, eventually becoming angry and shouting, and then this can escalate to physical violence.

They are just creating bigger and bigger effects in an effort to be acknowledged. Not an effective thing to do but that is the arc that can occur with the frustration of a failed communication.

If you want to calm someone down just let them know that you have heard and understand what they have been trying to say.

Repeatedly failing to acknowledge a police officer is a good way to get arrested!

So you see that acknowledgment is a very important element in communication. You are in effect letting the person know they were heard and understood and then they are able to end that segment of that communication and move on to the next part.

The 2nd error in acknowledgment is to prematurely acknowledge before the speaker is finished. This is an interruption that makes the speaker feel that the listener is impatient and unwilling to listen and wants to shut them up. If you have ever experienced talking to someone who keeps saying things like: *Uhuh! Yeah. Yeah. Yeah! Ok, ok, ok.* you will have experienced an uncomfortable desire to stop talking to them. So don't do this to others—just wait until they are done talking and acknowledge them so they know they have been heard.

### Be Flexible In Your Point of View

A vital step to conflict resolution is being able to view a problem from the other person's point of view. You cannot successfully negotiate with someone if you are not even willing to grasp their point of view!

Remember we are not discussing how to beat down an opponent in a deal here. This is not some manual about ruthless negotiation skills designed to beat someone into a pulp verbally!

We are talking about how to listen in a positive, therapeutic and spiritual way *that benefits both parties*. This is the only kind of resolution that will last and not produce a negative slap back.

When you are listening to someone, try your best to understand what they are saying and fully grasp and *assume their point of view*. This is practicing empathy. If you are willing to see and even adopt another person's point of view in place of the one you currently have, and when the other person is also willing to do this, then there is a possibility of complete resolution of conflicts, where the two can meet somewhere in the middle.

This means you have two people who are not communicating from the stance of ego, meaning they both have to be right and " win" an argument, but who are actually looking to adopt the most productive course of action, regardless of who came up with it. This is sane and unselfish negotiation directed to the best outcome.

But when one or both of the parties is only interested in

their point of view and in enforcing this from the motivation of being right (ego), or self-interest at the expense of other people (unconsciousness), then it is unlikely that their conflict will resolve, unless a skilled negotiator is involved who can engineer a compromise where each side gives up something, but still feels they kept enough to feel that they "won" and saved face and an agreement can be reached.

It is important that you are not egoically attached to your point of view in a conflict resolution process. If your goal is to achieve the *best* solution that serves everyone, then it doesn't matter who comes up with it. People who are stuck in their ego mis-perceive every conflict as an ego battle where only *their* solution can be acceptable, but their solution may not be the best one, so they are useless negotiators. They are incapable of intellectual generosity.

In the absence of this kind of maximizing approach, the resort is to the opinion of an impartial third person whom both sides have agreed to abide by—an ombudsman or mediator, or expensive lawsuits. Failing those, violent conflicts and in the case of countries, actual war, where if I can pound you into submission I am Right and you are Wrong.

War is of course another form of business and someone is always profiting hugely from any armed conflict, such as arms manufacturers and international banks who, if they are lucky, can fund and supply both sides. These kinds of enterprises have the most invested in the continuation of armed conflict across the planet.

If two people are in a relationship such as marriage, and cannot develop this skill of adopting each other's viewpoints, being unselfishly caring of each other's desires and welfare, and able to detach from their egos by not having to always be right, then they will either have a very painful relationship or they will eventually get divorced.

So if you wish to avoid suffering in your relationships— learn to let go of your own viewpoint long enough to see the other person's.

Have you ever talked to person with an intractable religious or cult viewpoint?

They are not interested in and cannot even entertain a new point of view—they really just want to trot out their fixed viewpoint.

Once you have heard it there is little point in talking further because they know they are right and entertaining a new concept would require a flexibility of thought of which they are incapable.

The desperation with which someone clings to a concept with utter inflexibility, is in proportion to the degree that conviction is the solution to an unresolved, emotional problem. It is the dam holding back the flood. Disturb the dam and the flood would overwhelm them.

The person who has no such heavily charged emotional problem however, can afford to be flexible in their thinking and entertain different points of view.

### Don't Take Other's Negative Communication Personally

Don Miguel Ruiz makes this point with great clarity in his wonderful book, *The Four Agreements*. As we have discussed, everyone lives in their own reality, based on their beliefs, experience, culture and so on. So they communicate from this reality. If this includes negative communication to you, realize how much of this is something they would be saying to anyone who is standing there—it just happened to be you.

Certainly if you have failed to do something well, take responsibility for that and correct it as best you can and learn from that experience. But if somebody is angry and abusive to you, realize that is coming from their unconsciousness, and you aren't responsible for that, so don't take it in.

I waited my whole life for my father to tell me he loved me.

At the end of his life he implied it, and I realized that was as good as he could do. When I saw that the issue wasn't that I didn't deserve his love, but that he had a big problem expressing it, or ceasing being judgmental long enough to feel it, I stopped taking it personally and so it stopped being a problem.

We see here how communication is inseparable from consciousness. And how conscious communication becomes a force for illumination in the world.

# 10th Habit of Transformation: Helping Others

## In Selflessly Helping Others We Also Help Ourselves

*I don't know what your destiny will be, but one thing I do know: the only ones among you who will be really happy are those who have sought and found how to serve. ~ Albert Schweitzer, German Philosopher and Physician,*

When we help others we create a bond with them, because we have invested our own effort in their survival. This builds a bridge that love can move across. This helps them and it also helps us.

Most of this book is focused on us, but again paradoxically, we are helped when we *selflessly* help others, not motivated by personal profit, and no ego boosting thoughts of how good or holy we are being.

It is OK if others exchange with us for our help—we all have bills to pay—but profit must not be our primary interest for helping others in this transformative habit.

Helping others also helps to balance our exchange with the help we have received from others, and helps balance our karma for the harm we have done others. So this needs to be part of our habit of love, made practical.

And so we must attach no expectations to our helping

others—that they should see things our way or change. We help, expecting nothing in return, demanding no result—just accepting life as it happens. Remembering our job is to focus on our own journey, not to enforce our beliefs or values on others.

Helping others helps us not be self-centered and narcissistic as we focus on our own evolution.

I once saw someone complaining bitterly about how betrayed she felt by a friend. These were two very wealthy women and the first had introduced the second to a jeweler. The second woman had then purchased a piece of jewelry similar to the first woman's, only more expensive, and worn it to an event that they both attended. The first woman felt so undermined by being outdone in this way that she was still upset days later.

We are talking about serious jewelry with the value of an expensive car, and someone with a great deal of wealth and comfort who had originally come from very modest circumstances. Yet all this affluence was not enough to prevent her from being upset by a friend owning something that was even nicer than hers.

This was suffering induced by ego and identification with an object, resulting in losing touch with reality. One of the best things this lady could have done to feel better about the situation would be to have volunteered at a soup kitchen or something similar, to help those who were homeless, and thus receive a reality check, and then realize her great good fortune, and become grateful for it instead of being consumed by insecurity and jealousy.

This is an example of when this teaching applies: *It is easier for a camel to go through the eye of a needle, than for a rich man to enter into the kingdom of God* ~ Matthew 19:24 KJV.

There is nothing wrong with affluence, but when we let it lower our consciousness through ego aggrandizement of how important, superior, and entitled we are, we are using it to our disadvantage. This was someone who worked out, ate the right things, looked after her family, but was being made unconscious by her possessions.

The concept of *noblesse oblige,* that the wealthy and privileged have a responsibly to help those less fortunate, goes back to Homer's Iliad, and this concept has been echoed by other prominent authors. The Christian tradition includes *service* to others.

I noticed I loved my dog more when I had taken him for a walk. I loved my children more when I had just helped them in some way. I liked my house more when I had cleaned it up or decorated it. I found myself loving or being more connected to people I was able to help.

Not that you have to continually support someone who won't take the responsibility to help themselves. Then help turns into a disservice.

We are all connected to each other, to all spirit.

What you do to one, you do to all.

*If you want to feel better within yourself—go and help someone else.*

But do it without getting involved in your ego by feeling superior or special because of what you did. The do-gooder who works away helping others, feeling satisfied with themselves for their good works, but judging everyone they help as being inferior to themselves, is sabotaging themselves spiritually.

However you do it, include your help to others as one of your routine habits of transformation.

# 11th Habit of Transformation: Empowering Ourselves—Not Blaming Others

The Empowerment Of Taking Responsibility— Ceasing To Blame Others—Karma—Attraction And Manifestation

*We can only be what we give ourselves power to be.~ Native American proverb*

**We exist in an interactive universe**. Whatever we believe— consciously or unconsciously, and whatever we think, feel, intend and do, all speak to the universe to say: *bring me this!* And the universe responds to what is in our hearts—our deepest loves and our deepest fears.

It is *always* our **free choice,** however, whether what we are asking for is **negative** or **positive**.

**Positive attracts positive. Negative attracts negative.**

**You have free will to choose which energy you wish to create.**

And it is *this choice*—negative or positive—that makes every bit of difference to our life experience, our evolution, our consciousness.

Every habit in this book is another aspect of turning how we internally think, believe and function in life from *negative to positive;* undoing negative habits and instead replacing them with deliberately created positive habits.

These are the keys to release us from the prison of suffering. This is our path to enlightenment.

And so **our internal past has created our external present**. And **our internal present will create our external future.**

This is one of the greatest realizations about the underlying functioning principles of the universe that we could have.

This is the basis of the teaching called *Karma,* which comes to us from Hinduism and then Buddhism. In modern language it is expressed as the phrase: *what goes around, comes around*

This is also the basis of what is referred to as *The Law of Attraction and Manifestation,* which we will shortly look at in more detail.

But first we must examine the mechanism of another of our great stumbling blocks which we must dispense with in our life:

### Ceasing To Blame Others

Blaming others for what is wrong in our life will stand in our way to attracting and manifesting the life that we want to have.

You may respond: "What? But other people have caused all kinds of problems that affect me negatively that I had nothing to do with. That makes no sense!"

Here is what you have to consider to change your thinking and empower yourself: When we *blame* other people and forces outside our self for what is wrong in our life *we take away our own power.* We are saying in fact: "I didn't cause my life, I am the powerless victim of another force that is greater than me, and I can do nothing about this." You are casting yourself to play the helpless victim of another's power every time you blame others for your situation.

And guess what the effect of that belief will be? The universe will oblige your request by reducing your power. Remember that everything turns on our choices, intentions, and where we choose to direct our energies.

The path back to our empowerment lies with taking responsibility. The moment we own our decisions and their consequences, we start to take back our power. The more we can assume responsibility for our lives, the less we blame others for our situation, the more we assume power and control over our lives.

Those who have been blamed and shamed a lot may view taking responsibility as threatening—nevertheless, they must reframe the subject of responsibility and lose its negative connotations and assume responsibility.

If all this seems far fetched, look at it this way: we have each been dealt a hand in life—the best we can do for ourselves is to accept it, stop complaining and playing the role of victim—and do the best we can with what we have to work with. Do you have a better approach to life?

As we start to grasp the reality that we are now experiencing our own past causations in life, or the lessons we now need to experience to increase our consciousness (which is more or less the same thing), we begin to stop blaming others for what is wrong in our life.

We stop moaning and complaining about others, we cease feeling hard done by if we don't have what others have, we stop feeling resentful if life isn't behaving as we expected it to. We stop seeing ourselves as a victim of anyone or anything.

Instead we begin to take responsibility for what we are creating, moment by moment.

None of what happens to us is *punishment* or *judgment*. Let go of the false concepts that God or the universe is vindictive, jealous, cruel, or random or out to cause us personalized punishment.

The only heaven and hell are the experiences we create for ourselves through our own consciousness or lack of it. Saint Peter is not waiting at the pearly gates to judge you after you die and send you to either to the happy place (if you have been good) or the place of endless suffering and torment if you have been bad. These are the misinterpretations of a spiritual system designed to bring you consciousness, viewed through the eyes of fear.

People who are chronic blamers, instead of taking responsibility for their actions, use a mental trick to try to keep the convoluted logic in place so they can avoid feeling guilt: they will often invert the sequence of events so that although they did something which caused a problem that others *then* reacted to, they will reverse the cause and effect, so that in their mind others did the reaction first, which gave them the justification for doing their negative action.

The revealing element in the person's life is that there will be a pattern of deep upsets and broken relationships due to the fundamental dishonesty.

In religious language Satan is sometimes blamed for evil in the world, an external cause we can point at to get ourselves off the hook for what we ourselves have caused.

There is no Satan, and there is no other external cause for our own suffering. There is only our unconsciousness, individually and collectively, that has caused the hell of our human experiences of pain and suffering.

And there is no one to save us from this unconsciousness and suffering except ourselves and our free choice to create only positively instead of negatively.

We were given free choice and this will never be taken from us. It is time to accept our free choice to create positively, despite every reason why not, and so escape the hell of suffering we have caused for ourselves, and instead create the heaven of love, forgiveness, non-judgment, acceptance, gratitude, connectedness, and positive manifestation.

I cannot stress how important it is to grasp and employ this principle continuously. The *moment* you start to blame and complain about another's actions or your life situation, you will sabotage yourself and close down your heart. To blame others and feel resentment for what they have done, however human and normal this is, is to miss the whole point of this exercise we call life.

You are here to heal yourself from all your own negative reactions to all the difficulties that life will dish out to you. At the point you have no more negative reactions but can maintain an internal state of peace and love *no matter what,* you will be in the graduating class of Life University. You are attracting to you the experiences you have because of what you are: because of what you love and what you fear. You are pre-selecting your life experience, attracting it to you. Your life is *your* causation, no one else's. The universe is simply responding to what you are consciously and unconsciously asking for. Therefore to blame anyone else when it shows up is to fail to realize the basic cause and effect of what is going on here.

Instead take responsibility for what you have caused, and look within you and deal with any negative reactions you have. See each problem as an opportunity to learn and advance. Because it is not the life situation that is the problem, it is our negative thoughts and feelings about it that is the real issue. When we no longer have those to deal with, dealing with the problem itself becomes far simpler.

The book *Zero Limits*, co-authored by Dr. Ihaleakala Hew Len and Joe Vitale, describes a version of an ancient Hawaiian healing technique, which embodies this same principle. One is instructed to take 100% responsibility for one's own negative emotions activated by life situations or other people, and dispel them by using the mantra: *"I love you. I'm sorry. Please forgive me. Thank you."*

### Choosing Positive Over Negative

Our spiritual progress is always based on one fundamental principle:

**Our ability and decision to choose positive over negative in any situation.**

There is a line in the bible from the Book of Proverbs:

*As a man thinketh in his heart, so is he.* ~ Chapter 23 verse 7 KJV.

Jesus taught: *Ask and it shall be given to you.* ~ Matthew 7:7 KJV.

We hear the same message of wisdom being repeated again and again.

In 1902, English philosopher James Allen wrote a book entitled *As A Man Thinketh* on this subject of the effect of one's own thoughts. It begins thus:

"Mind is the Master power that moulds and makes,

And Man is Mind, and evermore he takes

The tool of Thought, and, shaping what he wills,

Brings forth a thousand joys, a thousand ills:

He thinks in secret, and it comes to pass:

Environment is but his looking-glass."

Allen included in his book, further writings which spoke directly to this subject:

(some lines emphasized in bold type by myself )

**"Men do not attract what they want, but what they are.**

**A man is literally what he thinks, his character being the complete sum of all his thoughts.**

Cherish your visions. Cherish your ideals. Cherish the music that stirs in your heart, the beauty that forms in your mind, the loveliness that drapes your purest thoughts, for out of them will grow all delightful conditions, all heavenly environment, of these, if you but remain true to them your world will at last be built.

**The soul attracts that which it secretly harbors, that which it loves, and also that which it fears.**

It reaches the height of its cherished aspirations. It falls to the level of its unchastened desires—and circumstances are the means by which the soul receives its own.

**Men are anxious to improve their circumstances, but are unwilling to improve themselves, they therefore remain bound.** Every action and feeling is preceded by a thought. Right thinking begins with the words we say to ourselves. Circumstance does not make the man, it reveals him to himself. You cannot travel within and stand still without. As the physically weak man can make himself strong by careful and patient training, so the man of weak thoughts, can make them strong by exercising himself in right thinking."

This teaching reveals to us in a few lines what has been echoed by others time and again, that when we deliberately, by an act of will and persistence, turn our thoughts to positive, we transform ourselves into what we desire.

## *Manifesting*

Manifesting what you want is a matter of first defining clearly what it is you really *do* want. When you know what it is, announce it to the universe with all the intention you can muster. I absolutely want *this*… You can hold the intention in your mind by writing it down or having a picture of it.

And at the same time focus on the highest vibration you can create, the kind of feelings you experienced when something went absolute right, when you got something you wanted, when you were successful, when you felt empowered, when you felt at peace, when you felt great joy, when you felt great love, when you felt confident, when you experienced a state of *flow,* when you felt an appreciation of beauty, when you felt unstoppable, when you felt connected to another person or nature or to God, when you felt gratitude.

When you have recreated those kinds of emotions, and asked for what you want with that high intention and emotion, then feel gratitude that you have received whatever it is that you want to achieve in your life. Not with any opposite thoughts that express its absence or doubt that it will come to you, **but how you would feel as if it was already here**. Think all the positive things you would think if it really *was* here, without any negative thoughts that admit it really isn't. Imagine it has happened with all your senses.

It's like an actor creating a part, visualizing and imagining it until it assumes a reality of its own. Feel the relief, the happiness, the sense of accomplishment. The most powerful way to communicate what we want to the universe is to feel *as if we already had it,* with all the joy and gratitude that having it would bring. That is what we need to learn to emanate. That is what we need to visualize and create within ourselves.

Thinking as if it has *already occurred* tells it to come *now*, thinking of it *sometime in the future* leaves it hanging sometime in the future, and so not showing up now, or in the near future.

Jesus taught: *Therefore I say unto you, what things soever ye desire, when ye pray, believe that ye receive them, and ye shall have them.* (Mark 11:24 KJV)

Make this your new, consistent way of thinking, feeling, believing and bringing things into being.

It is important to also bear in mind this law:

**Anything the mind accepts as true becomes a law in the subconscious and manifests in the world of the one who accepted it.**

So if you have a strong conscious or subconscious belief that for example, you should *not* have money, you can do all the manifesting visualizations you want for affluence, but it will be sabotaged by your own existing belief *that you should not have it*, which is also broadcasting to the universe. Similarly if you hold a core conscious or subconscious belief that you do not deserve love, you can visualize and ask the universe for love, but it will be nullified by the negative belief version that you are holding.

Remember, we attract what we *are*, not what we *want* on the surface. So we see how important it is to rid ourselves of all negative beliefs.

Conscious beliefs are easier, we sit down with a notepad and write down every negative belief we are aware of on each part of our life, we decide to get rid of all those concepts from our belief system and we can reinforce this with positive versions by repeating affirmations and creating new neural habits.

And we can prove to ourselves in the real world, by

facing and overcoming our fears, that we are able to succeed where we previously believed we would fail.

*Whether you think you can, or you think you can't, you're right. ~ Henry Ford*

When it comes to our thoughts, we "Fake it until we make it." If we are afraid or anxious, we don't dwell on that, we take a deep breath, smile, and go forward looking and acting confidently, and expecting the best to happen. And we keep doing that while learning about what we are doing as much as we can and practicing our craft and honing our skills to become as good as we can at whatever we are doing, until suddenly we will find we have become the success we envisioned, and our fears have evaporated.

But our subconscious beliefs are more difficult because they are buried from us, usually under emotional or physical painful experiences. They usually require some digging to get to.

For example, years ago I did regression therapy with a girl who had been raped by a drunk man in a wood as she made her way home at the age of thirteen. This had scarred her life; although she was in her twenties and wanted to get married, as soon as a relationship would turn serious or physical she would bolt and end the relationship. This was the ruin of her life. We spent 4 hours regressing and re-experiencing the rape incident.

She went from fear and overwhelm to tremendous grief, to eventual boredom and then laughter as she finally recalled: "That is when I decided to never let a man get close to me again!"

This decision was meant at the time to prevent hurt from ever happening again. But, because it took a specific incident and tried to make a general rule about life, it became a false belief, hidden in her subconscious mind under a great deal of emotional pain. Once she confronted the pain and it evaporated, she located the false belief and brought it into her conscious mind, where she saw it was false, and let go of that too.

She got engaged 3 months later. As soon as she looked fully at the false belief, it lost all power to control her life adversely. This is the same with all false beliefs. *The truth will set you free.* ~ John 8:32.

### Karma

*How you treat me is your karma. How I react is mine.* ~ *Anon.*

As I have used this term several times in this book, I should define it:

The principle of Karma is included in Buddhism and came to Buddha from the ancient Indian teachings of Hinduism.

Suffering or karma is the spiritual universe equivalent of getting your hand burned in order to learn not to stick your hand in the fire in the future.

This isn't personal any more than the fire is being personal when it burns you. It's a system of cause and effect, perfect justice, NOT crime and punishment.

That is why blaming others, being resentful of other, or being angry at God for your condition or holding onto grudges with anyone is all so pointless!

There are laws to how all this works! We can either learn them and function within them or get burned and suffer! It is really that simple! The choice is always ours.

Part of the Law is that: *what you send out to others, favorable or unfavorable, returns to you.*

Anyone who sent a destructive thought or intention to

others in the past, and hasn't received it back yet, should know that it is on its way!

Though a superficial examination doesn't show it—undeviating justice does rule the universe, sometimes across incarnations. So you need to learn techniques of how to deal with it when it manifests.

The point of all this is not to punish us—the traditional Christian concept of endless suffering in hell as punishment for our sins as taught these days is a misconception. I have no doubt that Jesus understood this perfectly correctly however.

*Suffering exists in order waken us; for us to learn the laws of the spiritual universe. Never to punish us.*

We live in an interactive universe, so we need to learn how it works, or like a child playing with a loaded gun, we will get hurt. And like the gun firing, this isn't personal—it is the way it is constructed.

Jesus taught: *Ask and it shall be given to you. Matthew 7:7.*

This is the same principle being taught. Our *asking* is our every thought, emotion, belief and intention, positive or negative. *That* is why it is essential that we deliberately turn everything we create to positive, to end our experience of suffering.

A spiritual journey, from my point of view, has nothing to do with some pious goody-two-shoes view of life. I simply have no desire to suffer any more than I have to—I prefer joy to misery. It is really that pragmatic.

My personal journey has to do with stumbling over some principles that worked for me very well and so wanting to discover more. So learning the spiritual laws, such as the principle of forgiveness, from a book like this or elsewhere, and then putting them into practice in one's daily life so that you are not creating new karmic debt to deal with, while dealing with your past energetic issues, shortens the amount of karma you will have to wade through.

### The Obstacle is the Path

I found a Zen proverb just as I was pondering all this.

It said: *The obstacle is the path*—which means that the person or circumstance that gets in your way and drives you crazy is there as your teacher.

The life incidents and people that drive us nuts are actually revealing to us the areas of reactive, unconscious behavior that we still need to deal with. It is there that we are attached to our ego and it is able to take us over.

So instead of complaining about how irritating something was, or how obnoxious someone was, if we can change our viewpoint and realize that we are actually in school, then we can pay attention and learn our lessons.

Every situation, instead of being annoying, can become an opportunity to learn the lesson of: *How do I handle this without succumbing to my triggers, and descending into my ego, or becoming self-righteous, or descending into lower vibrations of negative emotions, thoughts or intentions?*

Becoming awakened includes becoming aware whenever life provokes a negative response from us of any kind. Before, when we are spiritually asleep, we are just reacting to life automatically: this happens and we feel angry, that happens and we feel fearful, something else happens and we feel resentful or jealous.

And if we believe that the external world is controlling how we feel and respond, and everyone else believes the same thing, this all seems normal to us and we bumble through life, complaining about this and that, and others agree with us—*yes that was so awful,they did a terrible thing to us, he was so bad*, and so on.

But when we wake up to the cause and effect of life and that everything is down to *us*, there is no one else to blame, and we have to pay attention.

This is a huge and fundamental shift in consciousness. I cannot emphasize too much how pivotal this change is: it is the shift from effect to cause. Life is continually offering us a way to observe all the negative patterns within us, and so we have the opportunity to change each one we discover, by deliberately changing our negative emotion, thought or intention to a positiveversion on the spot, and deciding to have that positive response the next time that trigger appears.

We can do the mentally creative exercise to deliberately feel and think and intend something positive where there was something negative before.

Each time we do this, we have undone another piece of our Grand Illusion that is keeping us imprisoned. As we are going through a process of gradually undoing all the false beliefs and attachments we have to the Game of Life we are living, as we realize the important thing is not how much we own, or how well set we are in life, but how are we responding to life, how conscious are we able to remain as life changes around us, and as our fortunes rise and fall.

Through this process we are gradually taking apart the underpinning to our own unconsciousness.

Each time we become aware of another Spiritual Law at a soul level, it is like removing the foundation of another wall of the fortress of unconsciousness that imprisons us, and with a little inspection another wall preventing our freedom, collapses.

We make the mistake of thinking that we are living a life according to our design, and that all this other stuff in life is inconveniently getting in our way. But once we make clear to the spiritual world that we have embarked on a spiritual path and are committed to it, our lives become a combination of: 1) the specific life directions that our guides are bringing us; 2) the karmic lessons we need to learn and have caused by the energy we have set forth in the past; and 3) that which we are attracting to us by our thoughts, emotions, and beliefs.

Remember all this is to serve our soul—not our ego or our physical desire and comforts. Our guides don't really care if our intent is to buy a new car or house or couch or remodel the kitchen, if that has nothing to do with our evolution. You will get that which best brings you your spiritual lesson at this moment in time.

People sometimes have a misunderstanding about the Law of Attraction: it is not there to provide you with a luxurious life so that you will remain trapped in the cycle of reincarnation forever—sorry—it is there to facilitate your Soul's awakening to its ultimate consciousness, so that you may reunite with Consciousness, or God.

And do not also make the mistake of believing that if you are going through suffering and hardship that this is karmic punishment for your misdeeds. Instead look to learn the lesson that you are being shown, and welcome it with acceptance and patience and as much grace as you can muster.

You may be up to your ears in some project, for example with timber, nails, and paint when your next lesson arrives. My last one in the home improvement department was trying to glue some hand-painted tiles with the wrong kind of mastic and watching them, instead of sticking, just sliding off the wall, leaving me with a pile of tiles and my hands covered with an incredibly sticky, but for my purpose, quite useless, substance...*that* was a test of my patience and acceptance.

However frustrating, if you *can* shift your attention from the task you are trying to do to your inner responses, and reframe the situation as a learning experience and a test, instead of a very annoying inconvenience, then these situations can become your next learning opportunity.

Then negative becomes positive.

### *Always Use the Positive Version*

It is important that we realize and practice positivity always, as we deal with negative issues that present themselves in our life: **opposing negative things with our negativity only creates more negativity.**

Thus when we *fight against* terrorism, we are actively creating more terrorism, we are focusing on the negative, and the universe obediently brings us more of the negative. Instead we should focus on *creating peace.*

When we *fight against* cancer, we are helping create more cancer. Instead we should focus on wellness. This applies to any undesirable situation—hunger, abuse, poverty.

"Isn't this just really the same thing—aren't you just talking semantics?"

No, the universe doesn't discriminate between what you focus on having a *yes* or *no, good* or *bad*, attached to it, it just brings you what you focus on. So: *I don't want poverty* brings you poverty, but *I want wealth* brings you wealth. *I don't want war* brings you war. *I want peace* brings you peace—do you see? Absolutely opposite results.

Your every thought is sending real energy into the universe and asking for a response. This is why becoming aware of, and disciplining your every thought, emotion and intention, and belief, becomes so important.

If we have fear about something, we don't resist it or try to deny it. We don't say "I am not afraid" because that is asking for the negative. Instead say "I have courage" which is the positive version we want.

We focus our thinking on the positive version: *We have courage, we can succeed, we will do well, we will receive what we need, everything will go OK, we are confident that the universe will support us and bring us what we need, and what we want. We believe in ourselves, that we are part of God, who wishes us success, and who is helping us to receive all we need.*

These are the positive thoughts we deliberately fill ourselves with until they become habitual for us. We visualize and emotionally feel ourselves achieving what we want. And we work as hard as we can to become as good as we can at what we want to do—so we are bringing the spiritual world and the physical world into concert.

And remember, if you wish to hold onto riches or power that you have attracted, use them for the benefit of others. If you use them to hurt others, eventually they will evaporate.

Sometimes the amount of negativity that life can stir up within us can seem overwhelming. We can feel lost, as if any kind of spiritual path is a fantasy. Just be patient, and rest and relax when you can, don't resist how you feel, just observe it. For negativity will eventually evaporate, the clouds will pass and the sun will shine again, and fresh hope and a sense of peace will blossom within you again, and you will feel your divine connection again. Your patience and persistence will be rewarded every time. Remember, the universe is constantly in motion, everything must change, and this too will pass.

And remember too, you are never alone or abandoned on your journey.

If you want annoying or upsetting things to cease in your life, learn to cease being annoyed or upset by them, and then you will no longer need to continue experiencing them.

We are attracting them to us by our own need to learn that lesson, by the negative thoughts, beliefs, and emotions that still remain in us—the part of the Grand Illusion we still need to locate, confront, and turn its stagnant, negative energy into positive life force.

When we learn that lesson, the need for the life situation evaporates.

Don't believe it? Try it.

# 12th Habit of Transformation: Daily Meditation

Observing Your Mind and Your Thoughts—
Becoming the Witness—Opening Your Heart—White
Light Meditation—Hesychastic Meditation—Stress
Reducing Meditation—Grounding Yourself—Who Is
My Teacher Today?

*Meditation brings wisdom; lack of meditation leaves ignorance.
Know well what leads you forward and what hold you back, and
choose the path that leads to wisdom.~ Buddha*

Meditation is a very simple practice that anyone can start immediately, with no preparation other than a quiet space in which you won't be disturbed. Its benefits are considerable: physically, mentally and spiritually. It doesn't require any beliefs.

***Why Meditate? Scientifically Verified Psychological, Health, Spiritual Benefits.***
    The health benefits of meditation have now been established in a number of studies. The Shambhala Mountain Center in Colorado for instruction in meditation and Yoga, also became a scientific laboratory in 2007 under the direction of a neuroscientist Clifford Saron at the University

of California at Davis. Findings of this Shamantha Project revealed that meditators experienced increased sharpened visual acuity, perception and attention that lasted for 5 months after the retreat had finished.

More surprising are the findings of Tonya Jacobs, a scientist at UC Davis's Center for Mind and Brain, who has reported online in the journal *Psychoneuroendocrinology* that those who meditate show not only improved psychological well-being, but that these improvements lead to biochemical changes associated with resistance to aging at the cellular level. Analysis of meditators' white blood cells showed a 30 percent increase in an enzyme called telomerase, a chemical essential to the long-term health of the body's chromosomes and cells.

The scientists stated the practice of meditation seems to give people an increased sense of meaning and purpose in life, which in turn gives them an increased sense of control over their lives and an experience of less negative emotions. This improved psychological and emotional well being results in the increase of telomerase, the anti- aging hormone, which repair frayed telomeres, the ends of DNA strands which have been likened to the tips of shoe laces. Stress damages telomeres, and shortened or damaged telomeres inhibits a cell's ability to divide and provide us with fresh cells, and this inability results in aging, and susceptibility to disease, cancers and death.

In the book *Power Up Your Brain*, by David Pearlmutter M.D. and Alberto Villoldo PhD. they also examine the positive relationship between meditation and cell health.

UC Davis psychological scientist Baljinder Sahdra reports in the journal *Emotion*, that meditation leads to a decrease in impulsive reactions—another health improvement linked to psychological positivity. Impulsivity has been tied to an array of health problems, including addictions and other risky behavior.

Clearly there is scientific evidence that adopting a regular meditation practice will reduce stress and benefit you emotionally, psychologically and physically.

With regard to our minds, meditation has the effect of calming down the amount of random and repetitive mental chatter that our brain generates.

The activity of simply noticing what your mind gets up to while you meditate, without trying to do anything to your thoughts or feelings, without judging them or resisting them, allows you to start to get space between you and your mind.

Someone I had recommended meditation to was experiencing daily fits of heavy grief that just turned up on its own without anything happening in his life to apparently trigger them. He was very upset and alarmed that this was happening, and thought it was a serious situation, because the negative emotion of grief was so very strong. Earlier he had self-medicated with marijuana on a daily basis, and used self-injury to calm his negative emotions down. First I told him that emotion was simply energy no matter how strong, and nothing to be afraid or alarmed about, not to worry about this, or take the emotion seriously, no matter how devastating it felt.

I then had him continue to meditate daily, and told him that when the emotion turned on, to just observe it, not resist it, or think it shouldn't be happening, or try to figure out what was causing it, or where it was coming from.

He just observed the emotion turn on, and then turn off. The result was he ceased to be alarmed about the feeling of grief and within a short while it stopped turning on altogether. He became much more relaxed and happy in his daily life, and no longer had any need to smoke marijuana or practice self-injury, because the negative emotions that these solved were no longer. He noticed chronic physical aches disappearing as he de-stressed daily through meditation. We can unknowingly hold stress in parts of our body which results in physical problems.

Meditation is the beginning of the end for the ego, and it will try to throw all kinds of sabotage in the way to prevent its own dissolution. Don't focus on the problems—just keep meditating and they will resolve.

Focusing your attention on what you are doing 100% while you are doing it turns that activity into a form of meditation and spiritual practice.

It helps to do this routinely all the time, or as often as you can. Letting yourself daydream with no specific purpose usually has the opposite effect: Rather than bringing you into the present moment, it tends to let your mind reassert itself.

When in the past I deliberately let some time pass without any kind of daily practice to see what would happen, I found that I returned to a mind-dominated consciousness but would spontaneously experience a heart opening from things in my life like watching a film, playing music, taking a walk, or spending time with family and friends.

But I also found that old habits of behavior were creeping back in, I was becoming irritated or frustrated more easily. Life became harder to get through, whereas maintaining a continual lifeline to my spiritual consciousness by reconnecting first thing in the morning and putting my attention back on my heart had changed how I operated in life completely. I found that I tended to slide around conflicts and dramas that would have hooked me into them as if now I was wrapped in Teflon.

I have found that when I abandoned my daily practice for a while and was working hard, I sometimes meditated for an hour with no apparent change at first. Then later in the day, I noticed a little lifting of heaviness. By the time I was ready to sleep, I finally felt my heart open. In the morning, I was back reconnected in just seconds of focusing my attention. Once you have the sensation of heart energy running in your body, stay focused on that continually throughout your day and as you fall asleep at night.

When you perform intellectually demanding tasks, take tiny breaks and refocus on your heart energy connection. Throughout your day take a moment to focus back on your heart energy. This will gradually become a habit and the energy will increase, until you are living most of your life with a flooding open heart, and you are continually in the present moment, and experiencing love, compassion and connectedness to Consciousness all around you.

The main thing is not to worry about how you are feeling. Acceptance of what is, applies to the emotions that arise as well. If you just observe them without reacting, they will arrive, and then leave.

The better I got at all this, by observing what I did caused me to lose my state of open-heartedness and adding those to my list of things to avoid, the longer I could stay in a state of continual open-heartedness.

I try to maintain my inner equilibrium and remain conscious of it as I go through my life experiences. If I lose consciousness because of something I experience, I pull back from that and reestablish my sense of peace as quickly as I can.

There is no sense of failure in this, no shame or regret. We just forgive ourselves and others, and resume, making mental notes not to fall for that trigger again.

It is all a gradual practice, and it gradually gets easier. The key is intention and perseverance.

## SOME MEDITATION TECHNIQUES

There are many meditation techniques. These are some I have found useful—as with everything, use what you find works best for you:

### *Observing Your Thoughts, Becoming the Witness*

What opens the door to our awakening is becoming the witness to our own minds. This means observing the *negative* thoughts, feelings, beliefs, and reactions that we have, not resisting them or judging them, not believing them to be true, not acting them out, but just simply noticing them as they pass through our consciousness.

As we start to observe, we start to separate from them, to get distance from them, to cease being hypnotized by them. This will take as long as it takes. If you have spent several lifetimes as a Buddhist monk it may happen more quickly. But this is not a contest.

I cannot stress the importance of *doing nothing* when you encounter negative emotions or other thoughts during meditation. You must not resist them, such as think thoughts like: *I wish I didn't feel like this, I should be over this by now*, and so on. Or judge them, by thinking thoughts like: *that is so immature*, or *that is so important*.

Meditation also has nothing to do with some kind of self-psychoanalysis, where you asking yourself questions like: *Where is this coming from? What is the significance of this?*

That is a guaranteed route to digging yourself into the endless minutia of suffering, received, caused and observed, in your history.

People sometimes make the mistake of thinking understanding their history holds the key to their happiness. Except for sometimes in locating and looking at certain traumatic incidents with a therapist, it doesn't. 30 years of psycho-analysis won't get you there. I have known overly significant people who have been looking to just understand that final part of their history that will change everything, for all their lives. It will never happen.

Because resolution and happiness lies in the opposite direction: when you stop identifying with your history altogether! Let it all go—when you realize that you aren't your history and that it doesn't define you—poof! It suddenly isn't very important. The present moment is where you should be living, not the past.

People in insane asylums who talk endlessly to themselves are trapped completely in this world of mental preoccupation and delusion. Psycho-therapy, to be effective, requires a trained and, insightful and emotionally uninvolved guide to take you into specific experiences and then bring you out and back to present time.

Trying to figure out *why* things in your life happened as they did, from the belief they should fit into some kind of mold, conforming to human logic and justice that makes sense of everything, will get you nowhere at all, but only dig you into a hole of self-pity and loss of personal power.

You do not have the perspective of the Big Picture at this time. Just trust that the universe knows what it is doing, and has been giving you the experience you need to learn a lesson of consciousness. The earlier chapters of this book are there to outline the steps that will lead you to achieving your life lessons.

At the point you have the awareness for things to make sense to you, your history will no longer be a concern to you, you will no longer need to heal from it. But until that point, trying to demand it make sense so you can "figure it all out" will only be a destructive path for you to pursue, which will make you feel more of a victim because you do not have the necessary awareness, *because you cannot see what you cannot see, until you can see it.*

It is a paradox. That is why you need to trust the universe and your spirit guides to have given you what you needed, even though it makes no sense now, and do your spiritual work so you can move forward.

You must understand you cannot *think* your way out of being hypnotized by your own mind. Believing your mind will give you *all* the answers is like being a hamster on a wheel—lots of effort but you won't get where you want to. Yes you need to empty your mind of false beliefs, and yes you need to learn to think sanely, logically and calmly.

But we are also talking about achieving a state *beyond mind,* of you, a spiritual being, separating from the tool which is your mind. It is awakening from identification with your own thoughts. This is not an idea, this is a state of consciousness which you must achieve and experience. This is an evolution from Homo Sapiens, and becoming a new, awakened kind of being on the planet, of whom there have been relatively few in the history of humankind. In achieving this, you will be at the forefront of human evolution.

*Doing something* about a negative emotion during

meditation will only serve to keep the mechanism of subconscious energy generation, which is creating the negative emotion in the first place, turned on, and keep you embroiled in it unknowingly. That is the opposite of this observation meditation. *Doing nothing*, but observation, will allow it to turn off and fade away, and eventually enable you to separate out from the entire mechanism of your mind and come fully into the present moment.

Emotions are, after all, just different wavelengths of energy, nothing to get excited or alarmed by. During this process, we can arrive at a point where we are experiencing strong emotions such as anger or grief but are also just observing the phenomena. And now, unlike before, we no longer believe them to be real or cause for alarm. We know they are coming from somewhere in our subconscious mind, and we watch them dissipate. They are tourists, just passing through.

But when we do anything to them, resisting them in anyway, we stop this from occurring.

Eventually, all these negative emotions and thoughts will calm down because you will spot them as they start to arise, and that will be enough to pop them as you can pop soap bubbles floating through the air.

We are not trying to end all thought. If you realize you have begun to think, or have become lost in a train of thoughts, just return to your focus, on your breathing or on your heart, just consciously being the observer of your thoughts.

**Doing this meditation** should be the first step before you do anything else. This will let you become aware of what your mind is up to and cease to believe your negative thoughts, or take them seriously.

1) Sit comfortably and upright in a quiet place where you won't be interrupted by phones or anything else. Consciously relax, let go of all the muscles in your body, let go of your jaw, and place your tongue behind your upper teeth. Smile.

2) Focus on your breathing: Breathe deeply and slowly. Breathe using your diaphragm so your stomach moves up and down and your chest stays relatively still. Close off the back of your throat so you can hear your breath clearly going in and out; it will make a rasping sound. This is known in yoga as Ujjayi breath. Doing this helps focus on your breath. Notice the space in between breathing in and out. Just doing this slow deep breathing using your diaphragm instead of your chest is very calming and also physically beneficial.

3) Watch your thoughts. Don't interfere at this point. Just see what your mind is up to. You will eventually see the same thoughts circle around in a loop.

*Be aware that you are not your thoughts.*

*Be aware also that you are the one watching your thoughts.*

*Be aware that just because you think something negative or feel a negative emotion does not make it true.*

Do this meditation until you are able to separate somewhat from your thoughts;

Until negative thoughts that keep returning—generated by your mind like a song that gets stuck in your head—are simply observed as just that and are no longer taken seriously by you.

4) When you can do this, start to bring your thoughts under control by emptying your mind and noticing the silence of *no thought*, the quiet space in between your thoughts and when you notice that your mind has started up again, bringing it back to silence again. Like a puppy on a leash, gradually work on getting your thoughts under your conscious

control. When your mind starts to go into the past or the future, bring it back to the present.

5) When you are first doing this, if things come up in your mind that you have to do in life, just write them down and make a list so you can take your attention off them and don't feel you have to remember them, then carry on with your meditation.

Then in life, when you notice negative thoughts arising about something, you can begin to stop them and deliberately replace them with positive thoughts.

Gradually, by doing regular meditations, and focusing on the present moment in life, you will calm down your mind and the random, out-of-control thinking will quiet down. It will be a tremendous relief and a big step towards enabling you to gain inner peace.

### White Light Meditation

This I have found to be very workable when I have been really "socked into" my head.

It is a technique that is referenced in many places.

Do steps 1) and 2) as in the meditation above.

3) Visualize yourself surrounded by white light. Each time you inhale, deeply, slowly and with your attention on your breath, "breathe" the white light into you through your crown chakra (the top of your head). Visualize it filling a different part of you with each breath until your whole body inside is filled with white light.

4) You may also wish to visualize each chakra being filled with white light.

You may then wish to go to the heart-opening meditation described in the 13th Habit.

In my experience, opening the heart is the first thing to do if you can, because it changes your experience of anything else you do. But if you cannot do it right away, don't fret; just work on meditating regularly and things will improve bit by bit

### Hesychastic Meditation

This meditation is taken from a book called *Meditation: The Bridge From the Apparent to the Real*, by Douglas Buchanan, who gave me his blessing to reproduce it. In it, the author details all the pitfalls and distractions that can derail one's meditation from real progress, and how the ego can sneak back in to a person's practice. He writes based on decades of experience with meditation, knowing what works and what doesn't. It is invaluable information, resulting from great experience and study, and can save anyone from repeating the same mistakes.

The author describes in detail the Hesychastic tradition of meditation, saying that it succeeds where other methods fail:

This is an introduction to this meditation:

1) Choose a sacred name that represents God or an enlightened being to you in whatever spiritual tradition you are familiar and comfortable with. It might be Jesus or Buddha or another spiritual name that is sacred to you personally. A name with two syllables is good. All sacred names will help you access the same consciousness, but it is important that it is significant to you and you are comfortable with it as sacred. Sit comfortably, with the spine upright, where you won't be disturbed.

2) Put your attention on your breathing. As you breathe in,

deeply, slowly with attention on your breathing, say the sacred name three times out loud. Then on the out breath, say the name three times out loud. As in: *Jesus, Jesus, Jesus,* or *Buddha, Buddha, Buddha,* or another name of an enlightened being of your choice. Do this for a short while.

3) Now hear the name three times on the in breath, then three times on the out breath, without saying it out loud. Continue the meditation.

4) Do your meditation for a specific period of time. This has the effect of aligning your consciousness with enlightened consciousness, and keeping your mind focused. It prevents your mind from wandering aimlessly. You can do this while performing tasks in life. I like to do it after I have done the heart-opening meditation described in the 13th Habit; it is a delicious combination. I have also sometimes combined the heart-opening meditation described in the next chapter with Hesychastic meditation and also self-Reiki directed to my chakras. The result has been blissful, and healing.

### A Science Proven, Stress Reducing Meditation—"Oh Well, Peace"

Dr. Herbert Benson of the Benson-Henry Institute for Mind Body Medicine in Boston uses a very simple meditation exercise which he has verified through blood sample testing has positive healing effects at a cellular level. He studied monks meditating in Tibet. He maintains that sickness is as much a product of our mind as our body. He believes that stress is a result of our brain's fight or flight response, when our brain's limbic system releases a flood of hormones. One of the effects of these hormones is to create inflammation in cells. If this inflammation is prolonged it can trigger heart disease, arthritis and Crohn's disease of the digestive system. To combat this effect of stress he developed a 15 minute a day, 8 week course of meditation to bring about a "relaxation response."

Meditate and when you encounter thoughts just think: **"Oh well....peace"** and disregard any other thoughts.

Blood testing before and after the 8 week stress reducing meditation showed that inflammation inducing genes had been turned off by this simple procedure. Dr. Benson's research proves scientifically that meditation can bring about positive change at a genomic level.

### Grounding Yourself

If you find yourself feeling very "spaced out" after a meditation, you can do this grounding meditation to ground yourself so you can better function in the normal world. Lie on the ground and put your attention deep into the ground beneath you. Become aware of the connection you have to the Earth and the energy involved in this. After a short while you should feel more grounded.

### Who is my Teacher Today?

Who is my teacher today? This is a phrase I ask myself after I have finished my meditation and opened my heart. It helps remind me to be ready for the lesson that is coming so I do not lose consciousness as easily with the surprise of its arrival in whatever guise it comes.

It could be anything: Someone dangerously cuts you off in traffic; someone takes your parking place; you're in line at the grocery store and discover you have no wallet; someone cancels a contract that had been orally promised; someone is rude, angry, officious, or tries to keep you from doing what you've promised to do; someone fails to keep an agreement, betrays you—anything that can make you irritated, angry, or resentful, or closes your heart and draws you into the drama of "real life" before you are aware it has happened.

The martial arts analogy is that someone is always able to pull you off balance just before you get thrown in judo. If you can keep your balance, you won't be thrown.

*We could say that meditation doesn't have a reason or doesn't have a purpose. In this respect it's unlike almost all other things we do except perhaps making music and dancing. When we make music we don't do it in order to reach a certain point, such as the end of the composition. If that were the purpose of music then obviously the fastest players would be the best. Also, when we are dancing we are not aiming to arrive at a particular place on the floor as in a journey. When we dance, the journey itself is the point, as when we play music the playing itself is the point. And exactly the same thing is true in meditation. Meditation is the discovery that the point of life is always arrived at in the immediate moment. ~ Allan Watts*

# 13th Habit: Opening Your Heart Chakra

## Opening Your Own Heart—What Keeps Your Heart Open—Avoiding What Closes It

*And now abide faith, hope, love, these three; but the greatest of these is love.~ Corinthians 13:13 NKJV*

*It is only with the heart that one can see rightly. What is essential is invisible to the eye. ~ The Little Prince. Antoine Saint-Exupery*

*The best and most beautiful things in the world cannot be seen nor even touched, but just felt in the heart. ~ Helen Keller*

*Shall we make a new rule of life from tonight? Always try to be a little kinder than necessary. ~ J. M. Barrie*

At a certain point as we learn to practice the other habits of: forgiveness, acceptance, non- judgment, being in the present moment, and separating from our ego, we can learn to open our own heart energy center, or *chakra* as it is called in the yoga tradition.

This is an important step, and part of *becoming centered*, because when we can open our own heart and experience the flow of love through us and our connection to the conscious universe around us, or God as others prefer to call it.

We are then released from the delusion that others are the cause of our joy, or that we cannot experience love without that special person, pet, place or whatever.

Once we can feel love all by ourselves at will, we no longer ascribe our own internal causation to the external world, and we are set free of the external world for our happiness. We are not longer a slave to others for our own happiness; we are no longer addicted to others because we misuse them as our portal to the divine.

Sanity then enters into all our relationships—compulsion, possession, jealousy, addiction, fear of loss or abandonment, and desperation all leave our relationships. We are now free to enjoy and love and receive love from others, because we no longer have to have an outside source as our portal to experience love. And so the outside world ceases to have power over us.

We are able to be joyful and at peace in isolation, if necessary, because we are able to be in connection with the divine.

There have been many attempts throughout various cultures to describe the architecture of the subtle energy body that exists within and around the human body with which we interact.

The energy centers known as chakras have been described in the ancient Indian Upanishads and became part of the tradition of Yoga and Tibetan Buddhism. The chakras are also part of ancient Mayan shaman teachings in the Andes region.

Chinese medicine has a version of chakras and the internal energy field and there are some differences that exist between these cultural interpretations.

Even some hospitals and medical establishments in this

country are now willing to train people in breath regulation and diaphragmatic breathing. It is important to note here that modern Western medicine has finally acknowledged what the yogis have known for thousands of years: that the breath is intimately connected to the autonomic nervous system and the mind. In other countries the fact of this connection has long been taken for granted.

In Western literature the heart has universally been accepted as the seat of human emotions. We speak of *having a broken heart* or *a heart bursting with love*. And if you observe what is happening to you when you experience intense love or the pain of lost love—you will notice it is happening in the area of the human heart.

What is occurring is a flow of energy from the heart chakra—an energy center located near the physical heart of the subtle energy body that exists inside and around your body.

And you can learn to open your heart chakra at will. You do not need outside sources to achieve this—not people you love, or pets, or great music. It is fine if any of these work to open your heart—but they are not a requirement, and you should learn not be reliant on them to do this for you.

**Because love is not an emotion. Love is your natural state**.

Love is what you naturally experience when you subtract the distractions that are acting as a veil, the Grand Illusions standing between your experience of what and who you naturally are.

When you feel love you are simply experiencing your own spirit.

It is of course perfectly all right if other things open your heart chakra naturally. What is *not* all right is to be *addicted* to all these kinds of things because you believe you *need* them to open your heart. This is an illusion.

Part of your spiritual evolution is to learn to become *centered*: which means to realize all that you are, and to take responsibility and control for creating or co-creating your human experience, and also of your heart chakra opening, so that you can routinely live with an open heart chakra. This is the state of *tender, loving heart* that is referred to in many spiritual traditions.

This is the gathering of yourself back together, which is touched upon in various chapters of this book. Learning the technique of opening your own heart at will releases you from dependence on outside agencies in order for you to experience the divine. This will change your orientation to everything in a good and profound way.

It is only the shadow of our mind and our identifications with mind and the physical universe, and the attachments we form, that cloud this state from you.

There may be many different activities that can open your heart chakra - relationships with those whom you love, holding a baby or a beloved pet, being in nature—all these are common for many people to act as heart chakra openers. The heart chakra energy starts to flow and we say we feel love.

Anything that moves us to feel love is always a wonderful thing. But there is a very important point to observe regarding this phenomenon:

*We can make the mistake of attributing the source of our experience of love to someone or something external to ourselves.*

*And we make the added mistake that without that external source—that special someone or something—we cannot feel that love.*

This mistaken identification renders people addicted to the person or thing that they perceive to be their portal to experiencing the bliss of an open-heart chakra.

Another person or experience may be what causes us to change our orientation so that we start to feel love—but it is us who is feeling it. *We are experiencing our own causation.*

This is the basis of many "conversion" experiences to a particular religion or cult. People mistake the circumstances under which it happened as the cause. They thereby become fixated on the opinions of the group among which it happened.

But correlation does not prove causation—which means that just because two things happen at the same time is not necessarily proof that one caused the other.

Hence all the high drama and romanticism associated with love. If we find a person or perhaps even a pet who acts as our portal to experiencing a state of bliss then we can make the mistaken assumption that we absolutely must have that person or pet to connect with our experience of love.

*Whereas the truth is we are experiencing the native state of our own spirit, revealed to us by the total acceptance, forgiveness and lack of judgment we have toward the one we love.*

It is important that this distinction is grasped: You view the one you love deeply without any judgments and with total acceptance—**and it is this change of viewpoint on your part that opens your heart chakra**. You believe it is the loved one that causes you to feel this way—no it is the way you choose to view them that does it. Yes, it is true that they may be wonderful but it is your appreciation of them and the subsequent suspension of judgment that you have that causes you to feel love. Do you see the distinction?

Not everyone feels the love for them that you do, because they are not suspending their judgments. Hence the observation of Dalai Lama XIV: *Love is the absence of judgment.*

This is why it is essential that we learn to cease judging everyone and everything around us, in order that we may learn to open our own heart chakra and live with it remaining open. Then we start to experience everyone and everything with love, not around just a select few.

It is this *lack* of acceptance and forgiveness, and the judgment that we usually place on the world around us, which prevents us from experiencing this same love all the time.

This is why we must make these 3 habits parts of our daily life: **acceptance**, **forgiveness** and **non-judgment** and added to these the 4th: **living in the present moment**. Whether we agree with this logically, or not, in various circumstances, is not the point—*if we wish to live in the experience of open-hearted joy and love, these are the conditions.*

When trying circumstances arise, our ego is always ready to jump in to convince us: We should be outraged! We should be competitive! We should withdraw our affection! How could they have done that! This time they have gone too far! I won't stand for it!

And if you inhabit those thoughts and emotions, your heart will close down.

So we have before us, the not insubstantial task of learning to navigate and negotiate through the complexities and outrageous fortunes of life, without letting our ego rule us and closing our heart again, once we have learned to open it at will.

This is the path towards enlightenment.

When we love another person, we are experiencing the beauty of our own spirit in its natural state which our love for another has revealed to us. Before we understand this, the loss of a loved one is utterly devastating. This is partly because of that mistaken assumption: the false belief that without them we cannot feel love. We assume that *they* are the reason we can feel love.

That mistaken assumption can result in people doing some unnecessarily destructive and obsessive things in the name of love.

But once we can learn to open our own heart chakra at will, then obsession and addiction to another person leaves, along with anxiety and jealousy.

We are then freed to enjoy our relationship sanely and more fully. It is very important to fully grasp this distinction—if you can do so you are a member of a very small group in the history of mankind—and if you can practice it you are among an even smaller group.

And when you do, your center then assumes its rightful place—in the center of one's own being, instead of being misplaced somewhere external, which is how most people exist.

In the light of understanding how to open one's own heart chakra, *Romeo And Juliet* becomes a charming story, beautifully written, of two people who simply did not understand how to manage their emotions or access their own individual bliss experience.

This does not mean that relationships or love or other people we care about become less—neither does it mean that we are becoming selfish, self obsessed, narcissistic or callous—on the contrary, with the addiction and obsession removed, your relationships are free to become far deeper and much less easily damaged.

Another human being is *eventually* not required to open

your heart chakra. Learning how to open your own heart chakra at will means you are no longer dependant on others to be your portal to your open heart: other people, pets, places, or activities.

And so we become released from our addiction to these outside agencies and we are able to become centered. This is a *huge* step in our spiritual evolution. It means that no one else has control over us to open our own heart chakra.

And this explains all the jealousy, possessiveness, drama, and despair that can accompany great love affairs. When we mistakenly believe that only another person will bring us this divine experience of love, and that is why we are with them, we are making someone else responsible for something for which *we alone* should be responsible.

So losing them represents not just losing that relationship—but also the loss of our portal to the divine! No wonder people can get crazy about breakups.

Once we can open our own heart chakra at will and experience our connection to Spirit and the love that accompanies this—some have called it the love of God—from that point on we are never alone or isolated even when by ourselves. And sanity can enter our relationships for the first time, because others are not being used as a portal—but as beloved friends and partners.

All of these—lovers, our children, our family, beauty, nature, music and all the wonderful things in the world, have been our portal to spiritual experiences for thousands of years. For some their religion may have allowed them to touch their spirit and experience joy.

In taking control of opening our own hearts, we are talking about our spiritual evolution, going further into our own consciousness. Remember, we alone hold the key to everything we have mistakenly believed external people, things and circumstances have held, which is just another aspect of the Grand Illusion.

The purpose of our relationships is to increase our consciousness. Learning to open our own hearts enables us to keep our loving relationships indefinitely. When we combine this with integrity on the part of both parties, then we have the formula to lasting, loving, sane and conscious relationships.

Anyone who can learn to open his or her heart at will, and then learn to live with that open heart, will be experiencing the joy of existence day by day.

### The Heart Opening Meditation

I will describe the method that I discovered works for me to open my heart:

I sit comfortably in a quiet room where I won't be disturbed by phones or other distractions.

I close my eyes and put my attention on my breathing. I close the back of my throat so I can hear my breath making a raspy noise as it goes in and out. In Yoga this is called Ujjayi breathing.

I put my tongue behind the back of my lower teeth, relax my mouth which means unclench my jaw, and then I generally relax my body.

I put my attention on the area of my heart, inside my chest. I visualize a smile on my heart.

Usually I can feel an energy there as a kind of aliveness, sometimes as a sense of love or joyfulness. As I put my attention on it, it is like a pilot light igniting a flow of gas in a furnace—if you have ever turned on your own furnace and watched that. Sometimes just visualizing my Ujjayi breath passing over my heart, in and out, is enough to open my heart chakra, and feel it flood with love.

My heart area may start to gently ache as the energy increases by placing my attention on it. Then I will imagine or will it to be pulled up to my throat, which will start to ache also. The energy can be pulled up further into my head where my gums may tingle and the spot on my forehead between my eyes will ache.

This aching is part of a very pleasurable sensation, not painful.

By now as this energy is being pulled up from my heart it usually starts to "flood"—there is a sensation of love overflowing from my heart. On occasion it has just flooded out into the space around me for some hours.

The sensation as one's heart opens up is exquisite, joyful, one of being bathed in love, of being connected to a universal love that is kind and nurturing. Fears vanish, as does any sense of isolation or being alone or separate. One is contented and peaceful.

This is the *bliss* experience that mystics talk of, or the *joy plateau*.

If you can avoid all the traps that will take you out of this state by practicing all the Habits described in this book: not becoming fixated on a mentally demanding task, not defending yourself and being right or comparing yourself to another and waking up your ego identification, avoiding impatience, anger, frustration, judging and condemning another, being resentful, and blaming, then you can stay in this state of bliss indefinitely.

So far I have managed several weeks at a time before becoming wrapped up in life and having to restart my heart opening with this meditation.

This is why these 20 habits have been listed in this book and why they are so important to master.

Another useful practice can be to focus attention on things that one loves: people, places, situations, music, art, dance, movement, skill, nature, animals, writings, concepts—whatever moves you. Feel gratitude for these things. Consider the beauty of these things that you love. Be aware of your positive internal response to these things.

When I first experienced this on the rainy night in the empty parking garage that I described in chapter six, *Here And Now,* it was overpowering, staggering.

When I would briefly lose the state by concentrating on a mind operation as simple as going into a food market and searching for an item that was hard to locate, I would panic slightly. Had the magical state vanished from me again?

I would repeat the instruction contained in Eckhart Tolle's master work *The Power Of Now,* to go inside the body, by putting my attention inside my body and especially my heart center as this seems to be the most effective for me. Sure enough the pilot light would flame and I would be back in the open-hearted state.

By returning the focus of my attention to my heart during the day as I completed each mind-consuming task, I found I could stay in an open-hearted state for weeks at a time.

When something happened to end my state—usually an arising of my ego when I felt I needed to defend myself, or if I became irritated and intolerant of someone's actions or behavior—my heart would close and I would lose the state.

So this became my new spiritual practice: to identify each button that I responded to with a flash of anger or intolerance or judgment or impatience or frustration or resistance or ego, which then closed down my heart. I then took out that "button" and thoroughly examined the false attitudes or assumptions or resistance or lie that was contained in it that gave it power by diminishing my consciousness when it was aroused.

And so what had been incredible became normal. But a whole new kind of normal.

Sometimes I find this whole meditation to be unnecessary—I can sometimes wake with an open heart which has been with me all through the night from the day before. Or other things can do it—a thought that is life affirming or that resonates with Truth can do it. Or a hug from my wife or my daughters.

There is a road I drive going from my house into the town of Santa Fe that faces me towards the Sangre De Christo mountains. Looking at these mountains and placing my attention on my heart can open it instantly very often.

Sometimes if I have experienced a strong disconnect from my heart energy because of something that has surfaced, this doesn't work immediately and when I have done this meditation it will be later in the day that I begin to feel a flicker of energy in my heart, like the embers of a fire being fanned by a breeze.

If you are doing this exercise as described but without success—check to see if there is anything that you are internally unwilling to accept? Is there a situation or person that you are actively resisting? If you locate what you are resisting and let go of it this will sometimes open your heart.

When one is living with an open heart and constantly putting their attention into their energy body to reconnect with their spirit as they go through their daily life, their orientation to life is dramatically changed.

They are in a state that some Buddhists refer to as *loving kindness*. They are experiencing their connection to others and automatically regard and treat others with love, kindness and compassion.

This is quite different to being in a mind-bound state and *trying* to feel love for others and treat them well. Those who are attempting to emulate Jesus from a mind- bound state have to work very hard to follow a code of behavior. Their mind-dominated attention has closed down their own connection to Spirit. We all know there is a huge difference between really feeling happy and trying to *look* happy when you feel awful inside. The difference is like that.

When you have a true open heart there is no effort involved. You cannot help yourself!

Learning to live with an open heart changes the vibrational frequency of your being. Love attracts love.

It is learning to detach from, let go of, and avoid all the future snares you encounter that would pull you down and lower your frequency—all this enables you to live with an open heart. This is why studying and learning becomes necessary even if you have managed to experience bliss and an open heart. Now you are learning how to maintain the state no matter what life throws at you.

You may well experience changes in your health when you live like this: you may cease becoming ill, or less often. Or you may not: there is also the matter of any karmic debt you are working out.

In order to ascend to the spiritual world and escape the pain of the physical world this is what you need to learn to practice.

This is what Jesus meant when he said: *The kingdom of God is within you.*

### Interconnectedness

Another aspect to this is experiencing the interconnectedness of all beings. You will not be able to stay in a state of open-hearted love if you are going to selectively hate others.

*You cannot experience love for one person while you are hating another.*

Your hate for *anyone* will close your heart. It does not work to say to yourself: *"Well I will love these people because I like them and they agree with me and they are nice to me. But those bastards over there are not good to me so I will hate and resent them!"*

You will quickly notice, once you have succeeded in opening your heart, that the moment you start to judge, condemn, or spiritually disconnect from certain people, that your heart has closed.

*All* people are connected spiritually. *All.* Not just the ones who look or talk or think like you. *All* people are divine spirits with the potential to attain total consciousness, no matter how unconscious they may be at this moment. No matter how destructively they may be acting now.

So our task is to learn to love, even when people are unlovable, so that we may remain with an open heart and experience bliss and our connection to the divine.

This is why Jesus taught: *Love your enemies.* (Matthew 5:44)

I realized that if I don't *condemn* the actions of another, I can remain open-hearted despite whatever destructive thing they are doing. I can *observe* their unconsciousness, and see that is where they are at in their progress in the spiritual class of life right now, but that doesn't mean that I like or agree with, or wish to be involved in their unconscious activities.

And I can take measures to protect myself and others from them. But I can still wish them well in their progress towards eventual consciousness, at which point they will wake up and say to themselves: *My God! What was I thinking? I need to change my life and never do that again!*

It has been observed that we learn to love God by learning to love others unconditionally. As we forgive and still love our children or pets even when they are destructive, as we still love our close friends and spouses or significant others despite their faults, and as we are loved despite our own. In this way our relationships become spiritual practices.

I found once my heart was opened, that unconditional love became effortless in a way it was not before, I no longer had to work at it—I couldn't help myself. Unless of course I violated one of the habits and managed to close my heart down, then I would have to realize what I had done, make a mental note not to repeat that, and go through the open heart meditation again and repeat the experience of trying to not be caught unawares by life and momentarily lose consciousness. It is the best training procedure, because once your heart is open, the last thing in the world you want is for it to close.

As I started to experience these spiritual laws at work within myself, various pieces of the teachings of Jesus with which I had been familiar since childhood, suddenly made sense to me for the first time in my life. Jesus was a spiritual mystic of the highest degree and that was the perspective from which he was teaching.

*Loving your enemies* does not mean that you do not observe the unconsciousness of others. This does not mean that you deny your perceptions of those who would do you or others harm, and when necessary take steps to protect yourself or distance yourself from energetic mayhem.

Jesus was willing to be crucified *after* he had completed his spiritual transformation. The rest of us still have to get there, and allowing others to randomly destroy or harm you will not help your progress. You have important work to do.

It means you separate the unconsciousness and the destructive behavior from the person who is performing this. You separate the unconsciousness from the spirit beneath it.

That is why you do not judge or condemn others by denying their underlying spirituality.

In the same way you must forgive others and let go of, resentments towards them for their actions.

This does not mean you allow yourself to be victimized or harmed. But you must forgive once the dust of action has settled in order to open your own heart.

Again the principle of spiritual interconnectedness applies: to receive divine love—meaning to be open to experience ever-present divine love—you must avoid those actions that you experience have the effect of closing you off from divine love.

To experience the bliss of divine love it is necessary that you raise the vibration level of your own consciousness.

You are then able to experience your own native state—which is pure love, kindness, and compassion.

It has been observed that Buddha was the enlightened being whose path was through the 6th chakra of intellect and mind/spirit relationship, and Jesus was the enlightened one whose path was through the 4th chakra of the heart and love. Or at least that was the focus of their teachings. I have no doubt that all their chakras were healed and balanced.

We can benefit from both their teachings in balancing and healing all our chakras, and then living with an open heart in our highest vibration of love. Simply silently repeating the phrase *I love you* over and over in your head and directing it to the people and things around you, even though you do not feel it at all at first, will eventually cause a shift and the feeling of love will follow.

# 14<sup>th</sup> Habit of Transformation: Prayer and Accepting Guidance

## Prayer—Asking For Help—You Are Not Alone—Guides—Synchronicity

*Once you make a decision, the universe conspires to make it happen. ~ Ralph Waldo Emerson*

*Therefore I say unto you, what things soever ye desire, when ye pray, believe that ye receive them, and ye shall have them. Mark 11:24. KJV*

You are never alone as you make your way through life. You have guides and angels who are helping you, and trying to give you messages. Become still enough and open your mind and you will be able to perceive them. Meditation is a good way to achieve this.

As you become firmly committed to your spiritual journey your guides will respond to bring you what you need. How much you can perceive of their messages depends on how open you are to them.

When things start to manifest in the world around you, it is important to acknowledge what you receive. It is important to be conscious of, experience, and express gratitude for what you already have and each new thing that appears to aid you. As you do this, you will increase the flow of gifts and blessings towards you.

### *Prayer*

One day I was doing a guided meditation in a class and I suddenly felt I made contact with a spiritual presence who felt to me like a long lost friend. That was the beginning of feeling that I had a guide with me.

Having profound openhearted experiences gave me a sense of being in spiritual contact with a loving and nurturing force in the universe that some might call God.

When I started to do Reiki healing on others I also felt the presence of other beings helping me. I was assisting my Reiki master friend for the first time in a healing session on my wife. He was also very psychic. He had his head down, eyes closed, and was focused. He suddenly raised his head, startled and said: *You have several guides standing behind you who are helping you heal your wife*. I have been aware of the presence of other beings helping me when I did Reiki healings since.

When I came out of an ego-dominated consciousness, I was able to sense the help and existence of a spiritual presence to which I was continually connected. I no longer felt isolated and alone. I had experienced this sense of connection in the past but it was a temporary experience that I didn't perceive for what it was. As I became more sensitive to my impact on others and wanted it to be positive whenever it could, I experienced a feeling of being supported by the world around me, and my anxiety about my survival went away. The universe ceased to feel hostile, instead it became nurturing.

When we start accepting, forgiving, and cease judging others, we are able to experience our connection to them. I had a realization one day that everyone was trying to make their way and figure things out just as I was. I saw it was just *my issues* that kept me from seeing this before. Just as *my issues* sometimes close down my connection to the spiritual matrix around me.

But if I just spot where I lost consciousness, where I defended my ego, where I became impatient, where I became judgmental, and vow not to make that mistake again, I could always make the reconnection. There is never a reason to panic—*you can always reconnect.*

So out of this overall experience of spiritual contact to the world around me I to started to pray, to give thanks, to express gratitude for all that I had in my life and all I wished to manifest in my life, and to ask for guidance. This was a natural progression of what had gone before. I no longer felt an ego-driven sense that it was just all me achieving things *by myself.*

It was no longer me against the world. It felt more like a group effort and I am pretty certain it always has been. Without this help, I might well not still be here to write this. Sometimes, just the act of prayer would flood my heart chakra with love and gratitude.

I had rarely prayed during the years since I was a small child because I wasn't able to sense this connection. It felt dishonest to do so when I could sense no spiritual contact. Now prayer provides a sense of connection with Consciousness immediately. It opens my heart now. I heartily recommend it. It is another of your spiritual tools.

*Ask, and it shall be given you; seek, and ye shall find; knock, and it shall be opened unto you: Matthew 7:7*

This fact that this book exists at all is evidence of the truth of this teaching. I asked, sought and knocked over the years—this book is the result.

There have been many scientific studies over the last 40 years that have all confirmed a positive connection between prayer and physical health. Harvard Medical School cardio-vascular specialist Dr. Herbert Benson, a pioneer in the field of mind/ body medicine, discovered what he calls "the re-laxation response," during periods of prayer and meditation, when positive physical such as a decrease in metabolism, the heart rate slows, blood pressure goes down, and our breath becomes calmer and more regular. A National Institutes of Health funded study found that those who prayed daily were 40 % more likely to have lower blood pressure results than those who didn't.

Other studies have established that prayer increased do-pamine production, boosted the immune system, increased longevity; a study showed that those with religious convic-tions were 3 times more likely to recover from heart surgery, another that prayer reduced the severity and recovery time from diseases.

Physical health benefits may be the least reason to pray, and there is far more going on than will show up in scientific studies, but establishing a scientifically proven benefit to prayer is another example of the worlds of spirituality and science coming closer together and meeting.

### Guides and Help

I used to think I had never experienced anything that I considered to be "supernatural" or out of the ordinary. After my experience with Allen's death, which undeniably fell into that category, I began to look back through my life to see if I overlooked any other of these experiences. It occurred to me that it might be important to acknowledge them.

After all, when I gave someone something nice or

did something good for someone but they seemed to be oblivious, it definitely lessened my willingness to give them more. My response to people who seemed to take no joy or gratitude in receiving from me wasn't so much that I needed to have them tell me how great I was—I just wanted them to *get it*, so that the communication was completed.

When someone was grateful and appreciative for something in life, my automatic response was to give them more. As if their gratitude and joy in receiving, turned on a tap or faucet of generosity within me. When they were ungrateful it closed down my desire to give them more. I would feel: *What's the point? They don't seem to get it. It's a waste.* If that response is automatic within me and it seems to be a common response within all of us, I felt it might also be within the rest of the universe.

We call it good manners and politeness to say thank you. We brought our children up to always do this and they have always been complimented for their wonderful manners. They are all lovely people and gratitude comes from their hearts. But I believe gratitude is something far more profound than we might think. It is part of the key to our receiving the bounties of the universe.

Gratitude includes consciousness and love. How can you fully enjoy that for which you are not grateful, but take for granted?

When I looked back to see what I might have taken for granted or dismissed as mere coincidence, chance, or luck, I realized there were a few extraordinary events that resulted in me even still being around here and able to write this. These are a couple:

When I was about eight years old I went on holiday with

my parents. One day we were at an estuary somewhere in Cornwall or Devon in South West England, I don't know the name of the place. There was a long, beautiful, sandy beach and a wide river very close to the sea filled with salt water. My parents stayed on the beach and I went swimming. I looked carefully all around me before I went in the water. I was amazed that we were the only people there. As I was not a very good swimmer, I swam a little way and put my foot down to feel the sand beneath my feet. I did this over and over.

It was my intention to stay within my depth. But by now, I was some distance away from the shore. I put my foot down again and this time there was no sand beneath me. I immediately panicked and my ability to swim instantly deserted me. I went under, swallowing water. I tried to call to my parents but only went under again, swallowing a lot more water. I tried to wave to them but they were sunbathing, laying on towels on the sand and didn't see me.

I went under a third time, swallowing more water and I remembered that someone had told me that you usually go under three times swallowing water and then you drown. I realized that I was actually about to drown and there was nothing I could do about it. I remember mostly feeling some regret, but not a great deal of fear, no real panic. It seemed a shame to me that I was about to die as I had hardly got anything going in this life, and that it apparently was about to be very short and rather pointless.

Suddenly, a calm voice next to me said: *Ok son, I've got you. You are ok, just relax.* And a left arm came around my neck, lifting me up so I was no longer swallowing water. With the ease of a trained lifeguard, a man was swimming with his right arm and legs and very efficiently pulling me to shore. He did this with complete effortlessness, as if he did this all the time.

He helped me to my feet and delivered me to my parents who were still laying down and quite oblivious of what had just happened. I was coughing and spluttering, trying to expel the water from my lungs and breath properly again. The man said one sentence very calmly to my parents: *Better keep an eye on him next time, you nearly lost him.* There was no drama or reproach in his voice, just a simple statement of fact. My parents stood up in shock as the full import of what had just occurred hit them. The man turned around, walked back into the sea, and swam away. That was it. I didn't even get a chance to thank him, I was still getting the water out of my lungs and I couldn't speak.

My rescuer looked middle-aged to me, maybe forty, with dark hair and a touch of grey at the temples with a trim, and fairly muscular body. He seemed to me like a hero character in a comic book. He had some hair on his chest. He was quite good looking with a square, shaven jaw and a dark shadow of a beard. He was wearing navy blue square-cut swimming trunks. I caught all this in a snap shot as I was coughing up salt water. I was impressed by how calm and in control he seemed. He had an air of authority about him and I could see my father accept him as the man in charge at that moment, which in itself was a very rare occurrence.

My parents fussed over me to make sure I was ok. My mother seemed horrified at what had almost happened. Even my father seemed shocked. I looked back into the sea again a few moments later and I could not see my rescuer. I carefully looked all around and I couldn't see him swimming away anywhere. There was no one visible in the estuary or the long beach except my parents and me. My rescuer had apparently simply disappeared as inexplicably as he had suddenly appeared.

The timing of this whole experience had been incredible: I was swimming alone, seeing absolutely no one else in the whole estuary until the precise moment I was drowning, when an expert life saver was suddenly right there next to me to save my life. If that was all "just a coincidence" it was one hell of a good one.

I had another experience I considered to be extraordinary when I was in my early thirties. I was working for a graphics studio in West Hollywood and I was in the very unusual situation for someone my age of just learning to drive. I had lived in a country full of busses and trains and not a lot of cars at that time. In London, like New York, it is far easier to take the subway, or the "tube" as we call it, or a cab, or a bus than drive. But in LA it is hard to buy a loaf of bread if you don't drive.

On this night, I had borrowed a car from friend who worked in the same graphics studio. It was an old AMC Pacer with completely bald tires—I mean they were totally smooth, no tread at all. I was making my way over to a photographic lab in City of Industry to pick up some 8 x10 duplicate transparencies. There were a great many 18-wheeler trucks in that part of the world in the slow lane of the freeway. That evening found me at the bottom of an onramp to the freeway about to make my move to join them.

I was feeling some trepidation about my second foray onto the great LA freeway system that night—with good reason as it turned out. I, a grown man, was about to have one of those kinds of experiences 16-year-old boys usually have as they try to master the mysteries of driving. All I knew was I had to get this old car moving fast by the time I hit the top of the onramp so I could merge with the 18 wheelers. I pushed the accelerator all the way to the floor. What I had failed to notice that dark night was that there was a broken water pipe nearby and my vehicle was standing in about 4 inches of water.

The totally smooth tires spun in the water and the old Pacer was thrown into a spin as it shot up the onramp. I found myself swerving off the ramp and up the grassy incline on the side of the ramp. The car was now about to enter the freeway at a 90-degree right angle to the oncoming traffic, where a stream of very large trucks would have crushed me and the car like a bug. The new driver that I was, I had no useful reaction to these rapidly developing circumstances. I sat frozen to the wheel, my foot still down all the way on the accelerator.

I was about fifteen feet away from broad siding the freeway traffic when my miracle occurred: the vehicle just stopped dead. My seat belt prevented me from bouncing around too much. The car was at an upward angle in the grass on the side of the onramp and unscathed.

I waited for a moment until I had calmed down and gently turned the ignition key. The car started right up. Nothing was wrong with the engine at all. So what had caused it to come to a dead stop so conveniently, allowing me so escape almost certain death?

I have no idea. I was aware something amazing had happened to intervene in the situation caused by my inexperienced driving, which was the only reason I was still alive. Why should a car that is accelerating at full speed suddenly stop? Especially when the motor starts back up again immediately when the key is turned?

I put the car in reverse and slowly reversed back down

the onramp, as other cars drove around me and their drivers gave loud assessments of my mental capacity and the legality of the circumstances of my birth. Reaching the bottom of the onramp I noticed the pool of water that had caused my skid.

I said a little prayer that even unbelievers will say in extreme circumstances, and tried again. This time, accelerating gradually, I made it safely onto the freeway. Eventually, later that night, I made it safely to my bed.

The most recent thing that made me sure there is sometimes much more to "normal" life than meets the eye, happened more recently. I was going to get my Reiki treatment. The person who was going to be giving it lived about an hour out of town in a new development that was gated and required an entrance code to open the gate. I had been rushing around getting things done so I could make my appointment and I arrived at the gate to realize I didn't have the code with me. It was on the same piece of paper that had his phone number, which I suddenly remembered I'd left on my desk.

At that moment, a big rainstorm started and the sky opened up. My wife wasn't home to read me the code from the paper left on my desk and she wasn't answering her cell phone. I was now in a remote area with only a few homes built so far and it could be hours before someone drove up to the gate who did know the code. I tried a bunch of guessed and half remembered numbers but nothing worked.

I ran out into the rain and waved my arms at the gate mechanism on the other side hoping to fool an electric eye somewhere to believe I was a car on the way out. Nothing happened except I got very wet. I certainly wasn't going to walk the two miles to his house in the now torrential rain, leaving my car at the gate. I would just have to drive all the way home an hour away to be able to phone him and tell him why I had foolishly missed our appointment. I didn't want him to think I was a flake who didn't keep appointments. This was ridiculous.

I looked upward and said out loud and with a lot of intention: *Hello! I could use some help here please!* I have no idea why I did this or what help I expected to receive. I do know that I really felt what I said with a lot of intention at that moment, it wasn't a casual request.

As soon as the words had left my lips there was a flash of lightning, a thunderclap and the big gate swung open. I called out: "Thank you!" as I drove through the gate and made my appointment. If you were directing this as a scene from a movie, the timing could *not* have been more perfect.

Just another coincidence? As I said before: then it was a damn good one. When I recounted this story to my Reiki master he didn't seem at all surprised. I am of the belief that I have had some assistance staying alive during my life as I tried to sort out the differences between bravery and idiocy, and fear versus the valid internal perception of foreboding and danger. It seems that indeed I have on several occasions been a very lucky man and for that I am very grateful, and I have expressed that gratitude in prayer.

Throughout my life I have come to realize that what I took to be pure luck, coincidence, and chance at the time, was no such thing. I think I may have had a lot more help than I realized and that I didn't do everything on my own at all, as I used to believe. Since I am no longer as dominated by my ego, this realization is no longer the threat to my self-esteem that it would have once been!

As I have mentioned, while I was writing this book, at

times I came to things I didn't really understand, and yet somehow as I wrote about them, things just became clear to me. When I got things right, I experienced a flooding of life energy and love. When I wandered off the path, this closed down and I erased what I'd written and started again. This was the internal compass mechanism that guided me through the writing of this book.

The first draft of this book was written in the state of open-heart chakra that I have described experiencing many times in the book. It was not written from a purely intellectual perspective. I am certainly not saying I channeled this book, but I am aware that I received guidance when needed while I wrote it. I was certainly able to tap into a well of wisdom that became accessible to me while writing in an openhearted and conscious state.

The writing of this book became an obsession and an exercise in wisdom and education for myself. Added to which, I was suddenly strongly motivated to track down my old spiritual mentor, Douglas Buchanan, an enormously educated man, who had introduced me to Buddhism and other spiritual traditions around the age of 13.

Although he was now living in another country than when I knew him, I located him at the precise moment I needed someone to edit this book and assure me I was on the right track and wasn't passing on any false spiritual guidance. He was the only person I knew who had also been, among his many other professional accomplishments, a book editor, and for most of his life a student, and teacher, of all the spiritual material I was writing about and far more, and also a trusted friend.

I charged him with the responsibility of correcting any statement that was inaccurate from the viewpoint of spiritual truth. The last thing I wish to do is give anyone a false direction. I am very confident that through all this guidance, internal and external, what is contained in this book is true. I still follow it myself on a daily basis. The principles always work for me to produce a positive effect.

I am quickly reminded these days when I violate the laws described in this book. I rarely get sick anymore, but the last two times I slipped into negativity I become physically sick immediately. It helps to keep me on the straight and narrow.

I let my guides know that I appreciate their help. It must have often been at times a frustrating job! I used to say that I had always had a small but select group of fans throughout my life who were kind to me, loved and helped me, and they are a most important part. I very much hope they continue to guide and protect me in the same excellent manner! Actually, I am very confident that they are doing so.

I recommend that you too give some thought to this subject. Have there been extraordinary circumstances in your life that you may have dismissed as chance or luck? Perhaps there was more to them than that.

We are all on a journey; we need to pay attention as to where life has been taking us, and to the messages we are being given. Our guardian angel is always with us. Once you start to separate from your ego and meditate regularly you may begin to become aware of the being or beings who are with you on your life journey. The more open you become to receiving messages and guidance the more open you will be able to receive.

You may actually hear a voice speaking to you very briefly on occasions. Your guide is trying to help you all the time—be open to messages.

## Synchronicity

*Synchronicity* is a term coined by psychotherapist Carl Jung. He defined it as: *acausal connection of two or more psycho-physic phenomena*. In other words, things that happen together in a significant way without any direct apparent cause. He was fascinated by those surprising coincidences that had no rational explanation and had discussed this phenomena with Albert Einstein before WW1, but coined the term during a lecture 1930, when he was referring to psychological insights gathered from consulting the *I Ching*.

His attention was drawn to this during a psycho therapy session with a woman who's extreme rationalization of thought was preventing her assimilating subconscious materials and progressing. She mentioned dreaming of a golden scarab beetle the night before, and an actual scarab beetle, rare in that area, flew into their psycho therapy session. Jung then followed this symbol—an ancient Egyptian symbol of resurrection—with his patient, unearthing the cause of the neurosis from which she was suffering.

Becoming aware of and acknowledging these special "coincidences" in our lives as the interplay between the physical and non-physical realms, instead of dismissing them as simple random luck or chance, we enhance our intuition and by expressing gratitude for them we encourage more of them into our lives.

In truth, you are not alone, and you are listened to. When you need help, for yourself or others, ask for it.

Pray for the assistance you need, always asking for the *positive* aspect of what you need, never the *negative*, as in: *I want to be well*, never: *I don't want to be sick*. If you pray in the negative you are likely to get *sick*, the opposite of what you are asking for. This is very important to get right.

Just ask for help. You will always be heard and helped. It has been said that the most powerful prayer in the world consists of two words: *Help me!*

And again: use the technology of prayer that Jesus taught: *"Therefore I say unto you, what things soever ye desire, when ye pray, believe that ye receive them, and ye shall have them."* KJV. Mark 11:24

**This is very specific about belief that you *have* what you are asking for, with all the emotion and sensory details imagined as if you already have it.**

You are a child of God. Your innermost consciousness is part of God. It is the pleasure of this universal Consciousness and all the other aspects of God, to whom you are telepathically connected, to provide you with all you need to help you on your journey to awakening and obtaining Consciousness.

Therefore, do not put distance between yourself and God, or believe you are small, unworthy, undeserving, or a person of no interest. Your consciousness and the achievement of your enlightenment are as important as anything in this universe. God desires your enlightenment, just as you do, so you may return home where you belong.

Everything is available to us; we simply need to learn to shift the focus of our attention away from the illusion, to the real.

### Asking For Guidance and Remaining Open to Answers

So when we pray we can ask for spiritual guidance: *What should we be focusing on? Where should we direct our energies?*

It is important that we remain open to the guidance we receive. If instead, we assume we know what we should be doing, what our next step is, or if we pray for a specific outcome, if we have already decided where we need to go and what we should be doing, then we have assumed we already know the answers to our questions. And we will only be open to answers that fit with our existing ideas. And if, having asked for guidance, we are actually receiving guidance in one direction, but we have already decided on another direction, we are going to experience unrest, and problems.

If we are truly in spiritual school, then we must have the humility to believe we have something to learn, and that we need to remain open to the wisdom we receive.

So we need to ask for assistance and guidance *but without demanding specific results or expectations*. We need to have faith in the superior wisdom of the universal Consciousness that we are invoking. And then we remain open to receiving that which opens our hearts and fills us with positive energy and love. But the main thing is, when you need help—ask for it.

### *Other Spirits*

As we are on the subject of other spiritual beings in our sphere of influence and us being in theirs, I should mention the subject of other spiritual beings who may be attached to you who have lost their way.

My wife and I had an experience with our last horse. My wife had a very strong link with her horse Breezie. She was there at her birth and helped pull her out of her mother and then helped her stand for the first time. If Breezie was in a paddock about 100 years from the house with her head down eating Vicky only had to stand at the window of the house and without making a sound, put her attention on the horse for her to stop eating and look up at the window, as if to say, " What?" If you know about horses you know they don't stop eating casually!

Breezie had a huge personality and was very smart—she was a larger than life presence.

Breezie got old and became lame and moving was very painful for her with no chance of improvement. Out of compassion for her suffering the vet put her down. Vicky was devastated.

A few weeks passed and I walked into the field and unmistakably felt Breezie's unique personality and presence. I mentioned this to Vicky. She had experienced the same thing. I said we should both go talk to her spirit and explain that although we loved her it was time for her to move on and get another body; I told her she was smart enough to be a human if she wanted to try it.

So we both did this separately and talked to her about this. I could feel her presence as I was talking to her.

A couple of days later I went into the field and this time I couldn't feel her personality at all. I mentioned this to Vicky—" I know," she said. "She's gone."

A friend had a grandmother who died. The two had been very close, her grandmother had always looked out for her. After she had passed away my friend still felt the presence of her grandmother from time to time, and this would result in a lot of grief. She told me about this.

I suggested she talk to he grandmother and tell her she was OK, she loved her and appreciated all she had done for her but it was time for her to move on in her journey. She did so and after that she never felt her presence again.

This isn't a strange or unusual occurrence and you may have had similar experiences of your own. It doesn't help spirits to be tied to us just because we may be safe or they may be disoriented or not even realize they are dead. Just communicate kindly to them as if they were still here with you when you feel their presence, and unless they are very unconscious they will move on.

When a women experiences a miscarriage or abortion the being who was expecting to be born can sometimes get stuck, confused about what happened and can hang around the woman who may continue to feel their upset, and so not recover from the grief of the experience. Contacting and communicating with the spirit and kindly guiding them to leave and seek another body to be born into can set the spirit free and allow the woman to heal.

# 15th Habit of Transformation: Cultivate Humor and Joy

Wisdom, Healing And Humor—Joy, Love And Manifestation.

*A person without a sense of humor is like a wagon without springs— jolted by every pebble in the road. ~ Henry Ward Beecher*

*Of all our responsibilities, the greatest is being responsible for our own happiness. ~ Nathaniel Hawthorne*

*Through humor, you can soften some of the worst blows that life delivers. And once you find laughter, no matter how painful your situation might be, you can survive it. ~ Bill Cosby*

*Follow Your Bliss and the universe will open doors where there were only walls. ~ Joseph Campbell*

Laughter is good for us for so many reasons. Laughter comes from our rejection of a situation or concept, and when we insert humor into emotionally charged subjects it can have the effect of prying us loose from emotional issues we are attached to and releasing stress and raising our emotional level. Laughter is in fact, therapy, and learning to face adversity with humor, a spiritual practice.

When we become free from the grip of negative beliefs and emotions, we naturally experience lightness of spirit and we readily see the humor in the insanity and contradictions of everyday life.

If you find yourself depressed or stuck in a bad mood, simply try watching some comedy to get unstuck from that which you have become fixated on.

*Dying is easy—comedy is hard. Attributed to Sir Donald Wolfit on his deathbed.*

Great comedians are great artists and magicians of a certain kind. They are able to communicate to us on a level that, like music and some of the other arts, often bypasses our analytical thought and touches us and elicits a spontaneous response over which we have no control and which raises our spirits.

Sometimes comedy can be profound wisdom that doesn't preach but circumvents our judgments because it's funny. Comedians do a great therapeutic service to society. Comedians can be some of the most honest and sane voices in our society. It is reflective of the insanity of our society in general that usually drama and tragedy or violence is most often considered worthy of awards in the filmic arts and yet comedy seldom is.

Historically the fool or jester was employed in medieval courts and charged not only to entertain but to criticize their master, mistress and guests. Although going too far could result in a whipping! The Joker in the deck of cards is a remnant of this role.

The Trickster figure that appears throughout mythology is a cousin of the comedian. He sometimes manages to succeed by unconventional intelligence where others have failed. Sometimes he merely entertains. But other times he is a messenger from the Creator with the powers of the Creator. He often breaks rules but usually through his games, he raises awareness. In Native American cultures he is Coyote. In Norse mythology he is Loki.

Norman Cousins was the editor of a publication called the Saturday Review. In 1964, he returned home from a meeting in Moscow in Russia experiencing severe joint pain and fever. A doctor diagnosed him with Ankylosing Spondylitis, a collagen illness that attacks the connective tissues of the body. He was told he had little chance of surviving his illness. He was hospitalized but while in hospital he used the research department of his magazine to gather information about the symptoms of his illness.

He read that stress could depress the immune system of the body, and about a theory that negative emotions could be detrimental to health. He surmised that if this was true, *then positive emotions could have the reverse, positive effect.*

He checked himself out of hospital and into a Manhattan hotel suite where he engaged a nurse to read humorous stories to him and play Marx Brothers movies for him.

The only other specific aid to his recovery was taking massive doses of vitamin C. The only reason the physician went along with this was that Cousins so strongly believed in the vitamin C supplement. This combination laughter and vitamin C treatment proved to be so effective that in very little time Cousins was off all painkillers and sleeping pills.

He found that laughter relieved the pain and would help him sleep. He would laugh, go to sleep for a couple of hours and when the pain returned and woke him up he would go back to watching the movie. With this regimen Cousins cured himself of a disease that was a virtual death sentence.

Norman Cousins returned to work and wrote about his experimental treatment in his book *'Anatomy of an Illness.'* Published in 1979, the book became a best seller and helped to raise awareness in the West that there was a connection between one's emotional state of mind and one's physical health.

In 1989, it was finally acknowledged in the Journal of the American Medical Association that laughter therapy could help improve the quality of life for patients with chronic illness and that laughter has an immediate symptom-relieving effect.

Consequent research about brain chemistry and how thought and emotion results in the release of neuropeptides and their effects on cells through out our body has shed scientific light on this same subject.

Simply forcing oneself to smile when one is depressed or upset—even though this is nothing more than an upturned mouth grimace at first—has the effect of changing brain chemistry and elevates one's mood. So smile often. Just altering one's physical and mental attitude by deliberately smiling can shift one's whole outlook.

Placing a smile on one's face and on one's heart when starting to meditate can shift us out of life's irritations and into a place towards serenity.

In the past, when I used to find myself upset about something or in a black mood, I would watch a few minutes of a comedy TV show because I discovered that simply shifting the focus of my attention away from my upset onto something funny, had the effect of making it impossible for me to continue to remain stuck in my dark mood. And the fact that I could find myself suddenly laughing in the middle of something I had thought was so terrible, demonstrated that maybe it wasn't that bad, maybe I was being dramatic about nothing much, which was usually the case.

I found that simply interrupting my own mental process of being stuck in thinking about something negative—the way we sometimes do with a child who is crying when we show them another toy and they stop and forget what they are having a tantrum about, was more effective than trying to reason myself out of it.

"Wait!" I hear someone saying. "Now you are saying we are like children to simply be distracted, and mindless entertainment is more useful than constructive thought! What nonsense!"

Well OK, let me be very specific: IF you are upset because of a situation that occurred, where careful analysis can yield some insights, and we can learn and make decisions about how to improve what to do next time we encounter a similar situation, then yes, of course do that. And *then* cheer yourself up.

BUT if you have no idea why you feel sad or depressed, or you were in a conflict, and your thinking about it consists of reinforcing why you were right and they were wrong, and so pumping up your ego, then all your thinking is a waste of time and will just dig you deeper in your hole.

Often when we feel sad or depressed for no reason we are aware of, our attention is subconsciously on past incidents of loss and we aren't going to be able to access them without skilled therapy. So it is far more helpful to interrupt this subconscious flow of energy of our attention and put it onto something comedic, which will break this attachment, and raise our morale.

Remember, we cannot *reason* our way out of our mind by endlessly digging through the minutia of our past in searc of the one significance that will finally explain what is wrong with us. I have known people who did this compulsively and got nowhere except to waste their life.

When what is wrong with us is that our attention is trapped on our mind, instead of being focused on the present moment where it belongs.

The *answer* is not in the past, it is in the present. It is not *in* your mind, it is *out* of your mind, meaning escaping from the clutches of compulsive thought, and into being focused on the present moment, with your mind peaceful. As you get better at all this, you will not need so many external things to help you—you will be able to look at what you are doing right as you feel upset, see the hook you took hold of, let go and your upset will all vanish. But at the beginning, we use anything that helps. *Anything* that produces a rise in our mood, an increase in our consciousness, is valid.

The secret is the shifting of attention away from something that is only an illusion in the first place. Eventually you can learn to do this by simply directing the focus of your attention, but until then this is a good way to start observing the effect.

"Gallows humor" or "black humor" was originally the attempt to relieve suffering by trying to find something to laugh at under the most dire of circumstances, such as imminent death during wartime.

So in view of all this I recommend cultivating humor!

I was once reading a very funny novel entitled "Wilt" by Tom ¬arpe that a great friend had given me, while flying ¬m England. At the same time the plane was screen- ¬entimental film that had many ladies on board ¬eir tissues. My gales of laughter resulting from k, some of which came at very inappropriate, sad moments during the film, got me many dirty looks, and no doubt categorized as just another insensitive man... which added to my amusement.

You can train yourself to have a sense of humor if one is lacking. Seriousness is evidence of being stuck in a mind-based or deluded and unconscious view of the world.

Spiritual awakening and humor go hand in hand. Notice how elevated you feel with people who can always make you laugh, who always put a comedic spin on the most serious issues and refuse to be bowed down by them. That is not a minor talent, it is symptomatic of someone who is awakening and does not fully believe in the reality and seriousness of the Game of Life.

Take what *you do* in life seriously—by which I mean do it with full attention and intention, and do it as well as you can, but don't be somber or pompous or humorless about it. Take aligning yourself with the laws of the spiritual and physical universe seriously, and live in harmony with them, and create no more negative karma for yourself.

But don't take the game of life itself seriously, always remember it is transient but that your consciousness will always exist. And above all, don't take yourself seriously, for seriousness is a lower vibrational level than when you are in your natural state, which is joyful, loving and naturally full of kindness and humor. You were the most your authentic self when you have been the most joyful in your life, and in those moments laughter came easily to you.

So watch those comedy movies, or read those comedic novels. Just tell everyone it's your therapy! Like the song says: *Smile, darn you, smile!*

*Always laugh when you can. It is cheap medicine.* ~ Lord Byron

Humor opens the door to joy and love. We need to resonate with high emotions as much as we can to manifest what we most desire. So we need to do those things that bring us joy as much as we can. Our internal compass is telling us the way to go when we experience joy. Joseph Campbell's famous advice to *Follow our bliss* was teaching us to pursue whatever brings us the most happiness in life.

Doing something that brings you joy or love just to experience that high emotion is not self-indulgent—it is an essential part of your life. It is part of your spiritual path because it is transforming your internal energy to its highest level.

We attract what we most resonate with, so make note of what consistently raises your spirits and pursue those things, and the universe will accommodate you.

We find God in our laughter, our joy and our love.

# 16th Habit of Transformation: Bringing Your Life Into Balance

## Balancing All The Aspects Of Our Life Creates The Stability To Generate Power

*The new form of insight can perhaps best be called Undivided Wholeness in Flowing Movement ~ David Bohm*

The more I have worked at this, the more I have become convinced of the importance of bringing our individual lives into balance in order to advance on a spiritual path. When our lives are out of balance our attention tends to be pulled continuously into dealing with drama and chaos. The fact is human beings are complex creatures and we operate on many different levels simultaneously, whether we are aware of it or not. Neglecting any of these areas will pull us out of balance.

The news is regularly covering the lives of people who achieved great success in one area of their life, but because other parts of their life were dysfunctional, their lives came tragically crashing down. It is not enough to have a successful career and make money. If that is all you put your attention on, it is unlikely that you will be able to sustain it for long and you will probably experience burn out because of a failure to nurture the other aspects of your existence, which will pull you out of balance.

I have also known people who were dedicated to a spiritual path, had regular spiritual practices, and read all the right books, but who failed to deal with the most fundamental details of normal life, and as a result their lives were chaotic and always in turmoil. They were spiritually adept but physically inept and as a result quite dysfunctional. They were completely out of balance.

For some years in my youth I devoted all my time to following what I considered to be a spiritual path. I made an overall poor choice in the path I took, although it did afford me many insights, but my life became very unbalanced as I abandoned my connection to my parents, my personal life goals and interests, my health, finances, education of other matters, and my general connection to the world.

At thirty-one, I emerged and began to rebuild my life and instinctively bring it into balance again: I got married to a beautiful, loving, and multi-talented woman, learned to drive a car, got a job, started to make money, opened a bank account, developed a career and extended my education, bought a house, rehabilitated physical issues in my body, reconnected with my family, and with my wife raised my own family, then reclaimed my personal goals in art and music.

I was so fortunate to have a wife who was conscious and supported me in all this, as I did her with her goals, and we formed a wonderful team and created a beautiful home. She never once belittled any of my goals or interests; in fact she always encouraged them. I told her I used to be a painter but hadn't done it in years. She went out and bought me canvas, paints, and brushes and told me to get busy. Eventually some years later, I was showing in galleries.

She got my drums sent to me from the foreign customs shed in which they had been languishing and I started playing again and eventually formed a successful band. For my part, I bought her a horse and she started riding again and also bred horses. When I formed a band I forced her back into singing, which after her brief initial terror she reclaimed with great success and satisfaction as the natural entertainer she always was. We worked to help each other rehabilitate our personal goals, pushing and encouraging as needed to help get each other over our hurdles.

As we raised our children, she developed her career with great success, and always found time to prepare her family delicious and nutritious food.

After my life was back in balance and I was living a functional life and had re-established my power to operate in the world, thirteen years later spirituality returned to my life as I described in the first chapter of this book.

This process of rebalancing my life took me those years of dedicated, hard work as I played catch up with all the parts of my life that I had let go. It requires persistence and focus to achieve the high levels of skill and achievement we need to function well.

We exist simultaneously in both physical and spiritual universes and each has its own laws, which we need to learn and abide by if we are to navigate successfully through both of them.

A good analogy for this interdependence of the human system is a mobile: In 1931 American artist Alexander Calder invented his kinetic sculptures, dubbed by fellow artist Marcel Duchamp as "mobiles." These sculptures are suspended and move in the air. Their stability is achieved by the fact that each piece is counter-balanced by the other pieces. If you were to remove any of the pieces the sculpture would collapse.

Our lives are similar: if we focus too much on some areas but neglect others, our lives start to shift out of balance and become unsustainable. So let us examine what are the different parts of us that require our attention. Keep in mind that we are a combination of body, mind, and spirit. Our life is a system that requires treating as a whole, and we in turn are part of human and planetary systems that require regarding as a whole if they are to be sustainable.

One of the greatest weaknesses in the way the human species generally tend to function has been described as not perceiving and acting holistically, but instead viewing things and operating in a fragmented way, which leads to imbalances which then cause collapse and destruction of whole systems: We manufacture but fail to notice the damage we are creating in the environment in so doing; we treat a disease but ignore the patient's preceding emotional crisis, and so on.

We tend, as a species, to be holistically perceptually challenged. In other words—we often fail to see the big picture.

However, anytime we try to function by just focusing on fragments of the whole, the system will suffer damage and eventually collapse. For evidence of this hypothesis I offer the current state of the planet.

So it is important we consider our own human life in its broadest sense and give adequate care and attention to all its component parts.

The following aspects are part of all our lives:

**Your body** and keeping it healthy and pain free so you can do what you need to unimpeded. Feeding it well, keeping it well hydrated, getting enough regular sleep, exercising regularly so that it stays strong and functional. It is your vehicle to spiritual enlightenment.

**Your mind** as well as getting it under control and free of the toxic effects of its negative aspects, there is its **education** and the gaining of knowledge, **learning to think** clearly and logically, free of bias or irrational reaction; **learning to study**, which is the gateway to empowerment in your life as you learn to acquire new skills;

**Your personal goals** that are expressed in **your career** and **your personal interests**;

**Your finances**;

**Your possessions**;

**Your family**;

**Your connection to society** around you; **your circle of friends and all the relationships**, which are important to you and need to be nurtured;

**Your relationship to the natural world** around you;

**Your relationship to your planet**;

**Your relationship to all human beings** in general;

**Your spiritual relationship to however you name God and the spiritual realm.**

As an exercise, review this list and note down any areas that you have either neglected or that are in trouble and need your attention. Make another list of the areas of your life that are doing well or that you are working on and are functional. Arrange the non-functional list in the order you feel you can best approach them. When one of them is working well, transfer it over to the functional list. Keep doing this until everything is going as well as you can manage.

This process may highlight areas of your life that you have neglected, or have difficulty confronting, and get you taking positive action on it.

You are, or need to be, operating on all these levels simultaneously, to a greater or lesser degree, in order to attain balance in your life. The point of this chapter is to identify that all these areas are part of your life and require your attention in order for you to bring them all into balance.

Back in the days of the Ed Sullivan variety TV show there used to be an act where a man had two rows of plates spinning on top of sticks. While Khachaturian's Saber Dance played furiously in the background, the man would run around spinning each plate. Just as the last one seemed destined to crash he would arrive and get it spinning again.

Minus the sense of frantic activity or the Saber Dance, my analogy is that we need to attend to *all* the parts of our lives in order to keep them all in balance, so that we don't neglect any and have our plates come crashing to the ground.

There are many, many excellent books and other sources of information on all of the aspects of life that are listed here. In an effort to restrain the size of this book I am not going to go into each part in detail.

The important point I am making is that we need to be aware of *all* these aspects and develop and attend to them *all* in order to live a balanced life so we aren't pulled down by an aspect of our life that we have neglected.

As in everything in life, it's one thing to know something intellectually, it is quite another to put it into practice on a regular basis.

In the same way, the habits of transformation outlined in this book are interdependent. If you practice some but ignore others you will experience being pulled down by the neglected areas in your life.

Eventually we come to think of all of them as one big functional, conscious whole, but initially we need to address them as bite-sized individual parts.

The 16th Habit then is to maintain all the aspects of our physical and spiritual life in balance, so we can proceed without experiencing the self-created chaos and distress resulting from the neglect of some parts of our life. From this stability we can then generate power to manifest what we want in our life.

# 17th Habit of Transformation: Changing Negative to Positive

Techniques—Keeping Your Attention Inside Your Body—Breaking Automatically Triggered Negative Reactions—Affirmations—Undoing Negative beliefs—Monitoring Energetic Feedback—Handling Great Loss—Reiki

*Life is an echo; what you send out comes back. ~ Chinese proverb.*

*There's only one corner of the universe you can be certain of improving, and that's your own self ~ Aldous Huxley*

*The mind is everything. What you think you become.~ The Buddha*

*Energy flows where attention goes. ~ Anon*

Happiness is a choice. It comes down to what you choose to focus on, what thoughts, emotions, beliefs and intentions you choose to put your energy into—negative or positive.

These techniques will enable you to deliberately transform emotions, thoughts and beliefs from negative into a positive version as you encounter them. We are all a work in progress, as we resolve one issue our consciousness shifts and deeper issues will present themselves. Sometimes we have a period of smooth success in life, then something will happen to reveal a new area that requires us to confront new emotions or fears.

What is positive in us is not a concern (and no I am not suggesting that blind, optimistic trust in the face of approaching malevolence is an advisable path), but it is the negative that contains the limiting false beliefs, the painful past emotions, the resentments, guilt, and fears, that attract to us the life circumstances we do not want.

These, along with meditation and anything else you have found to work for you, are these tools we can use to do work on ourselves to transform negative to positive:

### A) *Always Return Your Attention Inside Your Body.*

I cannot repeat this valuable technique too many times: Whenever you finish with a mentally demanding task, or when you take a few seconds break, always return your attention inside your body and onto your heart, and become aware of the energy there.

Keeping yourself mindfully in the present moment and connected to your internal energy will cause your mind to calm down, and old reactive mental patterns to start to fade.

### B) *Breaking Your Automatically Triggered Negative Reactions*

There is a very useful NLP—Neuro-Linguistic Programming—technique that I heard described one day on the radio years ago by an NLP exponent that I found very useful to get my own triggers under control so I wasn't piling up new incidents of negative behavior to have to repair.

Interestingly, it is also an ancient yogic technique; truth keeps re-emerging and being rediscovered.

It is application of your **Attention, Intention and Will**: Using creative intention to deliberately substitute a positive response where a negative reaction existed, and using your decision and will to change a habitual response from negative to positive.

Once you have *identified* a life trigger—something that happens in life that produces an automatic negative behavior response in you that you later regret, usually involving anger and drama, *notice* your negative reaction to it; then you can *create* a mental scenario for yourself in which you are reacting to the trigger situation in the way you would like to respond.

Figure out what you would prefer to say and do when that trigger situation shows up next time, and then create a mental movie of yourself acting in this more conscious way. The more detail and specifics you put into your creation the more accessible it will be in the stressful moment.

Then when the trigger situation occurs again you will have a split second in which to choose how to respond: either in your old unconscious mental pattern way, or in the new conscious way that you have mentally rehearsed. Choosing the latter will enable you to handle the situation and remain conscious and you will have broken the old patterned response. The more you handle this trigger in the new positive manner the less power the old pattern will have, until it will eventually fade away. You will have deliberately and consciously replaced your old neural pathway.

It is a bit like the old telephone jacks that were manually plugged in on a board by an operator when you made a phone call—yes it really used to happen that way!

You have "unplugged" neural connections associated with patterned behaviors and " plugged in" new neural pathways. This is a mental handling of a spiritual issue.

Of course this takes spiritual practice, or sadhana, to bring about, but I was amazed how effective it was in allowing me to stop flying off the handle about things that had previously angered me.

The point about positive, or *dharmic*, actions is that they result in greater consciousness, and negative, or *adharmic*, actions result in reduced consciousness.

These criteria really supersede questions of morality, ethics or customs.

As someone once wisely observed: *if you speak when you are angry you may give the best speech you will ever regret.*

I have found that when I treated everyone with politeness, respect, kindness and consideration, at the level I would my parent, a treasured friend, a valued client, or an "important person," I never regretted it. This maintains my internal flow of love and experience of divine connection.

But when I failed to be polite and respectful, or revealed anger or irritation, I always did regret it. because this cut my internal flow of love.

One cannot internally demand or expect someone to respond in a particular way, or blame them for not doing this. You are not behaving consciously for someone else's response, you are not doing it because they do or do not deserve it.

You are doing it to maintain your *own* internal state. If someone is aware and does respond in kind, it is an additional reward. In the same way, you are not "behaving well" to "earn" a specific result in life. So if you behave well to someone and they behave badly back, don't fall into the trap of then abandoning your conscious behavior just because it is not appreciated. Just as with forgiveness, you are *first* doing this for yourself, not others. Your model of behavior will teach others more than your words.

You are acting as consciously as you can, following the spiritual laws, with *faith* that the universe will bring you what is *best for you at that moment*. Not a *specific result* that you *expect* to receive. Grant that God has more wisdom for what is best for you than you do, and surrender yourself to that, accepting without internal resistance whatever comes your way, even if you choose later to change it.

If you momentarily lose consciousness and behave in a manner that you regret, see it for what it is: a learning opportunity. Life has revealed another piece of your Grand Illusion to be resolved.

Don't beat yourself up for not being perfect; apologize to anyone you hurt, make up the damage if you should, locate what triggered you, and do this exercise of creating the preferable and positive response and strongly associate that positive response to the trigger situation. Then next time choose to behave with the response you have mentally rehearsed, and keep doing this in life until it becomes your new habitual positive response. You will then have become free of one more real life, consciousness-reducing trigger!

### C) Affirmations

Affirmations are a technique of repeating positive thoughts to ourselves where negative thought patterns exist. This creates a positive habit of thought and belief which starts to replace the old negative habitual thoughts. If, for example, we have deeply imbedded thoughts such as: *No one loves me, I do not deserve love, I will never be happy, I am no good,* which come from past negative experiences in life, then we need to change these internal thoughts and beliefs to a positive version, in order to bring about positive change in our external life.

If we simply continue to think and believe the old negative thought loops about ourselves, we can become depressed, and life will oblige what we are focusing on by bringing us the negative experiences that "prove" what we have thought and believed.

If we create a series of positive affirmations such as:

I AM A CHILD OF THE UNIVERSE

I CAN GIVE LOVE TO OTHERS

I CAN RECEIVE LOVE FROM OTHERS

I DESERVE LOVE

LOVE IS MY BASIC NATURE

And we repeat these to ourselves standing at a mirror for 10 minutes in the morning when we wake up and 10 minutes before we go to sleep. In just 3 consecutive weeks we will have started to create a new positive habit of thought, and this can start a complete change in our outlook and resulting life experiences.

Louise L. Hay has a very useful book: *Experience Your Good Now!* which is full of useful affirmations and ways to use them.

### We experience what we believe and think.

In other words we all have our own version of the universe around us, based on our own personal beliefs, our thoughts and our chronic emotional level. We each have our own reality, based on our own beliefs. And the universe will oblige us by matching what we believe.

If someone believes, for example, that the world is a

dangerous, dog eat dog place, that everyone is only out for themselves, then that is exactly how the world will present itself to them. It will give them experiences so they can say with honesty: "See! I told you so!" If the emotions of fear and anger are chronically resonating within them, then what they will attract is others who are also full of fear and anger.

So their beliefs about the world become a self-fulfilling prophecy. **The universe will prove them to be right in how they think about and feel about life.**

So, if you desire for your life to change: **You must first change what you believe and how you think about your life**.

Now don't make the mistake of misunderstanding the mechanics of this:

This is NOT simply a matter of telling yourself that the world is always a happy place full of blue birds, bunnies and daisies, and so you are just talking yourself into feeling better about what is in reality sometimes a very violent and dangerous and selfish world.

I am also *not* saying we should be completely ignorant of the world around us or that we should put our head in the sand. But what point is there to fixate on every negative aspect of the world that we can do nothing to change? If we internalize every negative thing in the world we will become depressed and feel powerless and overwhelmed.

What I am saying is that we will attract to us, in the way that a magnet attracts ferrous metal to it, that which is similar to us in emotional resonance. And that our beliefs about the world determine what we are able to perceive of the world. How we listen is what we hear. How we think is what we see.

So this means that although everyone is living in the same physical world, what they experience of the world is entirely different—person to person—depending on themselves and their beliefs and emotions.

In other words—*we personally select the version of the world that we are experiencing*—positive or negative, violent and harsh, or nurturing and gentle. We are all aware that different people who may live near each other, even two siblings in the same family—can have completely different lives.

Yes, we as a species definitely need to collectively wake up and drastically alter how we are treating each other and how we are treating the precious planet that is our home, if we are to survive.

Sanity starts with each individual at a time. If we can start to love ourselves, then we can start to love and nurture each other, and our planet, and we will survive.

Our mind is just the tool that allows our spirit to have these material world experiences so that we may learn our spiritual lessons.

But we cannot experience spirituality when we are locked into a mental version of the world by false beliefs and a low chronic emotional level.

The way out of our negative emotional trap—which we experience as frustration, depression, anger, resentment, self doubt and so on: is to start to change our belief system, from negative to positive. If you wish to have a positive life—you must deliberately choose to think, feel, believe and intend positive things, not negative things.

And we must also discipline the focus of our attention—what we think about and give our emotional power to. **Energy flows where attention goes.**

### D) *Challenge and Undo All Your Negative False Beliefs*

Challenge every belief you have: Do you know that belief is true? Have you investigated it? Have you checked it out for yourself or is this just something you were told long ago? Read books, Google, ask people, investigate. Banish ignorance and superstitions. The giveaway for false beliefs is that they have negative emotions connected to them.

The route into uncovering our unconscious negative beliefs is if we ask ourselves—*what areas of my life are reoccurring problems for me? Where do I fail in life? What are my Achilles' heels?*

Make a list. Your life is acting as a mirror for you—the areas where you consistently fail to be successful, where you cannot seem to control things as *you* wish, that bring you unhappiness time and again—whether it is money or business or relationships or handling power or whatever—these are where you have unconscious negative beliefs. Your life is showing you the red flags that are saying: *Dig Here! Buried Negative Beliefs are waiting to be uncovered!* And our negative beliefs are always covered up with the energy of negative emotion and the unconsciousness that arose from the mistaken idea that *this is too awful to be looked at or experienced!*

It is our negative unconscious beliefs that are continually broadcasting to the universe for it to match their reality. They are asking for your life to manifest the reality they hold in place. So whatever you fear, whatever you hate, is being attracted to you in your life as the areas where you fail and where you experience pain. This is the cause and effect mechanism in motion, and your suffering is there to get your attention, so that you can awaken and do the necessary work to heal.

Once we know *where* to dig, by working back from our

problems and painful areas of life, we have many different techniques of digging that are available to us.

Different ways may work for different people at different times. The important thing is that we do the work to uncover *all* our unconscious negative beliefs and replace them with truth, facts, and positive beliefs—our spiritual progress depends on it.

### E) *Observing Emotional and Life Feedback*

A basic technique that is used in all walks of life is to **monitor feedback** to actions taken: You try something, and then observe if it was successful or not. If it failed, you try something else. If it succeeded, then you keep doing it! This is the basis of developing all successful actions in life.

Our emotions are not, as we usually think of them, unavoidable reactions to the pleasant and painful things we experience in life. *Our emotions are an internal response to how aligned or misaligned we are with the Laws of the universe.* They are a tool to assist us to become aligned with the universe.

The way to use them therefore is to observe what makes us feel happy, peaceful, loving, content, fulfilled, enthusiastic and joyful and do more of those things.

And similarly notice what *we* are doing or thinking or believing or intending when we feel angry, sad, hopeless, or any other negative emotions, and stop doing that!

Instead most of us usually look *outside* ourselves, instead of *inside*, and look to see what the world is doing to us that isn't OK, that we are justifiably upset about, and who we can blame for why we feel upset. It is the reverse of what is going to give us freedom from our own self- caused suffering. So ceasing to blame the external world has very far reaching implications.

We are always experiencing our own energy when we

feel emotions—whether positive or negative. Yes a piece of music may be exquisite and we are filled with joy when we listen to it. But it is *our* appreciation of it that enables us to create the energy of aesthetics and joy that we experience in response. Because guess what? The person sitting next to you in the concert hall may not be able to appreciate it and may feel bored out of his mind.

It requires a certain amount of intelligence, perception and honesty to connect what we do in life (even down to the level of thought, belief or intention) to the effect it creates. Those who fail to do this are stuck in negative situations, continuing to blame everyone but themselves, and failing to make positive change or improvements.

I approached all of this *not* from a religious or "holy" viewpoint, but purely from a practical viewpoint of:

**This works to make me feel much better so I will do more of it. This other thing works to make me feel worse so I will stop doing it.**

You are unlikely to experience anything for yourself if your mind is closed to it and you believe it to be impossible. So I say, at least open your mind to entertain the possibility—*if* you desire to increase your perception and experience beyond what it is now. As Aristotle observed: *It is the mark of an educated mind to be able to entertain a thought without accepting it.*

Do not be so arrogant as to believe you know all there is to know. Ignorance and arrogance are a deadly combination.

If you think you can just go on living any way you wish to, and that none of this has anything to do with you, I will say this: you are deluding yourself.

You might as well say gravity has nothing to do with you as you jump off the balcony…

But you have free will—it's your choice, and the consequences are yours to experience.

### F) Handling Great Loss

When you are reminded of a painful memory, such as the death of a loved one, it is your own energy that you are unconsciously flowing toward the negative energy stored in the painful memory. Your energy flow makes the old memory come alive, and it transforms the frequency of your energy in present time to the grief of the memory. Your energy, thus transformed to a low frequency then flows back to you and you experience it as a feeling of sadness or grief.

If you make the mistake of blaming the painful past event for re-feeling your grief again, it is because you are oblivious of your own part in unconsciously causing your own emotional pain.

Your emotional system tells you that you are out of alignment with the spiritual laws by this experience of grief: in this case your attention has drifted out of present time.

The solution is simply to observe the negative emotion you are experiencing and realize it is simply a low frequency of energy, and attach no more significance to it, not dig around to try to locate the cause by digging around in your past trying to see where it came from unless you are deliberately doing this with a trained therapist, or judging it with thoughts that "you should not be feeling this" and so on. The energy will swell and then dissipate.

Then refocus your attention on the present moment, and the memory will settle back into the past where it belongs. Negative emotions are just tourists passing through.

Some people can stay fixated on a past memory such as

the death of a loved one for months, years or even an entire lifetime.

People talk of this as "the grieving process" without realizing the mechanics involved, or the solution; not realizing they are creating their own pain, minute by minute.

The solution to great loss includes turning all thoughts of regret to acceptance of what cannot be changed. The thought *that this should not have happened, or if only we had done things differently,* and so on, is fighting with reality. Instead, focus on being grateful that we had that which we loved so much in our life at all.

The belief that we are entitled to have it for longer is false—because reality is showing us clearly that we do not have it anymore. Instead we must create new habits of behavior, to love and live with those who are still with us, and so recreate a new life for ourselves.

The idea that there is nothing to love now in our life is also false—the whole universe is around us waiting to be loved if we just allow ourselves to become open to it.

It is important to look at the physical implications of experiencing a great emotional loss and why it is so important to deal with it proactively rather than allow oneself to continue to wallow in pain.

We talk of people *dying of a broken heart.* Researchers have established this to be a scientific fact more than just a literary turn of phrase. Japanese cardiologists discovered a phenomena they named "stress cardiomyopathy." This occurs when an emotional upset, such as the loss of a loved one, puts such a stress on the body that it causes dysfunction in the ventricle chamber and brings about heart failure in people without any history of heart disease.

The heart muscle, impacted by the heavy release of stress

hormones such as adrenaline, temporarily weakens, causing it to physically break.

Researchers at Johns Hopkins found that women with this syndrome had none of the usual predisposing factors of heart disease. The fatal physical impact to their hearts was a result of purely emotional causes: losing a loved one such as by death or divorce.

St. Andrew's University in Scotland did a study of married couples and found that more than 40 % of men and 26% of women died within three years of their spouse's death. The causes were all over the place, but the statistics are telling. It was a surprise to many to see that men were the more vulnerable of the two sexes in the case of loss.

## Personal Experience

Years ago I had a very illuminating personal experience about all this: As a young man I thought myself in love with a girl, who while away on a trip suddenly broke off our relationship and then refused to talk to me about the reason when she returned from her trip. I didn't understand what had happened and as I couldn't talk to her about it I was also stuck in the unresolved mystery. I was very upset by what had happened and became quite ill with a fever and was in bed for three weeks.

I had never been in a situation like this before. I felt overwhelmed by my predicament and felt I had to get a handle on what was going on. I decided I had to try to see what I was doing in this situation.

Suddenly I saw the flow of energy that I was still sending to my ex-girlfriend coming out from my heart in a green pipeline. It was my energy of love and creation of our relationship and I saw it flowing as a tube up into the sky, but because it was being rejected by the girl through her decision to end the relationship, it was unable to connect to her and be received as it had been previously.

So now all my own energy was coming back to me and hitting my own heart. I saw clearly that *this* was the cause of the pain I had been feeling in my own heart! This energy flow had been received by her when we were together, but now that she had cut our connection it had nowhere to go and so it came right back to me.

I also saw that what I had to do was accept the situation that she apparently no longer wished to have a relationship with me and that I needed to cease sending that flow of loving energy and the desire to create a relationship with her.

And so I did just that. There was no ill will to her on my part or resentment involved. The energy I was sending to her was no longer appropriate. I was not even aware that I was still sending it. I perceived exactly how I was creating my own pain, moment by moment, and so I decided to cease sending her my love or intention.

Without any animosity and by an act of will I simply stopped flowing my energy of love and intention to create a relationship to someone who was no longer willing to receive it. I turned it off the energy like turning a tap. The instant I did so, I saw the pipeline of energy coming from me cease and disappear.

As I was no longer being hit by the energy of my own unrequited love and desire I also felt the pain in my heart cease instantly. I had gone from feeling tormented to feeling happy and light again in an instant!

The temperature I had broke very soon afterwards and I felt well enough to return to work the following day and shortly was back to feeling fully recovered.

Our love relationships clearly exist as creations of our intention and involve high level exchanges of high vibration energy, and we need to become aware of what we are actually creating and how this affects us and others.

Do not make the mistake of believing that just because you have continual attention on missing a relationship and having feelings of longing that these are just thoughts and emotions with no further impact on you. Every thought, feeling and intention is a real creation that has existence in the physical universe and has an impact on the universe and on you.

Your feelings of longing for a specific relationship are a real energetic creation of a relationship, and if it cannot be received by the intended person, either because they are now dead or they no longer want to have the relationship, this energy will return to you immediately and you will experience it as pain in your heart chakra. People talk about the "grieving process" as though it is something mysterious and beyond our control. It is not, but it will appear so if we refuse to learn and apply the mechanics of it.

There is another aspect to this subject that can confuse the issue: we have 2 different kinds of links to all those we love and who are significant in our lives. First we have a *spirit link* to all those people, or spirits incarnated as beloved animals too. Those come into our lives according to a planned purpose to aid our mutual consciousness. We cannot lose those links or our access to those spirits, although we may no longer be able to communicate to them in physical form at this time because they have passed on—and there is a lesson for us in that fact also. So our link to them is not something for us to be concerned about—everything is as it should be with regard to loved ones who are no longer with us. We do not disrespect or belittle a great love by ceasing to attempt to create it after that is no longer possible.

Secondly, there is an *energy link* we have to those we love. This is not the same thing as the spirit link. The energy link is how we create our relationships, by sending them love, caring, and positive intentions and visualizations for your future together, in all the ways that are possible to create a relationship. But this can only function in the physical universe. So if someone we love deeply dies and we continue to send energy on this link by longing to have a relationship which cannot exist on this plane at this time, we are unwittingly violating the laws of spiritual existence, and the result is that we feel great emotional pain. The greater the amount of unreceived energy we send, the more grief and pain we feel because we are experiencing our own energy—this is a matter of simple physics. If you are in this situation and choose to ignore and apply these principles you will continue to suffer. But suffering is always a result of choice.

The instant recovery that I described in my personal experience was all simply brought about by (A) examining what I was doing in this circumstance, (B) becoming conscious of it and (C) accepting the reality of the situation and responsibility for what I was doing. And then step (D) consciously deciding to change what I was creating at an energetic level.

**These four steps are essential in the ending of extended grief**. If I hadn't realized that energy was involved, I wouldn't have been able to do this.

Remember, we are energy channeling entities—we take it in, we change it according to our thoughts, feelings, desires, intentions and beliefs—and then we send it out. And then it returns to us.

In the case of my own loss experience that I have just described, if I had yielded to the temptation of *blaming* her for causing me pain and *resenting* her, *nothing* would have resolved. By discovering what I was doing to cause my own suffering, everything was resolved in an instant.

It isn't necessary to actually see the energy you are sending as I was able to in this case, to be able to do this. I was just very fortunate to have this extraordinarily revealing experience.

When we lose someone we love dearly it is important that we deliberately deconstruct the creation of a relationship, which no longer exists. If we continue to long for that which cannot be, realize that is manifesting in energy that we are actually creating and which is then affecting us negatively, because we are trying to create what cannot be created. And longing for them is doing that.

If someone has died we need to fully come to terms with that and cease trying in our minds to think of them as if they were still alive.

We need instead to focus on the living.

In these situations whenever we blame external circumstances for our own pain we are like a man who is hitting himself in the head with a hammer wondering why he has a headache.

It is your choice whether or not to suffer.

I will repeat the same spiritual laws again:

**We experience what we create.**

**Responsibility, not blame is the solution to our suffering**.

The other false belief that can tie us into continuing to suffer at the loss of a loved one to the detriment of our emotional and even physical well-being, is the belief that we dishonor someone if we don't grieve their loss for a long time.

This simply is not true. Express your respect and love for a departed loved one in any way you feel appropriate and respectful, but as in all things, do it positively: celebrate their life, be grateful that you had them for as long as you did. Accept the reality that they are gone.

Some people find the situation of suffering to be comfortable on some level: it gives them purpose, it may give them a sense of identity, it may bring them sympathy and attention. And so getting rid of their suffering is the last thing they are interested in. And so none of this information is likely to be well received.

This is a lot to grasp because it is the opposite of everything that possibly everyone around you probably has always done. But as we examined at the beginning of the book, statistically humankind is quite insane. If you wish to become functionally sane you will have to stop using "what everyone else does" as a workable model.

You have to become free of group consciousness, develop your own intuition, and become your own light in the darkness.

### G) Other Techniques

Various other therapies such as Reiki, Regression Therapy, Yoga, Pilates, Acupuncture, Massage, Lifeline, Body Talk, Reconnective Healing, Qi Gong, Psychotherapy, Tapping and other kinds of therapies that release old negative energies are effective and worth investigating to find what is a fit for you, to address what you need at any given moment to provide help.

I would recommend anyone to be attuned in Reiki, which

makes this healing modality available to use on yourself for physical and emotional/ spiritual healing, and anyone you care to help. I have never seen it fail to be of benefit.

I have also personally experienced Regression Therapy, Yoga, Pilates, Acupuncture, Massage, and Lifeline, and all have been very helpful at different times for quite different issues: physical, emotional, and spiritual. Which is the point. We are all a work in progress—we handle one issue and later another level of issue shows up which requires another approach. If something manifests physically then that is what needs to be addressed.

The important thing is to seek help when it is needed and keep trying until you find what works for you to handle the issue at hand.

# 18th Habit of Transformation: Controlling Your Internal World

## Deciding to Remain Internally Calm and Positive Despite the External World

*Let's not forget that the little emotions are the great captains of our lives and we obey them without realizing it. ~ Vincent Van Gogh*

*It's not what happens to you but how you respond that matters. ~ The Greek Stoic philosopher, Epictetus*

In this chapter I want to examine concepts we have touched upon already, but I wish to draw them into sharp focus here, because they are crucial.

There is a paradox about the relationship between our external world circumstances and our internal world experiences, which almost all of humanity has misunderstood completely since the dawn of our species.

This misunderstanding has resulted in one of the most damaging false beliefs we can have.

Most of us believe that our internal world of emotions and sense of peace, joy, and well-being *depends* on the state of our external circumstances. For example, if we have good fortune, if things go our way, or if we are doing well in life, *then* we feel happy.

If they are not, then we tend to respond to these circumstances by experiencing an array of negative emotions: disappointment, anger, fear, anxiety, and resentment.

If these unpleasant external circumstances persist, we form negative beliefs, such as: *the world is cruel, we are not loved, we have bad luck,* and so on. So we are making our internal state be *conditional* on an external world over which we know by experience we often have little control.

So then we spend all our efforts to create our *external* world how we want it, *in order that we can be happy in our internal world.* Small wonder then that most people experience life as full of pressure, stress, and suffering. Because no matter how much money or power we may have, there are always all kinds of things that can bring us to despair if we are dependent on the external world to tell us how we should feel.

Let us considering turning this cause and effect around: Instead of trying to change the *external world* so that we may be happy, why not simply change our own *internal world* and become happy, and then stay that way despite every external reason not to?

Magically, once we achieve this, we experience our outer world experience changing to accommodate us.

The truth is we have the relationship between inner and outer worlds exactly backwards and that is the paradox. When we make our internal world dependant on our external world, we make ourselves powerless—we become dry leaves to be blown around by any gust of wind that comes our way.

When we realize, however, that *we can create our internal state as we wish it to be by our decision to do so,* regardless and in spite of our external circumstances, we open the door to our power—to taking control of our lives and creating them as we wish. We used to refer to this as: *pulling ourselves up by our bootstraps.*

This requires developing our intention, and learning to control our own energy.

There *is* a relationship between our internal and external worlds—but it is not as we have believed. **Our external world is a mirror of our internal world,** so in order to change our external world we must *first* end our dependency on the external world to tell us how we should feel.

When we raise the vibration of our internal world, so that our chronic emotions and thoughts, and our beliefs, intentions and acts become positive, despite every external reason for them to not be so, then we have broken the grip of the external world upon us. We are not longer its pawn. Our own spiritual universe becomes more real to us than the illusory world of the external physical world.

This breaks the cycle of creating new negative karma in our future.

But when we react negatively to difficult present time events, we are in effect asking the universe to bring us *more* events in our future that match that low vibration of our negative emotions, thoughts, beliefs, intentions and actions. But when we remain *positive* internally, regardless of any negativity we are experiencing now in the external world, and we are creating only positive karma for us in the future.

This is the meaning of Jesus' teaching to love God, love our neighbors and even love our enemies (Matthew 5:44 KJV). He was saying we should remain in our highest state of vibration no matter what.

Buddha also told us:

*Peace comes from within. Do not seek it without.*

*What we think, we become.*

*We are shaped by our thoughts; we become what we think. When the mind is pure, joy follows like a shadow that never leaves.*

The reason the external world is difficult is so that our unhandled negativity is revealed to us, so that we are forced to do our spiritual work to avoid our discomfort and suffering. If everything was always comfortable and plentiful, would we ever change?

Ernest Shurtleff Holmes was an American writer and spiritual teacher (1871-1960) who wrote among many other books, *The Science Of Mind,* published in 1926. He has influenced many students of the metaphysical, and was acknowledged for his work and received a number of international honors. He wrote this about the power of belief and thought to manifest in our lives:

*As soon as we become rich in our thought then we will be rich in our expression. These are not mere words, but the deepest truth that has ever come to the human race. Hundreds of thousands of the most intelligent thinkers and the most spiritual people of our day are proving this truth. We are not dealing with illusions but with realities; pay no more attention to the one who ridicules these ideas than you would to the blowing of the wind. In the center of your own soul choose what you want to become, to accomplish; keep it to yourself. Every day in the silence of absolute conviction know that it is now done. It is just as much done, as far as you are concerned, as it will be when you experience it in the outer. Imagine yourself to be what you want to be. See only that which you desire, refuse even to think of the other. Stick to it, never doubt. Say many times a day, "I am that thing," realize what this means. It means that the great Universal power of Mind is that, and it cannot fail.*

Love is our highest vibration, it is what we are in our

natural state when the unconsciousness of the Grand Illusion is not impinging on us. Our spiritual goal is to remain in this state of love and forgiveness, no matter what is doing on around us.

Our internal world and the external world are only interdependent *if* we decide they are. Their connection—that external life circumstance A must automatically result in internal emotional reaction B, will remain true for us for us, *until* we decide otherwise. Once we decide that our internal landscape is under our control, and quite separate from the physical world experience we are in right now, we start to rehabilitate our ability to control our own experience of existence.

This may be going against the habit of lifetimes, but it can be done, step by step. We can *choose* not to react with anger, grief or negative desires for revenge when life does not go our way or others do us harm. This is what Jesus was teaching with *love thine enemies.* We can choose to stay positive internally despite every human logical reason not to.

It won't happen all at once but it can be done, one decision at a time, and by using the techniques we have discussed. This is how we become free of the physical universe.

This is where we again pick up the realization of Viktor E Frankl, the Jewish psychiatrist in Nazi Germany who was imprisoned in four concentration camps, including Auschwitz. His parents, his brother and his pregnant wife were all killed by the Nazis.

Viktor described in his book, *Man's Search For Meaning,* realizing that believing strong negative emotions were automatic and unavoidable human responses to suffering, was to surrender one's true power over one's own internal experience.

He described his realization as: *"Freedom is that point in time just after they do something to me and just before I choose my response to it."*

He realized that he could *choose* how he experienced the suffering he was enduring. In the midst of extreme suffering he was able to identify his ultimate freedom.

He emerged from his nightmare experience, not crushed, but in possession of a great wisdom.

This is a very profound realization—just to know that this is even a possibility is a bit like discovering fire, it has the potential to be so completely liberating—and something each person needs to practice until they have mastered this as a skill. Then we can separate what is happening to us in the external world from our response and the peace of our internal world. Each annoying and disturbing event in our life is another opportunity to practice remaining calm despite every reason not to be—there is no lack of those incidents!

Repeat this truth to yourself: **My internal experience of peace, love, and joy is in no way dependant on my external circumstances. I alone determine this by my decisions.**

Now change your focus to start living this truth.

We may not be jumping for joy. We may not be having the *best* experience of our lives but we are also not giving in to despair, anger, resentment, and fear. We make a deliberate decision of will to live according to our God-given ability to rule our own destiny and to create our own life as we wish to live it, in peace, joy, and love.

We say a prayer, ask for help, and trust that the universe will take care of us, aware that we are not going through this alone. It may be a hard lesson to experience, but this too shall pass.

You may have known people who experienced a difficult situation and staggered a bit from the initial shock, then said things like: "Oh well, no point in being upset about it, that won't help, what is done is done, better to cheer up and make the best of things, life goes on". Someone may make a joke and there is laughter and they start to raise their spirits by sheer force of will.

Compare it to being in a theatre watching a movie—we can enjoy the experience and perhaps even learn from it, but we seldom lose *all* ability to control our own emotions and become completely taken over by it. Just as we can say to ourselves: *That was just a movie,* we can also say to ourselves: *This is just a life experience, don't take it so seriously.* View it not as tragedy, but as an opportunity to learn a valuable lesson to aid your consciousness—because that is precisely what it is.

One day your life will come to an end, but you will still exist and so will your consciousness. So what is the worst that can happen? We can die. But we are all going to die anyway, guaranteed. So why not maximize your current life experience while you are here? You really have nothing to lose and everything to gain.

Once we have decided to take control of how we feel internally, and not allow ourselves to be controlled by reactive negative emotions whenever things don't go well in our lives, then we have started to create a base on which we can manifest what we do want in our lives.

Our next step is to create and visualize what we do wish to experience in the outer physical world, in our internal mental world. Having defined what we want and visualized it, we hold onto it persistently with intention, with high positive emotional vibration, and without contrary negative doubt, beliefs and emotions that will sabotage us. We think of it as if it has already happened with all the emotions and thoughts we have. We are creating a full mental reality in order to cause the physical universe to respond to us. *Then* we will experience our external world changing to our desires.

This is the meaning of Jesus' teaching: *Ask, and it shall be given you; seek, and ye shall find; knock, and it shall be opened unto you.* Matthew 7:7.

This is what some call the Law of Attraction—remember, *we attract what we are.*

As some of you are reading these words, you may find yourself in the middle of some kind of negative karmic experience that you have created in the past, or it is simply coming to you just because there is a lesson of consciousness in it for you, which is the same thing in practice.

You have to go through this experience. You have no choice. However, if you can resist the temptation to fall completely into negative emotions and find the strength to accept what you are going through without collapsing into self-pity, resentment, or denial, then through *acceptance* you can decide to shift your internal landscape from negative to positive by the power of your will.

You can do this by remaining aware—and this may require continual self-reminding—that the "real life" physical experience you are having at this moment is, at the level of eternal spiritual reality, illusory in nature. Meaning it is temporary and physical, and you are at your core eternal and non-physical. Then you will experience this detachment of the external and internal worlds.

### Meditation

So in order for us to play the game of life as well as we possibly can, we must never lose sight of the fact that it is only a game, just another of the spiritual paradoxes.

We have to detach ourselves from this dependence on the vagaries of the outside world for our inner emotions.

We have to tell ourselves: **It doesn't matter what is going on around us, we are going to maintain our internal equanimity, regardless.**

Our physical reality can become pretty intense and stressful—it can demand our attention and reveal all our fears and insecurities and grief buried deep within us—it can say: "Look! This is real life! You can lose all that you love! Be afraid! Weep!"

And this is exactly why daily meditation is important—it is our daily reconnection to our divine reality beyond our temporary physical reality. This is the way our physical reality does not become our only and dominant reality, because if we slip back into the false viewpoint that this physical reality is all there is, any disaster that comes along can overwhelm us.

Meditation can restore our inner peace within the storm.

Cause comes from within us, our own God Consciousness—the external world is the effect of our internal cause. When we falsely believe ourselves to be the effect of *external* cause, we lose our ability to cause and we become only effect.

All people who are able to cause effects in the external world grasp this principle, at least in part. They practice the trick of detaching their emotions from what is around them, and internally envision and create positivity regardless of what is out there—with the result that things start to improve. That is the magic technique!

These are the people who get struck down by disaster, brush themselves off and start to rebuild and recreate what they visualize internally. They don't allow themselves to be crushed by internalizing the negative events in the outside world.

The reverse is when we believe in the absolute power and reality of the physical world and the insignificance of our thoughts and beliefs, as well as believing our own inability to create or cause positive change. This is the depression and powerlessness of total effect. We see this in some who are locked in depression and believe they need mood altering medication to get through life.

Depression which is *not* the result of physiological imbalances, such as those which can occur after childbirth or in the case of bipolar disorder, but which have a *mental* cause, is the result of believing and being dominated by one's own negative false and limiting beliefs.

The solution is not giving medication to those without actual medical conditions, although this is practically epidemic in America now with more than 1 in 10 people on antidepressant drugs, which is enormously profitable for drug companies. Even when medication is used it shouldn't be the only approach—combine meditation with it.

The solution is for us each to awaken from the paralyzing grip of our own mind and its negative false beliefs.

Meditation, not medication! And inspection of each belief to see whether it has any foundation in reality and science, and if not, let it go.

### Remain Focused on Inner Peace and Love

When someone treats you with great negativity they are creating negative karma for themselves. But how you choose to respond to that negativity determines your karma: positive or negative—it is your choice. If you truly wish to live with inner peace, joy, and love, **you must make a decision to refuse to abandon them each time a difficulty arises in the physical world.** To do so is to mistake this temporary physical reality as more real than your own inner reality, which shall persist even though this physical reality has changed and ceased to exist.

As you begin to master this, you will cease to attract the same tests to hinder you, and those tests that show up will be less of an issue for you. Then, where you were Velcro, sticking to every problem, you will become Teflon and slide through trouble, calmly handling things but not being impacted internally by them.

This may seem to be a small, bumper sticker-worthy piece of jingoism, but it is a simple, very profound, and very workable principle.

You can decide to *refuse* to lose your inner sense of calm, peace, happiness, and love.

You can refuse to take refuge in your ego and become outraged, defensive, important, and intolerant: "Do these people realize who I am? These people are morons! I can't stand these idiots!"

You may think: "Well that would just be insane!"

Really? More insane than wasting a lot of energy jumping up and down, raising your blood pressure, bombarding your cells with all kinds of harmful biochemicals because you've convinced your body the world is about to end? That kind of stress is tremendously hard on your body.

Try it. Try not reacting, not complaining, not swearing, not getting upset at all. Being patient. Staying calm, not ranting and raving. Just try accepting what is happening and then get on with fixing it calmly.

Create a new habitual behavior of *not* getting frustrated and acting out when life goes wrong.

I know a young singer who has amazing calm. I asked her where she learned it. She replied that her two parents handled problems in completely opposite ways: her father, a minister, always remained calm—she only ever saw him lose it twice in her entire life, no matter what was going on. Her mother on the other hand, *always* got mad, yelled and screamed and made a big fuss. So as she grew up she had two opposite examples of how to respond to life's problems being demonstrated in front of her by her calm father, and her emotionally reactive and dramatic mother.

She said that she decided, when she was young, that she wanted to remain calm like her father, and not react like her mother. It just seemed to make more sense to her. I told her she was absolutely right and that she was a living example of a very profound principle, and never to lose that awareness.

She achieved her inner calm by a decision and a practiced habit to do just that no matter what.

**Maintain your inner peace and love—no matter what.**

### *Decide To End The Drama*

Make a decision to end your own drama today. Don't give into it yourself, don't get upset and feel sorry for yourself when things go wrong, don't get caught up in other people's drama, don't listen and engage in gossip about others, don't allow you inner peace to be polluted by watching reality TV shows of people acting out ridiculous bouts of conflict, ego and drama.

**If you can learn this one simple trick, it will transform your life**.

You *can* decide to be calm and happy, regardless of what is going on around you. It is a decision you can make. Not because you are mindless zombie and not because you are a fool who is unaware of reality. But because you realize that "reality" will *always* be challenging—it is designed that way. It is a test to see if you can remain connected to your divine awareness *despite* every logical reason not to be.

*That* is the paradox, *that* is the way out of the trap. Remember, you are in school—your lesson is to learn that your inner landscape is of your own making, under your control, that you can create it to be filled with calm and love. You have the right, *the duty* to yourself, to pursue your happiness. If you can detach from the false concept that the "real world" out there should dictate to you how you should feel in here, you can walk out of your prison cell and into the garden.

The world as a whole has always been a mess: wars, famines, pestilence, market crashes, disasters of one kind or another. Read some history if you don't believe me. There have been bubbles of things going Ok here and there for a while—then things happened. Winston Churchill's observation was: *Life is one damn thing after another!*

If you are going to wait for your life to be perfect before you can be consistently happy then you will stay locked in your cell—trapped on the endless wheel of incarnations and suffering.

There has never been a better time than right now to change everything by **deciding** that you will remain peaceful as you encounter the problems and difficult people of the world and remain connected to your inner joy, love and happiness that is the essence of you.

Situation A does not mean reaction B must automatically follow.

Problems, difficulties, and losses *do not* require that you freak out. There is no law of the universe demanding that.

Instead, see yourself in life as being in a classroom. This is your Life Test for the day: Here comes difficult situation A. Can you maintain your inner peace while you deal with it and pass the test? Or will you once more bristle, become rigid in your attitudes, get upset, blame others, and fail the test? Because that is why these difficult things keep happening; they are happening to teach you this lesson. Once you learn it, notice whether your life starts to calm down and run more smoothly, with that particular difficulty no longer showing up in your life.

Change your inner landscape and you will transform the world around you in ways beyond your understanding. This is the most valuable thing you can do for yourself, and others.

This does *not* mean that we abandon our responsibilities to deal with the world around us as well and as intelligently as we can.

Cultivate your inner calm. Make the decision now to empower yourself to continually maintain the peace, calm, love and happiness of your inner consciousness. Because *that*, not the world around you, is what is really real. That is the Truth.

It is the physical world outside of you, that is the illusion, the dream.

But can it really be as simple as that? Yes, it can. It is.

Our inner landscape does not depend in any way on the outer landscape.

Only when you decided that there was a relationship did one begin to exist.

So you can undo that decision so that you remain at peace and connected to Spirit or Consciousness, regardless of your current external circumstances in the physical world.

### *Worrying is a Waste of Our Effort*

This does not mean that we abandon our responsibilities to deal with the world around us as well and as intelligently as we can. And this does not mean we are adopting insensitivity or callousness—this is living in the viewpoint of timeless reality and non- identification with the temporary, illusory physical universe we are currently experiencing.

This is exerting your power of choice as to how to respond to life. Your choice is one of the greatest powers you have. You can choose to remain positive despite every apparent reason why not.

Every thought, emotion and intention you have shapes your future, as positive or negative—it's your choice.

Once you accept this as a worthwhile habit to strive for, then the rest of your life, no matter what you are doing, becomes an invaluable spiritual practice to put this into effect every day.

At the farthest point we can take our thought process about survival and disconnecting ourselves from anxiety is the realization that if we simply let go of any necessity to survive, then we can experience an enormous freedom from fears.

The human experience could even be characterized as an

attempt to control that which cannot be controlled! No matter how successful a person is in controlling their external life, there will still be aspects that are beyond their control and that impact them greatly. We are all going to die—guaranteed. So are we going to waste the life we do have worrying about the moment and manner of our death? It is simply beyond our control! Why not instead, focus on learning to control the only thing we can—our internal life.

And have faith that a Conscious universe will give us what we need to experience so we can become more conscious.

# 19ᵗʰ Habit:
# Letting Go of Attachments

## An Exercise To Assist In Letting Go Of Attachments

*By and by comes the great awakening, and then we find out that life itself is a great dream. All the while, the fools think they are awake as they chase suffering and cling to what is bound to change. ~ Chuang Tzu, Taoist sage, 400 B.C.*

*If you realize that all things change, there is nothing you will try and hold on to. ~ Tao Te Ching, verse 74.*

The truth is that everything around you is impermanent. One day you will die.

One day everyone you know and love and hold dear, will die. All your prized possessions will be lost to you. Everything must pass. Nothing stays the same.

The most basic law of the physical universe is change. Everything in the mundane universe is constantly changing, down to the smallest particle. The very existence of the physical universe is dependent on the motion of all its particles.

Only the consciousness of being is eternal, your awareness of existing; all you are aware of and all the wisdom you have learned, this is what you will take with you. This is the "I am" in Exodus 3:14 in the Bible.

The lessons that expanded your consciousness are the gold of your current existence, the only valuable thing you will take with you from this life, none of your physical possessions— does that change your perspective about living your life?

When we try to hold on to parts of this ever-changing universe, with the belief that they should be permanent, we are simply not aligned with reality. We are living instead in our fantasy, mentally created world.

It is our attempt to assert our mental version of *what should be* which comes into energetic conflict with the reality of *what is,* that causes us to suffer.

The *only way* for us to remain sane and joyful and at peace during our physical existence is to realize the truth of the impermanence of all that is around us, and to let go of all our false attachments to it, and simply enjoy it while it, and we, are here.

The universe is an incredibly beautiful dance of conscious energy in motion. By being part of it we are able to experience this beauty, and take part in creating our own beautiful forms and appreciating the creations of others: the face of a new born baby; a body; our family; a beautiful piece of music; a pet; a tree full of blossoms; a sunset; a landscape; an ocean; a piece of architecture; a painting; a piece of sculpture; a film; a car; a plane; a city...

There are endless forms to play with and from which we can experience wonder and joy. We can experience gratitude for what we experience—but still not be attached to it, not believe *we are it,* or delude ourselves that this is anything but *temporary.*

We can all experience gratitude that we can be part of this experience. If you need a reason for the existence of the universe, surely you need look no further than the pure joy of creating forms, either yours or appreciating the creations of others. I have experienced joy by creating paintings, playing music, writing, experiencing events and environments.

And I have experienced joy from appreciating many kinds of creations by others. If I could create planets and an entire universe I would do that for the sheer joy of it.

And would I prefer to share my creation with others who could appreciate my creation as well? Absolutely! Well there is the original reason we have a universe and humankind.

Do I believe God created the universe for the joy of creation, and then created the illusion of separate consciousnesses through individual minds, so that there would be others to enjoy and admire his creations? I can think of no better reason. I love to create. And I love to share what I create with friends. Doesn't everyone? I do not see why God would be any different.

But to argue with the motion and continual change of the universe, is foolishness.

When I became aware of my own fears—fear of all the people and things I might lose, I realized I was arguing with the universe.

Although logically I knew that when I died I would lose everything in my physical experience anyway—there was no way to avoid it. We all die.

There are also various activities that I love: making art, making music, looking and listening to art of all kinds, being with friends and family, being in nature, eating, having sex, dancing, different kinds of physical activity and so on—all the sensual pleasures of the physical world. And at one point in my life I was very attached to them.

You may have a different set of activities you are attached to. The list can be different but the principle and the goal of no longer being attached beyond your control to things that are external to you, is the same.

And this has nothing to do with not loving life or not loving other people deeply.

It has to do with 1) being able to go beyond your love of others and things in life which acted as a portal to a heart opening experience for you, because you are now able to experience bliss by opening your own heart, and so no longer being addicted to these things.

And 2) not having fears or compulsions about all the things that control or have power over us because we haven't confronted them full on.

So I decided to try to attempt an exercise of envisioning losing everything I held dear in my life—a menu of my worst nightmares: losing my wife; my children; my friends; my possessions; my favorite activities and finally my life. I was attempting to let go of my fears of losing all I loved. First I sat down on my own and meditated and opened my heart.

Then I mentally envisioned losing everything I held dear and desperately loved in my life.

I did this one at a time—imagining that each person, each family member, each thing, was no longer in my life. I saw myself losing them, burying them, and saying goodbye to them.

And as I imagined this with each one I asked myself this question: would I be able to accept this loss? Could I still live my life? Could I find a reason to live?

If I was penniless and alone—would I still want to live, could I re-create a life? Would there be purpose to my life with all that taken away from me?

And the answer I found was—yes.

That was my experience.

I had been able to experience enough connection to people in general, to life around me, to a sense of connection to universal spirit, that I no longer felt isolated.

I noticed that once I was able to experience opening my own heart and experience that connection to bliss, all these ceased to be addictions or compulsive attachments—I no longer *had* to have them to make my life purposeful. I enjoy them and I'm glad to have them and have no desire for them to leave my life—but the compulsive aspect of them and the associated stress of that compulsion has gone.

That is why being able to open one's own heart and have a profound experience of connectedness and love and bliss is absolutely pivotal to our evolution and becoming centered. Otherwise all this sounds like unattainable nonsense. It did to me from the time I read about non-attachment in Buddhist books as a teenager until my own heart-opening at will experience, decades later.

This exercise allowed me to let go of my fears that I couldn't live without any of the people and things I love as well. And that was very liberating.

It is important that if we are to be set free from our addictions to the physical universe itself, which are part of the reason we are compelled to return here, that we can naturally let go of our clinging to all the aspects of it, because of our bliss experience which eclipses it. Our bliss experience is our view past the physical universe experience to what awaits us in an enlightened state.

So why did I put myself through that and what was the point?

I was simply trying to break mental attachments that I had to the way things are now. To accept the inevitability of what, in the fullness of time, would definitely come to be.

Using the principle of **what we can completely face cannot hurt us**, I wished to undo the mental fears I had about loss, by facing the idea of loss.

The result for me was that I didn't feel anxiety about losing those people and things that were precious to me afterwards.

I'm not saying that I was then completely immune to any experience of suffering of real loss. But I am confident that, as in the case of my parents dying, I would be able to handle it.

So I was able to let go of the fear of loss.

Anxiety about something that may happen, but is not actually happening, stems not from a real event itself, but from the anticipation of an event. It is the mental model of the possibility of an event in the future which we create, prior to something happening, and which we then use to terrify ourselves! It is not the event itself—but our *thoughts* about the event that cause us to suffer.

It is another example of future *what-if* scenarios—the result of not being fully in the present moment.

Once I had completed the exercise I let go of these thoughts completely. Because we tend to attract to us that with which we resonate and continue to think about.

And that is why to dwell on one's fears—*"I must never lose my money, my house, my family etc."*—is to eventually attract those very events to oneself.

This is important: After I finished the exercise I spent time deliberately feeling gratitude for all that I had in my life and feeling the love and joy I have for all of them.

So this would have the effect of attracting them in a positive way, to cancel out my mental exercise, so that I didn't leave a residue of the losses I had envisioned to create a negative event.

*If you can face the idea of losing everything you have, without feeling fear of that idea, then you will become more free to enjoy all you have around you while you have it. Your joy and peace of mind and gratitude is increased. You can then love all you have more fully, without the fear of loss.*

### Exercise:

Ask yourself: What are you afraid to lose?

Make a list.

Visualize losing them all. One at a time.

After each one ask yourself: Can you accept that?

And: Would life still be worth living? Could you continue to create your life?

Then, at the end of this exercise, go over your list and experience gratitude that each is in your life, and realize that each one *is* in your life and you are happy and appreciative for that, so you do not leave a residue of telling the universe you do not want them all.

Say a prayer of gratitude for all you have in your life that you love.

# 20ᵗʰ Habit of Transformation: Becoming Centered

Follow Your Inner Compass—The Answer Is Inside You, Not Outside You—Don't Require Approval From Others—Overcome Your Addictions

*Your vision will become clear only when you can look into your heart. Who looks outside, dreams. Who looks inside, awakens. ~ Carl Jung*

*To be yourself in a world that is constantly trying to make you something else, is the greatest accomplishment. ~ Ralph Waldo Emerson*

*What other people think of me is none of my business.~ Dorothy Parker*

*Man struggles to find life outside himself, unaware that the life he is seeking is within him.~ Kahlil Gibran*

If you have read this far in this book, because at least some of it is resonating within you as true, then you are an "old soul" who has had many incarnations, and undergone many, many experiences, and learned many spiritual lessons that reside within you as innate wisdom with which you entered this life. The great amount of your learning has been done—you are close to the final shifts in consciousness that will release you from the trap of endless incarnations.

Becoming centered is one of those shifts. This is a phrase I use to describe the moving of one's universe inside oneself, which occurs as we realize that we are causing all we experience, that we alone are responsible for ourselves and our life, that we alone can change things for the positive, that we alone can reach enlightenment. When we realize that the power and consciousness we seek is inside us, and we cease to search outside ourselves.

As we begin to become more and more aware that we are responsible for causing what we are experiencing in life, we begin to assume more and more control over what we do, say, and allow our minds to think.

We cease to blame others, luck, chance, the planets, our parents, ex-spouses, current spouses, boyfriends, girlfriends, high school teachers, college professors, coaches, bullies, bosses, siblings, the competition, the government, foreign dictators, aliens, God, the universe, and the world in general for our condition!

The final realization about forgiveness is that we caused ourselves to have the experience we are blaming others for, and this somehow is the experience we need to have right now until we learn its lesson, so what is the point of blaming anyone?

We see the futility of all that. We see that we got ourselves into this situation, and only by taking responsibility and taking back our power can we extricate ourselves from it. We stop fighting reality because we see that we created the reality we are experiencing. If we want to change our external reality, we first need to change our internal reality.

So our gaze shifts gradually from *out there* to *in here* for solutions.

The outside world gradually ceases to hold the promise of fulfilling us, ceases its magnetic and mesmerizing hold on us. Places, possessions, other people, wealth, power, the admiration and approval of others—all these external things that used to hold us captive, begin to fade like a child's toy that loses its magic appeal when we start to awaken from the Grand Illusion.

As we learn to open our own hearts, learn to experience our connection to others and to universal consciousness, we begin to see that the Kingdom of God does indeed reside within us.

I found my relationship to the external world changing in this respect. I have always loved aesthetics in all forms: music, films, art, beautiful objects, beautiful locations, nature, beautiful women, beautiful physiques—and I still do—spiritual consciousness manifesting in the physical universe as aesthetics. It takes great awareness to bring great beauty into the world. Great artists create that which proceeds from their perceptions and consciousness.

But what changed for me was that I ceased to immerse myself in these things in an attempt to find that perfect painting, that perfect piece of music, that perfect film, or that perfect person, who would be my portal to the divine.

In fact, the moment I discovered I could open my own heart and access my connection to Spirit, everything changed.

I ceased looking *out there* for the answers, and started looking *in here*.

As we learn to access portals to the divine within *ourselves,* we cease to be addicted to the people or activities outside us that used to provide our portals. And so the external world and those around us assume their correct roles in our lives. Things become things, other people become other people, whom we may love and treasure but whom we no longer use for an incorrect purpose, to whom we are no longer *addicted.*

We are really in relationships to become more *conscious,* not because we have any illusions that it is another person's job to make us *happy.*

This gradual process of discovering our own inner portal is what enables us to relinquish the hold the external world had over us.

Desire becomes transformed into love as we become more conscious.

Piece by piece, the world around us ceases to hold sway over us, because the fires within us desiring everything in the physical world cease to burn.

The more conscious we become, the less desire we have for anything but for connection with the divine and to live with an open heart. Everything else pales in comparison.

Thus we become centered. We are still operating in the world, but our attention is no longer fixated *out there* because we have discovered that the resolution of all our issues lies within ourselves.

This is a major piece of the puzzle in undoing the Grand Illusion. As we cease to mistakenly look *out there* for the solutions to all our issues and shift our focus to *in here,* we are finally able to achieve change and resolution. We are able to be *in* the world, but no longer believe ourselves to be *of* the world.

We finally see that our solution is not to be found in the perfect mate, the perfect house, car, job, city, situation, achievement, or anything else out there. Yes, they are all wonderful, magnificent and can be great fun and provide distraction for a while and we embrace them with enjoyment and gratitude as we dance the dance of life.

But eventually, the fun will fade and you will come back to the same place you started out. People often assume mistakenly that this return to their chronic emotional set point is because they just haven't found the perfect person or experience or possession yet, and so they go off again in search of it/him/her, wondering why they keep having the same lack-of-fulfillment experience.

I was amazed to realize that it took about three months for any new experience, situation or possession to become just "normal" and part of the landscape. That included living my ideal, luxury existence, owning a magnificent car and a beautiful house. Some people waste a whole lifetime chasing after that elusive external thing or person that they think will change everything, and then die disappointed, wondering what went wrong.

I discussed this exact experience with someone on one occasion, and he described observing the exact same thing, but it made no difference to him. He still went off in search of the next perfect possession that would change his life, and rejected my suggestion that the answer lay within himself. The external world needs to fail us completely before we will explore the internal world. This is the function of suffering—it is the impetus that causes us to look for answers to escape the pain.

This is a truth, like all the others, that we have to experience ourselves before we *know* it. He needed to experience the failure of more possessions to fill the need within him before he came to the realization that none of them ever could.

This is the answer to the age-old question: why would God allow us to suffer if he loves us? Because if we did not experience pain when we violated the spiritual laws we would never evolve. Our suffering is the alarm bell that tells us: *wrong direction, try another path.* Our emotional pain is not punishment—it is the divine gift that enables us to find the path to Consciousness. The right direction is always rewarded with an experience of peace, contentment and love. Life is not random or chaotic—we are lost in a labyrinth and if instead of railing against the world for its harshness, we pay attention to what brings us emotional pain, or peace and bliss and follow the latter, we can find our way out.

Many years before I understood all this, I had read that I needed to let go of all these things in the external world, and I tried. But I found it impossible because I believed the external world held all that I truly desired: excitement, glamour, beauty, love, sex, achievement, acclaim, and possessions—the list went on and on! How could I relinquish what I truly believed I needed? I couldn't.

I thought there must be other things outside of me that would make me feel complete, at peace. And so I spent decades doing, possessing, and achieving all kinds of things, and they were all wonderful, but once I had achieved them, possessed them, experienced them and the thrill had died down, the same feeling would return—that I was missing something. It would nag at me. I couldn't figure out what this restlessness was.

We each need to exhaust our personal search among the physical world for that perfect thing, and be failed by the external world, until we are finally ready to look beyond the physical world, into our own internal world to find our true answers.

This continued all through my life until the experience that night in the London parking garage I described in Chapter 6.

Our journey becomes a series of these desire/disillusionment experiences until we find connection with our own spirit and, through that, all Spirit. The bliss of this experience surpasses all our worldly experiences or ego fulfillments.

Until we become centered, we are always making the mistake of looking outside of ourselves for our solutions: relationships, possessions, achievements, all of which can be very rewarding but will never be able to give us the peace and understanding we crave.

We will always be left restlessly looking for the answer, trying to achieve that perfect relationship, possession, or activity. And so, of course, we will never find them—which is why some people get married six times, or endlessly date new people, or compulsively do whatever they do.

Despite that line in the movie, *Jerry Maguire,* someone else can never complete us. Only we can complete ourselves.

Each new person or thing eventually must fail us in providing what we have to provide for ourselves. Until we grasp this, there will always be an issue, because we are using our relationships or possessions to supply something only we can give to ourselves, which is contact with our own spirit.

If we are on our spiritual path, we gradually become disillusioned with things outside of us, one by one, as "the solution" for the experience which only we can provide ourselves through our own awakening. But we probably have to go through this elimination experience ourselves in order to believe it. When I was a teenager I certainly didn't believe it!

In this way, we gradually *experience* our way to becoming centered. Which is why this journey can take quite a while, and many lifetimes.

And in this way, our eventual arrival at our own center is effortless, although it may take a lot of life experience to get there. And then we experience no loss of anything or feeling of having to give up anything. Rather the opposite.

The most important law of all is this:

**Our own consciousness contains all the power that we, in error, give to circumstances and other people.**

This is another way of stating Jesus' teaching: *The Kingdom of God is within you.* (Luke 17:20-21)

Another person who expressed this same truth was the Persian mystic Rumi: *You are searching the world for treasure, but the real treasure is yourself.*

In my case, my lifelong *addiction* to music disappeared, and I found that I also loved silence—and anyone who knows me well will know that this was a giant change. Music assumed its proper position as simply *music*. It was no longer a mood-altering source of *addiction* for me, because it was no longer needed as a portal.

As we become centered, how we feel inside changes. Feeling happy, contented, not anxious, and calm, has less and less to do with the world around us. Before, I needed continual stimulation from outside to feel good, and if my planned series of events went awry, it could wreck my mood for hours. Instead, now I found myself happy to do something else—it was not that big of a deal. In fact, I found that when I was completely in the moment, just about anywhere at all became the best place, because my external environment was not the source of how I felt.

I was fascinated to read, after I had experienced and

written about this personal transformation, the Hindu principle of *sannyasa*, or renunciation: the giving up of worldly attachments in order to focus on one's spiritual nature. In my own experience, it has never worked to try forcing this divestment of attachments—I seem to have too much enthusiasm for the things I love, when I love them. But I have been amazed to witness my own obsession and desire for things evaporate naturally from within, as my understanding and consciousness increased, and I was able to see so many beloved objects, activities, and relationships as temporary, and found myself willing to let them go when the time came. For me, that feels more natural.

I have lived at times with plenty of money and very nice things, and I have also been practically penniless. Each situation was a result of my own choices at the time. And neither made a huge difference in how I felt emotionally, beyond experiencing a level of comfort.

In their way, I felt that all these experiences were valuable. Every experience we have along the way helps bring us to the understanding we have today. There is no reason to feel that life was wasted, or regret one's past once we contact our own spirit by becoming free of our mind's hypnotic hold on us.

We may have all manner of plans for our lives, but once we have awakened and are on our spiritual path in earnest, and have declared our intention as such to the universe, life will conspire to provide what we need to teach us our next lesson. We only realize looking back that the journey that brought us to awakening was perfect and exactly what we needed to experience. But at the time all we may see is disaster and ruin, as life foils our best laid plans.

Out of things that seemed like the worst that could be happening at the time, can come the best *if* we are open to them.

Like my back pain that went on non-stop for six months—
that forced me to try restorative yoga and Pilates—that resulted
in my experiencing blissful subtle energy changes—that led me
to reading Eckhart Tolle's Power *of Now* to try to understand
what I was experiencing—then the devastation of my parents
becoming very ill and dying within a short time of each other—
out of all these painful and difficult events came the perfect
circumstance that opened me up and made me receptive to applying and experiencing the spiritual technique that revealed
all I had been trying to understand my whole life.

Looking back, I could see that I had been dragged and
forced by external circumstances to that precise moment of
realization. Left to my own devices, I would have chosen,
as most of us would, to remain comfortable and untroubled,
and I would never have realized what I needed to realize
and experience.

My guiding angels may have danced that I *finally* understood! Before that, they must have been pulling out their
angelic hair, so to speak: *What else do we have to do to get this
guy to really understand what is going on? He still isn't getting
it! OK, let's try this...*

This is why you cannot apply human, normal-life stan-
dards of good and bad, success and failure to these things.
You cannot see where you need to go; if you did, you would
be there already.

Once you have declared with full intention that you are
serious about waking up spiritually, you are on a journey
that may not make a lot of sense to you until you arrive. You
may think it's all about getting a BMW or that promotion or
marrying that special person.

But if you keep your spiritual goal of awakening always
in your heart, things will work out eventually. And then

the journey, no matter how crazy it seemed at the time, will make sense. You will see why you had to experience what you experienced.

There will be no regrets at that point.

You do not get graded at the end of your life on what car you drove, how big your house was, or what your income averaged. And if you caused others harm to get what you wanted, you will have achieved nothing but to dig yourself farther into the hole of unconsciousness and negative karma. That is why you do not have to desire revenge on those who deliberately harmed you—the perfect justice of the universe will function all by itself to balance things as others eventually experience their own negative energy returning to them.

When you die, all you take with you, aside from your energy body, is your consciousness—your lessons learned while you were here, and the issues you have yet to deal with, are all that go with you.

When we each arrive at our own center, we cease needing the approval or agreement of others. It is fine to please them and have them agree with us if it is about something positive and productive that does not awaken our ego. But it doesn't make any difference to our viewpoint.

This is not the same as ego or arrogance or callousness. It is simply a peaceful and un-boastful condition of knowing what one knows. When a person becomes centered, the inner compass is functioning to tell us what our right course of action is. Things that are true and will lead toward greater consciousness are rewarded by a swelling of life force within us, a flooding of the heart, an increase in compassion, and feelings of connectedness and kindness toward others.

I am not talking here about issues where money or a job

is involved—then, agreement about one's actions, performance, services, or product is an essential prerequisite to the exchange of cash.

Nevertheless, things that we consider to be wrong actions have an immediate negative effect on us: a closing of the heart, a feeling of isolation, of disconnection, seeming to ourselves smaller and less alive. So we find that we have to earn our living in ways that serve and are positive to other people and cause them no harm.

This internal positive and negative feedback effect becomes our primary motivation, because once a person has experienced the love and nurturing of our connection to universal Consciousness, becoming disconnected by our own actions, intentions, thoughts, beliefs, or emotions gives us the greatest motivation to realize what we did wrong and reverse it.

No one else is going to give us enlightenment but ourselves, so we had better get down to confronting our issues and resolving whatever is still bothering us while we have the opportunity. Dying won't solve our problems, and it seems that we need to be in Earth spiritual school at this time to learn our lessons.

This is a very good time in history to be holding this book or others on this subject. There is an unprecedented amount of information available everywhere now if you are just open to receiving it, ask for it, or look for it.

Only a few hundred years ago, writing a book like this would have meant being put to death as a heretic by the Church. The gates of wisdom are now wide open to those who are aware enough to walk through them. There is nothing more important we can do.

I don't like to suffer any more than I have to—feeling

better is my entire motivation for the work I have done as described in this book.

I cannot believe how much I have *finally* learned in the last few years that I have been trying to understand for so very, very long. The transformation and contentment has been indescribable. I am so very grateful.

## Overcoming Your Addictions

*If you are an addict, you live but you don't learn.* ~ James Taylor.

If external substances, activities or people have control or authority over you, then you cannot become centered.

When you have negative emotions that overwhelm you, or when your life is out of balance so that what you feel you really want is being thwarted, whether because of a bad relationship, an unfulfilling job, failure to pursue something because of lack of courage, or guilt or whatever unresolved issue is eating away at you, then you will likely be addicted to something.

Your addictions are a *symptom* of an imbalance between your chakras. They are acting as a long-standing issue that requires your attention. They aren't the most *basic* issue, as consuming as they may appear.

You will turn to any addictions that sufficiently impact you and have the ability to distract you and so temporarily ease the pain—whether it is alcohol, drugs, sex, shopping, eating, smoking, stealing, self-injury such as cutting, working, exercising, gaming, gambling, or anything else that you compulsively *have* to do to feel OK.

Now there may be habitual behaviors that have to be overcome, and physical dependency and bio-chemical problems as the result of taking substances that need a medical doctors help to get over.

But unless you also address the underlying issue that you are using the addiction to suppress, whatever therapy you use to address the addiction is likely to fail because the root cause is still there. So be honest, follow your pain or discomfort to its source and do the work necessary to handle it. Only when you cease to be addicted will you be able to become centered.

I realize that overcoming addiction can be the continual work of a lifetime, using whatever therapeutic methods work for you. But I do know that handling the underlying issues that the addiction has been a solution to is an essential step. Like every difficult life circumstance, overcoming addiction is an opportunity to learn lessons of consciousness.

It can be a very tough lesson, but remember—if it is in your life, it is only there as an opportunity for learning and consciousness.

### Don't Require Approval From Others

Your sense of self worth should not depend upon approval from others. Learn to be proficient at whatever you do and always do as well as you can every time. That way you are not reliant on other's opinions to tell you are good at what you do. You know yourself. By all means react to feedback you receive to improve what you do as it relates to a business, that is an essential business skill, but that is not at all the same thing as always craving approval from others to feel good about yourself.

If you find yourself requiring other's approval, then your center has become misplaced outside of yourself.

If you love yourself you will naturally assume that others will likely love you too, and that you are deserving of love. But your motives are not based on a desire to have others like you. If someone does not like you just because of who you are, it really doesn't matter. If it's a problem, then the problem is theirs, not yours. That isn't arrogance, it is just the way things are.

You cannot in truth be anything other than you are. You can certainly become aware of and considerate of other's concerns. You can become helpful and kind to others. But as you progress on your path to become less identified with all that you are not, how can you become anything other than more of what you are. And that transformation has nothing to do with anyone other than you. It requires no one else's approval.

I am not referring to *personality*, or *ego*, I am referring to the essence of you—that which doesn't require an identity.

I used to sometimes morph into an outward appearance of someone I thought others could accept. I was often aware from a young age that the way I perceived things was not what a lot of other people agreed with or understood. Then one day I decided I wasn't going to do that anymore, I was going to be as true to myself as I could. I realized it wasn't my job to be someone *others* could understand—it was my job to be someone who *I* could understand.

Unless they were employing me, another's opinion of me was not my business or something I could do much about. I found it to be a lot less stressful way to live.

Some people can be judgmental, jealous or feel threatened by talent, competence, strength and success. If for instance, you are a confident and very capable woman, then you are going to scare a lot of insecure men. But those kinds of reactions are their issues, not yours. You just happen to be there. You should never be less than you are to make others more comfortable.

If you have to have some kind of relationship with someone who is antagonistic for no apparent reason, you might try asking them if you had done something to upset them. If they can't come up with anything that is real, then you may just fall within their idea of how people shouldn't be. That is their false belief. It really has nothing to do with you.

As a life habit, never make yourself into something that others can accept that is contrary to your own nature. Just decide how you should live, and then follow your own code. When you aren't attached to a mind-based image of who you, or others think you are, then the opinions of others no longer seem important. That is an enormous freedom.

Now do not confuse personal integrity with narcissism, self-centeredness, or arrogance! Do not confuse "Integrity" as an excuse to extend the domain of your ego!

You may discover a difference between what you prefer to do and what others will pay you for.

If someone is paying you to perform a service, then their opinion becomes relevant to the quality of the job you do, because otherwise you may not get paid and you may also find yourself fired. If the job description doesn't conflict with your integrity, then do the job you are paid for to the best of your ability, as that is the agreement you have made. If a job description does conflict with your integrity—don't agree to do the job in the first place!

If you have agreed to do something and be paid for it, and it has passed your integrity test, then honor your own agreement and do it as well as you can.

Don't feign interest or affection. Be honest about your emotions. Follow your own internal compass, no one else's.

Cultivate love for yourself—don't *require* love from anyone else. That way you are open to receiving and giving love, because there is no compulsion or addiction standing in the way. When you can love yourself you can love others.

Remember that we are all spiritually connected; so achieving bliss consciousness for yourself has a positive contribution to all of humanity. Whereas living in personal suffering only contributes to the collective pain of all.

So living in peace, love, joy, and compassion is the most valuable thing you can contribute to everyone. Your individual consciousness contributes to the consciousness of the whole.

Practicing these habits will take you where you desire to go on your journey.

Blessings to you.

# Summary—The Spiritual Laws

1. There exist spiritual laws, that govern all beings, which are universal and supersede geographic boundaries and cultures, in the same way that the physical laws of the universe, such as gravity and the speed of light, do. They underlie all religions and philosophies.

2. Spiritual Truths and laws must be experienced. They are beyond mere intellect.

FREE CHOICE

3. We have each been given free choice in how we think, believe, feel, intend and act, and this will never be taken away from us. It is each person's choice and free will whether to continue to suffer through lack of knowledge of these spiritual truths, or whether to awaken to their own true spiritual nature, learn these laws and live in alignment with them, and thus end their suffering.

4. Changing your life in a positive way requires first changing your ideas in a positive way. You must first become the change you wish to see around you.

5. Human beings are a composite of A) an immortal, invulnerable spirit B) a temporary, mortal, physical body, and C) an energy body that occupies your physical body and some space around it.

7. You are in essence an immortal spiritual being who exists outside of space/time. You existed before you were in this temporary body and you will continue to exist after it has died. You also have an energy body that is your link between the non-physical and the physical realms that carries records of your past incarnations.

8. Your energy body contains your chakras that store the past experiences that still require resolution to convert their negative energy to positive. These will follow you from life to life until you resolve them. This is the energy body you take with you from lifetime to lifetime. It is the portal between you as an immortal spiritual entity that exists outside of space/time, and your physical body, which exists in the space/time of the physical universe.

9. The physical universe is not an illusion, it is composed of conscious energy. But it is illusory in the way we perceive it through our 5 senses and the equivalent models created by our brain. What we perceive as physical reality is not actually what is there. Our involvement with the physical universe is illusory and temporary. Our consciousness is real and timeless.

## PRESENT MOMENT

10. All that ever occurs happens in the present moment. The past no longer exists; the future has yet to exist. Therefore the past, future and present are not equal. To regard them as though they are is to believe a delusion.

11. Do whatever you do in life with the full focus of attention, without allowing your mind to daydream or wander.

12. Fear results from having attention focused on the past. Anxiety comes from being focused on the future. Inner peace comes from continually focusing on the present moment. There is value in imagining future events as thought forms to aid with constructive problem solving and planning. But the future has yet to actually exist, and so to scare oneself with "what if" scenarios is a pointless waste of energy that only results in worry and stress. Training your attention to stay in present time results in worry and anxiety fading away. When one is fully in the present moment and one's heart is open, there is a bliss experience of connection to nurturing love and peace which dissolves fear.

## MIND

13. Becoming aware of and then observing the endless and repetitive generation of thought forms, many of which are repetitive loops, is the beginning of separating one's consciousness from one's mind and awakening from being hypnotized by one's mind. Becoming free from this tyranny is achieving the state of Witness of one's mind.

14. We can awaken from our mind's tyrannical grasp by consciously focusing our attention on the present moment, learning to still our mind by consciously focusing on our breath and observing the negative thoughts, emotions, and beliefs it generates, and accepting them, no longer worrying about them, believing them, or trying to do anything about them. They will then fade away. This practice will give us distance from our mind and allow us to become its master and it becomes our servant, which is the correct relationship. The mind makes a wonderful servant but a terrible master.

15. We achieve positive changes in relation to our mind by directing the conscious application of our **attention, intention, will,** and **intuition**. These are our tools in our work to achieve Consciousness.

16. We are not our thoughts or our mind. We are the one observing our thoughts and our mind. Our mind is just our tool and belongs under our control.

17. Just because we have thought, felt, or believed something negative does not make it true. We should never make permanent decisions based on temporary emotions.

18. Any activity that focuses your attention away from a mind-dominated experience onto the present moment and brings you into greater connection with Consciousness is a valid spiritual practice.

19. Everyone exists in their own reality based on their own beliefs, thoughts, and emotions.

20. Your mental version of reality, created by the filter of all your false beliefs and negative emotions, is not the same thing as reality itself. This mental version is the false reality that most people live in, and it is the source of many of their problems and suffering.

21. The focus of our attention is under our control and will. It is the gaze of our spirit into this world. We can choose to consciously focus our attention on the present moment around us, instead of being hypnotized by the continuous projections of our mind, which cause us to experience a second-hand, false version of reality.

22. When we awaken from the false illusion of reality projected by our mind, we are able to experience life in all of its intense and vibrant beauty. If we cease to label and judge that which is around us, we can experience it directly.

23. A practice of daily meditation first thing in the morning will help you stay connected to all you have realized thus far and prevent your mind from reasserting itself into a dominant position.

24. Prepare yourself for life after you have finished meditation each morning by asking: Who is my teacher today? In this way, you will better be able to hold onto your inner peace when adversity shows up and you will be able to deal with it calmly without losing your consciousness in a knee jerk reaction.

EMOTIONAL PAIN

25. Emotional pain is a signpost for us that we are out of alignment with the universe at some level. Instead of blaming the external world for our pain, the solution to our pain is to uncover how we are out of alignment and adjust ourselves internally so we become aligned with the architecture of the universe, at which point our pain will resolve and be replaced by positive emotions and internal energy. If we reframe and welcome emotional pain in our lives as an opportunity to discover and become free from another uninspected identification and falsehood, instead of trying to ignore or suppress our pain or just complain about it, then a negative experience becomes positive. We can use this feedback of our own emotions and internal energy to guide us in our life choices.

EGO

26. You are not your name, your body, your family, your history, your nationality, your culture, your possessions, your profession, your affiliations, or anything of the physical universe. Identification with these physical and temporary entities results in a mental construct of a false identity, which is called Ego.

27. Identification with your Ego, and identification with the endless projections of the human mind, and identification with the temporary aspects of the physical universe, leads to suffering, and is the basis of human insanity.

28. Identification with Ego isolates you from your experience of connection to your own spirit, and to the universal Consciousness, Spirit or God. It is what causes you to experience the world as separate, isolated and alone.

29. Separation from Ego allows you to experience your true, natural state of love, kindness, compassion, and your connection to life, to others, to Spirit, Universal Consciousness, or God—these are different terms for the same entity.

30. The Ego tends to arise and reduce our consciousness when we encounter conflict and attack or when we engage in an attempt to defend ourselves by being right and making others wrong.

31. Identification with a group Ego consciousness: that of family, groups, nations, and so on, otherwise known as Tribalism, is another aspect of Ego.

32. Our fixation of our attention on our own Ego, or on other negative mental forms such as negative emotions, thoughts, or beliefs, prevents us from being able to experience our own native state of love, which we experience when our heart chakra is open, and our connection to the divine. Shifting the focus of our attention away from ego and negative mental activity allows us to experience this always-accessible spiritual state of bliss.

33. The desire to be right and make others wrong will cause you to maintain a victim role and continue to recreate and re-experience past painful experiences in order to show others your suffering and that you have been wronged.

34. You can only be hurt by another's emotional attack if you take the situation personally, become defensive, identify with your ego, fight back, and become involved in a right/wrong conflict. This will close your heart and break your connection to Spirit and you will lose consciousness.

35. Identification with either side of a pair of polar opposites that make you right and others wrong is another aspect of Ego and results in loss of consciousness. Many professions involve taking one side of a dichotomy and opposing the opposite side. Any identification reduces consciousness. In pursuing any profession or life goal it is therefore important to remain conscious and avoid identifying with the profession or goal.

36. None of us are any more important, superior, or entitled than any other, regardless of social standing, because at our essence we all have the same God consciousness, and we are all here learning lessons of consciousness. The false belief that we are superior or inferior to someone else is symptomatic of ego identification.

37. Everything other than the laws of the physical universe and the laws of the spiritual universe, and that which is constructed upon these laws, is merely a matter of preference and opinion. Arguing with someone or trying to convince them that you are right and they are wrong about something that has no basis other than opinion is pointless.

38. Instead of arguing and seeking conflict, it is more productive to attempt to learn about and understand another's viewpoint. This opens the door to tolerance, empathy, and

peaceful co-existence, which we all need to learn to achieve while we are here.

39. Our spiritual evolution is a journey from a mind and ego bound experience of isolation and fear, to a mind and ego free experience of connection to One Consciousness and Love.

PAINFUL MEMORIES

40. That which you accept resolves. That which you resist continues to affect you. What you resist persists.

41. When we resist something that happens in our lives because we are unwilling to accept or fully experience it as it is happening, that resistance reduces our consciousness and creates a toxic memory that can continue to affect us negatively until we face and accept it. At that point, the negative aspect will cease to exist. In this way, we can become free of the emotional traumas and the related false beliefs in our past.

42. When we experience emotional pain from a past memory, we are unconsciously creating this suffering ourselves by flowing our own energy at the memory. Our own energy is changed to the negative frequency that is held in our memory, which then returns to us and we experience as pain. We are unaware of the causation of our own suffering. When we believe the falsehood that this is occurring independently of us, or that we are not involved in creating the pain we feel, the situation persists.

43. When we raise our willingness and ability to confront painful experiences in the past by looking at and re-experiencing them at their basic source, old negative energy is at last changed to positive, and we become released from the memory's ability to cause us any further pain.

44. There is nothing we have ever experienced that is so painful as to render us incapable of eventually fully viewing and accepting it without resistance, and forgiving it completely. It is only our unwillingness to face our experiences completely and accept them without any resistance that gives them power over us to cause us pain, and makes them persist in a toxic state.

45. Similar painful experiences can join together and their negative energy can become connected. The negative energy of the earliest experiences can prevent the energy of the later experiences from resolving when looked at. However, when the earliest of these similar experiences has been fully viewed, accepted, and forgiven, the toxic energy of the whole string of experiences will evaporate and cause no further problems.

46. Acceptance, forgiveness, and responsibility will set you free from the painful effects of past experiences.

47. If you feel guilt over a past action, make up the damage to the people you harmed or if they are unavailable, people like them, with love and forgiveness. Then you will heal from it.

48. You are the source of your own negative emotions and you are unconsciously creating them as you are experiencing them. The act of consciously ceasing to create them in the present moment will result in ceasing to experience them.

49. Becoming free of your past does not mean you have lost any of the wisdom and Truth you have discovered from your past experiences. These remain with us after the negative energy of the past has been transformed to positive.

ACCEPTANCE

50. Refusing to accept reality causes us to suffer. Acceptance of reality dissolves our suffering. Accepting reality without any internal resistance on our part enables us to experience life without suffering. Learning to accept the reality of what is, instead of internally protesting and resisting it, opens the door to peace and the experience of living fully in the present moment.

51. The universe is always in a state of continual change. To resist any part of this change is to cause ourselves suffering.

52. What we refer to as time is actually change in the physical universe. Time is not a linear stream consisting of the past, present and future. In our universe all change occurs in the present moment.

## FORGIVENESS

53. It is necessary to forgive others and yourself for all past wrong doings and painful experiences in order to recover and heal from them.

54. With work you can eventually forgive and let go of all past resentments and hurts done to you by others so that nothing in your past has any power to affect you negatively. We are here to learn, and we cannot learn without making mistakes, so we need to let go of the significance of what we, or others, did that was "right" or "wrong," but instead focus on what was learned from each experience, because the purpose of life is not to be right, but to learn. If a wrong action produces learning and increase consciousness, it has served its function, so at a spiritual level it cannot be wrong.

55. If you forgive each new troublesome incident as it arises, and respond to hurt only with acceptance, forgiveness and love, you will avoid any further entrapment or loss of consciousness. You will cease to create future negative karma for yourself.

## RESPONSIBILITY and BLAME

56. Assuming responsibility for our own actions puts us at cause over them and enables us to assume our power and leads to consciousness. Blame reduces our power and consciousness, and casts us in the role of victim. Blaming others causes us to remain at effect and trapped.

## GRATITUDE

57. Cultivating gratitude for the positive things in our lives shifts our attitude from negative to positive, and attracts more of the same to us.

58. Cultivating gratitude for what we have, or had—rather than longing for, or feeling resentment or jealousy for what we do not have, opens the door to experiencing peace and the magnificence of the present moment and connection to Spirit, universal Consciousness, or God.

59. If we change our viewpoint about a situation of great loss from one of resistance and resentment to acceptance and gratitude for what we had, then we can shift from a negative to a positive outlook and healing can occur. The underlying belief that we should still have what has left us is a lie—we know this because it is no longer with us. Fighting reality always causes us suffering.

## JUDGMENT

60. Love is the absence of judgment. Judgments of others reduce our connection to them and prevent us from experiencing love. Our focus should be our own journey of achieving Consciousness, not on other people's journeys. We are in no position to judge their path or condemn others, that is not our business. Our own consciousness is our business. When we practice non-judgment, non-condemnation and tolerance of others and the world, then we establish the connection to others and to Spirit, Consciousness or God, that allows us to feel love.

61. Judging, hating, resenting, being angry at, or refusing to accept another person or situation will close your heart.

62. When you see someone else behaving unconsciously, perceive the unconscious behavior, protect yourself if necessary, but do not condemn or fail to acknowledge the spirit that exists beneath the unconsciousness. Because that will close down your heart and your connection to others. We are all connected at a spirit level, regardless the degree of unconsciousness that may exist in someone.

63. The idea that anything external to ourselves is responsible for us feeling love or negative emotions is false. Everything we feel, positive or negative, emanates from ourselves. We feel love for others by changing our considerations towards them and deciding they are worthy of our admiration and love. By ceasing to judge them, and instead forgive and accept them, we are able to connect spiritually with them, which we experience as love.

64. You cannot love others while you simultaneously hate even one person. We are all connected. So our task is to still manage to love others when they are being unlovable. In this way we maintain our connection to Spirit, God, universal Consciousness.

INTEGRITY

65. Failure to live according to your own code of personal integrity will separate you from others and your own connection to Spirit.

66. We are all spiritually interconnected. So what you do to someone else, positively or negatively, affects you also. The energy of the thoughts, intentions and acts you do to others return to be experienced by you. What you do to others you do to yourself. So always treat others as you would have them treat you.

67. As we exercise our free will we must maintain awareness of our interconnectedness to others, and treat others as we would have them treat us, then we maintain consciousness and remain empowered. When we violate this spiritual rule and do harm to others we condemn ourselves to a loss of consciousness, a loss of our power, and a karmic debt.

68. The only way to hold onto power and increase our empowerment in all its forms, is to not use it to harm others, or profit at their expense, but to use it only to help others.

69. Failure or unwillingness to exchange with others will create an energy imbalance that will eventually separate you from others.

70. Your true power stems from your ability to control yourself in all things, not in controlling others. As you develop your will to bring into being that which you have decided and envisioned while in a state of love, kindness, compassion, and joy, you will enlist the power of Spirit.

## FALSEHOODS

71. Our natural state is love, joy, peace, gratitude, compassion, kindness and connection to others. This is what we

are. Only our identification with our mind or the physical universe prevents us from experiencing this all the time.

72. All negative emotions, thoughts, and beliefs are based on falsehoods. Thinking them, feeling them, and believing them does not make them true. When you find yourself thinking or feeling negative thoughts or emotions, consciously use techniques to change these to positive.

73. We need to achieve freedom from the uninspected, false, and negative beliefs about ourselves, others, and the world that are held as hidden programs in our conscious and subconscious minds.

74. Fear is always based on an illusion, and a falsehood. If you can fully confront that which you fear, at its genesis, your fear will evaporate. It always comes down to trying to hold onto something that is impermanent and cannot really be held onto anyway.

75. You can re-program your negative beliefs with repeated positive affirmations, which will create new, positive, habitual neural pathways.

76. Your 6th chakra aspect of intellect requires clearing of all false, ignorant, illogical and irrational thoughts and beliefs, so that your aspect of intuition can function unimpeded, and your integrity will not be compromised. Through inspection, you can gradually divest yourself of all false beliefs, thoughts, assumptions, and generalities and learn to verify each belief before you accept it as true. Replace ignorance and superstition with science and facts. Learn to

think logically without irrational or ego-based ideas or negative emotions clouding your judgment with bias, prejudice or self-deception.

77. Do not ever make assumptions. If you do not know, ask. Always get accurate information.

78. Life occurs in specifics, not generalities. Don't allow a specific incident that occurred once to become a general belief about life, because then you start believing unsubstantiated, false generalities about people, events and situations. Because something happened once is not scientific proof it will always happen.

79. Observing your own negative thought patterns will enable you to cease identifying with and separate from them.

80. If you are still upset about something, you have not yet fully looked at all the aspects and falsehoods about it. At the point where all the falsehoods have been removed and you have confronted it fully with complete acceptance, any negative energy it retained will be transformed into positive.

## KARMA

81. The energy and intention we send out to others returns to us, positive or negative. This is the law of Karma. We are therefore creating our future experience, positive or negative, moment-by-moment, with every thought, belief, emotion, and intention we have in the present moment. It is therefore our choice whether we create a negative or positive future for ourselves.

82. When we violate the spiritual laws of the universe we experience suffering. This is not personal and this is not to punish us. This positive or negative feedback we experience in the form of our personal emotions and energy when we either violate or align ourselves with the universal laws when we act, think or intend, are in place so that we may learn the laws of the spiritual universe and so become Conscious. This learning mechanism is also referred to as Karma. When we take responsibility to consciously pursue a spiritual path of awakening, we start to undo negative karma. The conscious approach to suffering is therefore to become aware of how we are out of alignment with the laws of the universe and make adjustments that bring us into alignment, which will end our suffering.

83. The function of suffering in our lives is not punishment but consciousness. It brings us to a point of becoming aware of the spiritual laws and the consequences of violating them, which allows us to shift our awareness to become more aligned with them.

84. The purpose of karma is understanding and consciousness, not punishment.

85. We take on karmic debt at the rate we can deal with it.

86. The purpose of every experience in your life is to teach you something. Learning the lesson contained in each experience will remove the necessity for that experience to remain in your life, or be repeated.

87. Taking a spiritual path and proactively awakening consciousness in your life, to learn lessons, align with the spiritual laws, and ceasing to create further negative thoughts, emotions, beliefs, intentions, and actions, can dismantle the attraction of future karmic experiences.

## OPENING OUR HEART

88. We can learn how to open our heart chakra and experience love and connection to the divine without requiring another person or any external portal, at will. Adding to this is not requiring outside approval from others, and the realization that our solutions are within us not outside of us, which enables us to become centered. This means the illusion that the solutions to our evolution can ever be external to us has been removed, and our attention has shifted from outside ourselves to inside. Becoming fully centered means the external world ceases to have authority over us.

89. Learning to open your own heart and no longer needing someone else to be your portal, removes addiction from your relationships and introduces sanity into them.

## COMMUNICATION

90. Use your communication only to forward truth, love, compassion, support, tolerance respect and accuracy in order affect situations positively.

91. Communicate only in specific terms, never generalize about life occurrences because the single specific truth then becomes a generalized falsehood, as when "that person" is

extrapolated to become "those people," with no research to substantiate it.

Established rules or conventions in society or proven scientific facts, such as "door handles open doors," or "Firefighters fight fires," or "objects when dropped fall to the ground," are the only time generalities can accurately be used.

INTERDEPENDENCE

92. All these spiritual laws are interdependent and interlock like pieces of a jigsaw puzzle. If you employ some of the laws but neglect others you will create an imbalance in your life that can create instability that will eventually impact you negatively.

HUMOR

93. Laughter can help heal us emotionally and physically. Humor always exists in the absence of identification with the delusory drama of the physical world around us. Laughter and spiritual insights go hand in hand. Humor assists us in ceasing to be identified with negative emotions or drama and raises our emotional vibration.

BALANCE

94. We need to bring all the various parts of our lives into balance in order to achieve stability and remove drama and chaos from our lives, and enable us to focus calmly to achieve our goals. These include: your body, your mind- including its discipline and its education, your personal goals, your

career, your personal interests, your finances, your possessions, your family, your involvement with society, your circle
of friends, your relationship with the natural world, with all
human beings, with the spiritual world, God or universal
Consciousness.

95. Male and female energy must become balanced in society
for social sanity to be achieved.

## EXTERNAL/ INTERNAL WORLDS

96. No external experience requires you to react or experience
it in any other way than the manner that you choose. The
only apparent connection between our internal landscape
and our external world is due to our false belief that the
former is dependent on the latter. Your response and your
internal landscape are always yours to choose and under
your control alone, no matter what the external situation is.
You can choose to remain internally positive, peaceful and
loving no matter your external situation. In this way you
create no new negative karma for yourself.

97. Your spiritual consciousness is more real than the physical universe around you. Do not make the mistake of being
willing to abandon your consciousness for the sake of the
physical universe circumstances around you because you
believe they are more real than you are. The physical universe always changes and physical forms pass away, but
you are immortal. You cannot achieve inner peace if you
are willing to abandon it every time a problem or difficulty
arises.

98. You will not experience the continuous peace and con-nection to Spirit that you yearn for until you respect your own spiritual consciousness and start to operate in the Truth that you are more real than the "reality" of the physical universe around you.

99. Change your viewpoint so that each difficult person or circumstance becomes your new teacher to reveal to you what you have still to learn to deal with without becoming pulled loose from your connection to the divine. If you wish truly to live with inner peace, joy, and love you must refuse to abandon them each time a difficulty arrives in the physi-cal world.

100. The paradoxical truth is that our external circumstances are dependent on our chronic internal emotions, thoughts, beliefs, and intentions. But it is not true the other way round—our internal state is not dependent on our outer circumstances. Our internal state is dependent only on ourselves.

ATTRACTION and MANIFESTATION

101. We are attracting things to us through our chronic emo-tional level, our thoughts, beliefs, and intentions, that which we love most, and fear most in our heart of hearts. What we put out to others returns to us to experience—positive or negative.

102. We are currently experiencing in our present that which we have created in our past. And we are creating our future experiences, in each present moment, by our thoughts,

emotions, beliefs, intentions or actions. What we create returns to us, negative or positive, it is always our choice.

103. Our outer physical life is the refection of our inner spiritual life. If we do not like what we see we should change our creations, not blame the mirror.

104. We preselect the version of reality that we experience. We do this through our beliefs, our thoughts, our emotions, and intentions. What we think is what we see, and what we see is what we get.

105. Anything the mind accepts as true becomes a law in the subconscious and manifests in the world of the one who accepted it.

106. Life will always contain challenges and hardships until the day we no longer bring them to us by our false beliefs, negative thoughts, negative emotions, negative intentions and negative actions. The difficult situations that we are currently experiencing, which we created in the past, we must learn to experience without relapsing into negativity in order to break the cycle of creating more we will then have to experience in the future.

107. That with which we chronically resonate, comes towards us, whether it is positive or negative. You attract those things to you of a similar vibration wavelength to that with which you yourself resonate. If you are angry you will attract anger. If you are joyful you will attract joy. If you live in fear of certain things you will attract those things to you. If you are filled with love and abundance you will attract that to you.

In this way the universe becomes a self-fulfilling prophecy. You are attracting into your life that which you love and that which you fear.

108. The external world situation we are experiencing in the present is the result of the beliefs, thoughts, emotions intentions and actions we created in the past. Just as those we create in the present will result in the external world situation wewill experience in the future. Our external world situation is a mirror of our internal world. What we create comes back to us, positive or negative

109. When we have cleared away our conscious and sub-conscious negative beliefs and are able to practice a positive internal and external response to even negative life circumstances, we are then able to manifest powerful positive situations in the physical world. This is because we are no longer sabotaging our intentions with contrary negative beliefs and thoughts.

110. Manifestation can occur by defining clearly what we want and asking the universe for it with complete intention: visualizing already having it now in your mind, you can reinforce this by assembling pictures and writing it down, and experiencing all the emotions, gratitude and sensations of having it now. Sustaining all this, then letting it go with the knowledge that it is on its way. Then working on all the physical universe actions that will allow your intention to manifest.

## ONENESS

111. There is one consciousness throughout the universe. At our very core, we all share the same consciousness. My innermost consciousness is the same as yours, and every other being. What is different is our bodies, our minds, our experiences, our beliefs, our unresolved issues from the past, and all our present circumstances including our culture, all of which act as a filter to our available consciousness, and so we may appear completely different on the surface. But at our core we are exactly the same. Hence we are connected— and what I do to you I do to me, and we all respond to the same spiritual laws. We are all truly part of God, and desire to be reunited, and we will be. This is the meaning of the ancient teaching "We are all one."

112. All life is connected; we are all from the same source, at our core we are all the same, so when you close your heart to one human being you, close your heart to all. Conversely, when you help one person, you help yourself.

## BECOMING CENTERED

There is a state of existence that can be referred to as "becoming centered" that occurs when one recognizes that the resolution of all our issues lies within us, and so the outside world ceases to have authority over us. We cease to look to the outside world for solutions and instead look inward, realizing that we are experiencing what we create, and therefore only we can change our situation and our consciousness. We cease to be ruled by desires for the outside world, or by illusions that it holds the key to our evolution.

113. The most important law is this: Our own Consciousness contains all the power that we give to circumstances and other people

114. Do not require the approval, permission, or admiration of others. When you become centered, others cannot take your internal peace away from you or control you.

115. You must overcome any addictions in order to advance spiritually and become centered. You cannot become centered if something external to yourself has control over you.

116. Addictions are an attempt to mask or cause distraction from unresolved emotional issues. These issues must be resolved in order for the addiction to be resolved. What you feel, (the 4$^{th}$ chakra–heart) and what you think (the 6$^{th}$ chakra–intellect) must be in accord for the will (5$^{th}$ chakra–throat) to be empowered and in balance.

117. As you develop and live within your own code of ethics you will become increasingly aware of your own internal compass, directing you to that which increases your con-sciousness and away from that which decreases it. You will cease to require the authority of others in determining your path. This is part of becoming centered.

GUIDES and GUIDANCE

118. Become aware of, acknowledge, and express gratitude for the spiritual gifts and miracles that enter your life. Also, acknowledge your spirit guides and the assistance and mes-sages that you receive from them.

119. We all possess an internal compass of intuitive awareness or knowing that we can develop to guide us to that which is positive for us and away from that which is negative.

120. Develop your awareness of your internal emotional and energetic feedback response to everything, so it can guide you as to what is true, what to pursue, what is positive for you and what is negative and to avoid. What brings peace or relief is true, and what brings negative emotion and disturbance is false at some level.

PRAYER

121. Prayer is our communication with the divine; it enables us to ask for assistance in achieving our goals, in being healed, in gaining help for ourselves and others, in guidance, and in achieving wisdom and connection with universal Consciousness or God. The most powerful prayer is to simply ask for help.

CONSCIOUS RELATIONSHIPS

122. Conscious relationships can be a spiritual practice in themselves. They can help us to locate and become conscious of what we have still to deal with. That which makes us upset is a signpost that we have something buried nearby that we need to deal with.

ENLIGHTENMENT

123. The path to enlightenment is a reductive, not additive process. Consciousness is gained by removing false beliefs,

negative thoughts, negative emotions, identifications with, and attachments to, the physical universe and our history in it. The positive aspects of love, kindness, compassion, tolerance, peace, joy, creativity and the power of manifestation arise naturally, because these are what you are naturally, and they are revealed as layers of unconsciousness are removed.

124. No one can achieve enlightenment for you, because you have free will. Only you can achieve this through your spiritual work. We can pray for guidance and help, but we must still do the work of transformation ourselves in order to achieve wisdom and enlightenment.

125. Your spiritual journey is yours alone. No one can learn your lessons or have your awakenings and realizations—only you. Your first responsibility is to your own journey toward your spiritual awakening. That is why you are here.

126. You are actually playing a temporary game in the physical universe. Forgetting that you are only playing a game has resulted in your experiencing pain and suffering through identification and attachments with that which you are not.

127. The road to the ending of human suffering is through de-identification with the physical universe—the awareness that as a spiritual being you are not the physical forms around you that are temporary, and by their very nature constantly changing, and by letting go of all your attachments to the physical universe. Our identifications and attachments reduce our consciousness, keep us bound to

the physical universe, and prevent us being able to move freely through it.

128. Your spiritual progress is dependent on your ability to de-identify from mental thought forms, and forms in the physical universe itself.

129. When you are able to play the game of being in the physical universe with complete awareness, without further identification with it, then your compulsion to be involved in the physical universe ends and you are able by your high vibration to be reunited with Consciousness or God, your true source.

130. When you are reunited with Consciousness you will still keep the unique knowledge you have earned through your experiences in many lives, this will not be lost.

131. True spirituality is that which brings about a closer experience of love, forgiveness, peace, joy, kindness, compassion and connection to others and to God. True spirituality never involves the antithesis of these.

132. You have existed in many lifetimes before in many identities and different bodies and personalities, but always with the same internal you as the basic essence. Although your physical body dies, as this one will, you are immortal. You take with you into each new life your energy body which contains all the records of your past incarnations and any issues you still need to learn and heal. The way to escape the necessity for endless future incarnations and further suffering is to become fully conscious and awaken

to your true spiritual nature and embody the spiritual laws of the universe.

133. We are here on Earth having a physical experience so that we can progress in our spiritual consciousness. Everything else we are engaged in is secondary to that purpose. Our daily life is our spiritual school, and our daily experiences are our spiritual lessons. This current life has no more significance or reality than watching a three dimensional, full sensory instructional film or a high-grade ride in a fairground.

134. The purpose of our life is that we are in spiritual school and here to learn spiritual lessons of Consciousness. Our daily experiences are our spiritual lessons. We have agreed to the curriculum of our life experiences before we incarnated, so to this extent our life is predetermined. But we also always have free choice, this being our God given attribute which we can never lose, so if we learn a lesson from a life experience our curriculum changes and we will not have to experience that same life situation again. But if we fail to learn the lesson contained in a life situation, it will be repeated, beyond this life if necessary, until the lesson is learned. So paradoxically, predetermination is meeting freewill in an interactive universe.

135. Our own consciousness should be our primary focus. We are capable of deciding that our internal landscape of peace, consciousness, compassion and love is our reality.

136. The final lesson is to learn to exist maintaining your own internal state of love, peace, perception, and Consciousness, no matter what is going on around you. When nothing

and no one is able to reduce your consciousness and drag you back into believing the drama of life is real, or cause you to become identified or attached to the physical world regardless of what you are experiencing, you will no longer need to experience adverse life circumstances. At this point Life School has nothing more to teach you. You will have graduated. Your enlightenment removes your compulsion to continue to return and experience endless reincarnations.

# Recommendations:
# Other Books, CDs and DVDs

Here are additional works that may be of value to anyone interested in further study. The first 3, in bold print, were the ones that were instrumental in triggering my experiences described in this book, which fueled my interest in studying the remainder.

<u>General</u>

*\*The Power Of Now—by* **Eckhart Tolle.**

*\*Living The Liberated Life—by* **Eckhart Tolle (CD Lecture)**

*\*Living A Life Of Inner Peace—by* **Eckhart Tolle (CD Lecture)**

*Practicing The Power Of Now—by* Eckhart Tolle.

*Stillness Speaks—by* Eckhart Tolle

*The Four Agreements—by* Don Miguel Ruiz

*The Mastery of Love—by* Don Miguel Ruiz

*Zerolimits—*by Joe Vitale and Ihaleakala Hew Len PhD.

## Chakras

*Energy Anatomy—by* Caroline Myss PhD. *CD Lectures (includes information on chakras)* www.myss.com

*The Wheels Of Life—by* Anodea Judith PhD. *(chakras)*

*Pathways To A Radiant Self—by* Kathy Pike *(chakras)*

## Reiki

*The Reike Touch Kit—by* William Lee Rand *( Book, DVD, CDs)* www.reiki.org

*Advanced Reiki: Topics For The Advanced Practitioner—by* Douglas V. Buchanan. www.gatesofhorn.com

*Essential Reike—by* Diane Stein

## Meditation

*Meditation: The Bridge from the Apparent to the Real—by* Douglas V. Buchanan

*Wherever You Go There You Are—by* Jon Kabat Zinn

*Openness Mind—by* Tartang Tulku

*Caroline Myss' Meditation Music. CD—by* Stevin McNamara

## Therapy

*Loving What Is—by* Byron Katie. www.thework.com ( false beliefs)

*A Thousand Names For Joy—by* Byron Katie

*Experience Your Good Now!—by* Louise L. Hay *(affirmations)*

*How To Forgive When You Can't—by* Jim Dincalci M.D. www.forgivenessfoundation.org

*Awakening To The Secret Code Of Your Mind—by* Dr. Darren Weissman *(the Life Line method)* www.drdarrenweissman.com

*The Healing Power Of Water—by* Masaru Emoto *(referenced in Darren Weissman's first book)*

*The Silva Mind Control Method—by* Jose Silva & Philip Miele. www.silvamethod.com

*Leadership And Self Deception—by* The Arbinger Institute

*Shaman, Healer, Sage—by* Alberto Villoldo

## Religion / Philosophy

*Man's Search For Meaning—by* Viktor E. Frankel M.D. PhD.

*Hermetica, The Lost Wisdom of the Pharaohs, Penguin Books—by* Timothy Freke and Peter Gandy.

*The Jefferson Bible: The Life and Morals of Jesus of Nazareth—by* Thomas Jefferson, introduction by Forrest Church

*Who Was Jesus Really?—by* Douglas V. Buchanan.

*The Gnostic Gospels—by* Elaine Pagels

*Misquoting Jesus: The Story Behind Who Changed the Bible and Why—by* Bart Ehrman PhD.

*The Mystic Christ—by* Ethan Walker 111

*Buddha—by* Jon Ortner

*Buddhism Is Not What You Think—by* Steve Hagen

*An Introduction to Zen Buddhism—by* D. T. Suzuki

*Masterpieces Of World Philosophy—edited by* Frank N. Magill

*Yoga And Pilates For Everyone—published by* Hermes House

*The I Ching, Or Book Of Changes—by* Brian Brown Walker

*Analects of Confucius, translated by* David Hinton.

*Advanced Energy Anatomy—by* Caroline Myss PhD. *CD Lectures. (about archetypes)*

*Beyond Religion: Ethics For The Whole World—by* The Dalai Lama

*Autobiography of a Yogi—by* Paramahansa Yogananda

*Spiritual Liberation—CD lecture series by* Michael Bernard Beckwith

*The Science Of Mind—by* Ernest Shurtleff Holmes (1926)

*I Am - documentary film by* Tom Shadyc

*George Harrison, Living In The Material World—documentary film by* Martin Scorsese

*The Prophet—by* Kahlil Gibran

*The Essential Rumi—by <u>Jalal al-Din Rumi</u>*

*The Secret Teachings of All Ages: An Encyclopedic Outline of Masonic, Hermetic, Qabbalistic & Rosicrucian Symbolical Philosophy—by* Manly P. Hall

*Supernatural: Meetings with the Ancient Teachers of Mankind—by* Graham Hancock

*Modern Magick—by* Donald Michael Kraig. (includes an address of Kabbalah)

*The Empathic Civilization—by* Jeremy Rifkin

## Science/ Philosophy/ Metaphysics

*Physics of the Soul, The Quantum Book Of Living, Dying, Reincarnation And Immortality—by* Amit Goswami PhD.

*The Holographic Universe—by* Michael Talbot

*The Field—by* Lynne McTaggart

*The Elegant Universe—by* Bryan Greene *(Book 1999 & DVD 2004)*

*The Hidden Reality: Parallel Universes and the Deep Laws of the Cosmos—by* Bryan Greene (*Book 2011*)

*NOVA: The Fabric of the Cosmos—by* Bryan Greene (DVD, 2011)

*A Science Odyssey: "Mysteries of the Universe". A WGBH Science Unit Production in association with La Cinquiéme. Video for PBS TV.*

*What The Bleep!? Down The Rabbit Hole. DVD*

*Earthdance: Living Systems in Evolution—by* Dr. Elisabet Sahtouris

*Abundance—by* Peter Diamandis

## Psychology/ Brain/ Learning/ Language/Logic

*The Biology of Belief—by* Bruce Lipton PhD.

*My Stroke Of Insight—by* Jill Bolte Taylor PhD

*Non-Violent Communication—by* Marshall B. Rosenburg PhD.

*Power Up Your Brain—The Neuroscience Of Enlightenment—by* David Perlmutter M.D. F.A.C.N. & Alberto Villoldo PhD.

*Change Your Brain Change Your Life—by* Daniel G. Amen M.D.

*Brain Power—by* Michael J. Gelb.

*Change Your Thoughts, Change Your Life With NLP—by* Richard Richardson

*Introducing Neuro-Linguistic Programming—by* Joseph O'Connor & John Seymour

*Emotional Intelligence—by* Daniel Goleman M.D.

*A Brief History of Everything—by* Ken Wilber. www.kenwilber. com http://wilber.shambhala.com

*Levels of Human Existence—by* Clare W. Graves PhD. www. clarewgraves.com

*Synchronicity: An Acausal Connecting Principle.—From Vol. 8. of the Collected Works of C. G. Jung*

*The Power Of Positive Thinking—by* Norman Vincent Peale

*Anatomy of an Illness As Perceived by the Patient: Reflections on Healing and Regeneration—by* Norman Cousins

*The Ultimate Lucid Dreaming Manual: Basics and Beyond—by* Marc Vandekeere

*Logic Made Easy, How to know when language deceives you—by* Deborah J. Bennett

*Science and Sanity, an Introduction to Non-Aristotelian Systems and General Semantics, published 1933—by* Alfred Korzybski

*The Mastery Of Learning—by* Melvin Lewis Thomas

*The Personal Efficiency Program—by* Kerry Gleeson

## Mythology

*The Power Of Myth—by* Joseph Campbell with Bill Moyers, *Video interviews and book*

*The Hero With A Thousand Faces—by* Joseph Campbell

*The World Of Joseph Campbell—( Video lectures )*

*The Body of Myth—by* J. Nigro Sansonese

## Reincarnation

*Children Who Remember Previous Lives, 1987—by* Ian Stevenson PhD.

*Edgar Cayce on the Akashic Records: The Book of Life—by* Kevin J. Todeschi

*A Select Library of the Nicene and Post-Nicene Fathers of the Christian Church—*P. Schaff and H. Wace editors

*Encyclopedia Britannica, article on Origen (a prominent early Christian)*

## Nutrition and Health

*Eating Well for Optimum Health: The Essential Guide to Food, Diet, and Nutrition—by* Andrew Weil M.D.

*Why Our Health Matters: A Vision of Medicine That Can Transform Our Future—by* Andrew Weil M.D.

*Super Immunity—by* Joel Furman M.D.

*Wheat Belly: Lose the Wheat, Lose The Weight—by* William Davis M. D.

*Renewal, A Way Towards Healing Cancer—by* Claude V. DeShazo M.D.

*The Science of Breath—by* Yogi Ramacharaka

*The Breathing Book: Vitality & Good Health Through Essential Breath Work—by* Donna Farhi

## History

*Alice, Dancing Under The Gallows—a documentary film about Nazi concentration camp survivor* Alice Herz Sommer

*The Vanished Library—by* Luciano Canfora

*Decline and Fall of the Roman Empire—by* Edward Gibbons

*History Begins at Sumer: 39 Firsts in Recorded History—by* Samual Noah Kramer, Hiroshi Tanaka.

*The Two Babylons—by* Alexander Hislop

*Decoding the Heavens: A 2,000-Year-Old Computer—and the Century-long Search to Discover Its Secrets—by* <u>Jo Marchant</u>

*P.B.S. DVD, Michelangelo Revealed, Secrets of the Dead Series,—*Based on the work of Art historian Antonio Forcellino

## Fiction

*The Alchemist—A novel by* Paulo Coelho

*The Way Of Wyrd—A novel by* Brian Bates

*The Little Prince—A novel with pictures by* Antoine Saint-Exupery.

*My Dinner with Andre—a 1981 film starring* Andre Gregory and Wallace Shawn, *written by* Gregory and Shawn, and directed by Louis Malle.

# Bibliography

Allen, James. *As a Man Thinketh*. USA: Tribeca Books, 2012.

Amen, Daniel G. *Change Your Brain Change Your Life: The Breakthrough Program for Conquering Anxiety, Depression, Obsessiveness, Anger, and Impulsiveness*. New York: Three Rivers Press, 1998.

Anthes, Emily. "Natural Immunity." *Scientific American*, October 4, 2010. http://www.scientificamerican.com/article.cfm?id=natural-immunity

Bennett, Deborah J. *Logic Made Easy: How to Know When Language Deceives You*. New York: W.W. Norton & Company, 2004.

Buchanan, Douglas V. *Advanced Reiki: Topics for the Advance Practitioner*. Morrisville: Lulu Enterprises, 2006.

Buchanan, Douglas V. *Meditation: The Bridge from the Apparent to the Real*. Morrisville: Lulu Enterprises, 2006.

Buchanan, Douglas V. *Who Was Jesus, Really?* Morrisville: Lulu Enterprises, 2006.

Campbell, Joseph., and Bill Moyers intro: *The Power of Myth*. New York: Doubleday, 1988.

Canfora, Luciano. *The Vanished Library: A Wonder of the Ancient World*. USA: U of Cal, 1992.

Conway, Flo., and Jim Siegelman. *Snapping: America's Epidemic of Sudden Personality Change*. New York: Stillpoint Press, 2005.

Cook, Michelle Schoffro. "Study Finds Diet Soda Increases Risk of Stroke." *Planet Green*, May 2, 2011. http://www.alternet.org/newsandviews/article/577063/study_finds_diet_soda_inc eases_risk_of_stroke

Cousins, Norman. *Anatomy of an Illness as Perceived by the Patient*. New York: W.W. Norton & Company, 2005.

Cutie, Albert. *Dilemma: A Priest's Struggle with Faith and Love*. New York: New American Library, 2011.

Davis, William. *Wheat Belly: Lose the Wheat, Lose the Weight, and Find Your Path Back to Health*. New York: Rodale Inc., 2011.

DeShazo, Claude V. *Renewal: Finding Your Path to Self-Healing in Cancer*. Seattle: Pacific Institute Publishing, 2009.

Diamandis, Peter H., and Steven Kotler. *Abundance: The Future is Better Than You Think*. New York: Free Press, 2012.

Dincalci, Jim. *How to Forgive When You Cant: The Breakthrough Guide to Free Your Heart and Mind.* Chapel Hill: The Forgiveness Foundation, 2010.

Ehrman, Bart. *Misquoting Jesus: The Story Behind Who Changed the Bible and Why.* New York: HarperCollins Publishers, 2005.

Emoto, Masaru. *The Healing Power of Water.* USA: Hay House, 2004.

*Encyclopedia Britannica Online,* s. v. "Origen", accessed August 27, 2012. http://www.britannica.com/EBchecked/topic/432455/Origen.

Farhi, Donna. *The Breathing Book: Vitality & Good Health Through Essential Breath Work.* New York: Henry Holt & Company, 1996.

Frankl, Viktor E. *Man's Search for Meaning.* Boston: Beacon Press, 2006.

Freke, Timothy., and Gandy, Peter. *The Hermetica: The Lost Wisdom of the Pharaohs.* New York: Penguin Group, 1999.

Fuhrman, Joel. *Super Immunity: The Essential Nutrition Guide for Boosting Your Body's Defenses to Live Longer, Stronger, and Disease Free.* New York: HarperCollins Publishers, 2011.

Galilei, Galileo., Stillman Drake ed., J.L. Helibron intro., Albert Einstein forw. *Dialogue concerning the Two Chief World Systems: Ptolemaic and Copernican.* New York: The Modern Library, 2001.

Gelb, Michael J., and Howell, Kelly. *Brain Power: Improve Your Mind as You Age.* Novato: New World Library, 2012.

*George Harrison: Living in the Material World.* DVD. Directed by Martin Scorsese. Santa Monica, Ca: Grove Street Productions, 2011.

Gerbode, Frank A. *Beyond Psychology: An Introduction to Metapsychology.* Palo Alto: IRM Press, 1988.

Gibbon, Edward. *History of the Decline and Fall of the Roman Empire.* USA: Adamant Media Corporation, 2005.

Gleeson, Kerry. *The Personal Efficiency Program: How to Stop Feeling Overwhelmed and Win Back Control of Your Work.* Hoboken: John Wiley & Sons Inc., 2009.

Goleman, Daniel. *Emotional Intelligence: Why it Can Matter More than IQ.* New York: Bantam Books, 1995.

Goswami, Amit. *Physics of the Soul: The Quantum Book of Living, Dying, Reincarnation, and Immortality.* Charlottesville: Hampton Roads Publishing Company, 2001.

Graves, Clare W. "Levels of Existence: An Open Systems Theory of Values." Journal of Humanistic Psychology, 1970.

Greene, Brian. *The Elegant Universe: Superstrings, Hidden Dimensions, and the Quest for the Ultimate Theory.* New York: W.W. Norton & Company Inc., 1999.

Greene, Brian. *The Elegant Universe: Superstrings, Hidden Dimensions, and the Quest for the Ultimate Theory.* DVD. Directed by Joseph McMaster and Julia Cort. Arlington: PBS, 2004.

Greene, Brian. *The Fabric of the Cosmos.* DVD. Directed by Paula Apsell. Arlington: PBS, 2011.

Greene, Brian. *The Hidden Reality: Parallel Universes and the Deep Laws of the Cosmos.* New York: Vintage Books, 2011.

Hall, Manly P. *The Secret Teachings of All Ages: An Encyclopedic Outline of Masonic, Hermetic, Qabbalistic and Rosicrucian Symbolical Philosophy.* Pacific Publishing Studio, 2011.

Hay, Louise L. *Experience You Good Now! Learning to Use Affirmations.* USA: Hay House, 2010.

Hinton, David, trans. *Analects of Confucius.* Berkley: Counterpoint Publishers, 1999.

His Holiness the Dalai Lama. *Beyond Religion: Ethics for a Whole World.* Boston: Houghton Mifflin Harcourt, 2011.

Hislop, Alexander. *The Two Babylons.* Ontario: Chick Publications, 1998.

Hoffer, Eric. *The True Believer: Thoughts on the Nature of Mass Movements*. New York: Perrenial Classics, 1951.

Holmes, Ernest. *The Science of Mind*. New York: SoHo Books, 2011.

Jefferson, Thomas et al. *The Jefferson Bible: The Life and Morals of Jesus of Nazareth*. Boston: Beacon Press, 1989.

Judith, Anodea. *Wheels of Life: A User's Guide to the Chakra System*. 2nd ed. Woodbury: Llewellyn Publications, 1999.

Jung, C.J. *Synchronicity: An Acausal Connecting Principle*. The Collected Works of C.J. Jung Volume 8. Princeton: Princeton University Press, 1973.

Kabat-Zinn, Jon. *Wherever You Go There You Are: Mindfulness Meditation in Everyday Life*. New York: Hyperion, 1994.

Katie, Byron., with Mitchell, Stephen. *Loving What Is: Four Questions That Can Change Your Life*. New York: Three Rivers Press, 2002.

Korzybski, Alfred. *Science and Sanity: An Introduction to Non-Aristotelian Systems and General Semantics*. USA: Institute of General Semantics, 1994.

Kraig, Donald Michael. *Modern Magick: Twelve Lessons in the High Magickal Arts*.Woodbury: Llewellyn Publications, 2010.

Kramer, Samuel Noah. *History Begins at Sumer: 39 Firsts in Recorded History.* Philadelphia: University of Pennsylvania Press, 1981.

Levitt, Steven D., and Dubner, Stephen J. *Freakonomics: A Rogue Economist Explores The Hidden Side of Everything.* New York: HarperCollins Publishers, 2009.

Lipton, Bruce. *The Biology of Belief: Unleashing the Power of Consciousness, Matter, & Miracles.* USA: Hay House, 2008.

Lovelock, James. *Gaia: A New Look at Life on Earth.* Oxford: Oxford University Press, 1995.

Magill, Frank N, trans. and Roth, John K. *Masterpieces of World Philosophy: Nearly 100 Classics of the World's Greatest Philosophers Analyzed and Explained.* New York: Harper Collins Publishers, 1990.

Maloney, Mack. *UFOs in Wartime: What They Didn't Want You to Know.* New York: The Berkley Publishing Group, 2011.

Marchant, Jo. *Decoding the Heavens: A 2,000-Year-Old-Computer-and the Century Long Search to Discover its Secrets.* Philadelphia: Da Capo Press, 2009.

Matousek, Mark. "Is the Way You Breathe Bad for Your Health." *O Magazine,* November, 2011. http://www.oprah.com/spirit/Deep-Breathing-Methods-How-Breathing-Reduces-Stress

McLuhan, Marshall. *Understanding Media: The Extensions of Man.* Cambridge: MIT Press, 1994.

McTaggart, Lynne. "All Die of Heartbreak." *The Intention Experiment,* November 19, 2010. http://theintention-experiment.com/all-die-of-heartbreak.htm

McTaggart, Lynne. *The Field: The Quest for the Secret Force of the Universe.* New York: HarperCollins Publishers, 2008.

Myss, Caroline. *Advance Energy Anatomy: The Science of Co-Creation and Your Power of Choice.* Sounds True, Incorporated. ISBN 978-1564559081. CD. 2001.

Myss, Caroline. *Energy Anatomy: The Science of Personal Power, Spirituality, and Health.* Sounds True, Incorporated. ISBN 978-1564558800. CD. 2001.

*Mysteries of the Universe: A Science Odyssey.* DVD. Hosted by Charles Osgood. Boston: WGBH, 2005.

"Nurse Reveals Top 5 Regrets People Make on Their Deathbed." *Arise India Forum,* December 22, 2011. http://www.ariseindiaforum.org/nurse-reveals-the-top-5-regrets-people-make-on-their-deathbed/

O'Connor, Joseph., and John Seymour. *Introducing NLP Neurolinguistic Programing: Psychological Skills for Understanding and Influencing People.* San Francisco: The Aquarian Press, 1990.

Panne, Jeanne-Louise, Andrzej Paczkowski, Carol Bartosek, Jean-Louis Margolin, Nicolas Worth, Stephane Courtois, Mark Kramer ed., and Jonathon Murphy trans. *The Black Book of Communism: Crimes, Terror, Repression*. USA: President and Fellows of Harvard College, 1999.

Park, Alice. "What the Gay Brain Looks Like." *Time*, June 17, 2008. http://www.time.com/time/health/article/0,8599,1815538,00.html

Peale, Norman Vincent. *The Power of Positive Thinking: A Practical Guide to Mastering the Problems of Everyday Lives*. New York: Ishi Press, 2011.

Perlmutter, David., and Alberto Villoldo. *Power Up Your Brain: The Neuroscience of Enlightenment*. USA: Hay House, 2011.

Pike, Kathy. *Pathways to a Radiant Self: A Journey of Growth and Discovery with the Chakras*. USA: PTR Publishers, 2002.

*Pink Smoke Over the Vatican*. Directed by Jules Hart. DVD. Carmel, Ca: Eye Goddess Films. 2011.

"Professor Ian Stevenson." *The Telegraph*, February 12, 2007. http://www.telegraph.co.uk/news/obituaries/1542356/Professor-Ian Stevenson.html

Rand, Willam Lee. *The Reiki Touch: Complete Home Learning System*. Boulder: Sounds True Incorporated. 2005.

Richardson, Richard. *Change Your Thoughts, Change Your Life with NLP.* USA: BT Elite Publishers, 2010.

Rosenberg, Marshall B. *Nonviolent Communication: A Language of Compassion.* Encinitas: Puddle Dancer Press, 1999.

Sahtouris, Elisabet. *EarthDance: Living Systems in Evolution.* Lincoln: iUniversity Press, 2000.

Saint-Exupery, Antoine De. *The Little Prince.* San Diego: Harcourt Inc., 2000.

Samet, Matt. "The Benzo Trap." *Natural Solutions,* July/August 2008. http://www.benzosupport.org/Benzo.pdf

Sansonese, J. Nigro. *The Body of Myth: Mythology, Shamanic Trance, and the Sacred Geography of the Body.* Rochester: Inner Traditions International, 1994.

Schaff, Philip., and Henry Wace. *A Select Library of the Nicene and Post-Nicene Fathers of the Christian Church, Vol 5.* Grand Rapids: WM. B. Eerdmans Publishing Company, 1988.

Schiffman, Richard. "Why People Who Pray Are Healthier Than Those Who Don't." *The Huffington Post,* January 18, 2012. http://www.huffingtonpost.com/richard-schiffman/why-people-who-pray-are-heathier_b_1197313.html

*Secrets of the Dead: Michelangelo Revealed.* DVD. Directed by Fabrizio Ruggirello. Arlington: PBS, 2009.

Sommer-Hertz, Alice. "Alice Dancing Under the Gallows Official Promo." YouTube Video, 12:11, posted by batteriehaufen, April 6, 2011. http://www.youtube.com/watch?v=KMfxU3fCobw

Stein, Diane. *Essential Reiki: A Complete Guide to an Ancient Healing Art*. USA: Crossing Press, 1995.

Stevenson, Ian. *Children Who Remember Previous Lives: A Question of Reincarnation*. Jefferson: McFarland & Company, 2000.

Talbot, Michael. *The Holographic Universe*. New York: HarperCollins Publishers, 1991.

Taylor, Jill Bolte. "STROKE of Insight." *Ted Talks*. YouTube Video, 18:42, Posted by TalkDocumentary, March 11, 2012. http://www.youtube.com/watch?v=QTrJqmKoveU

Taylor, Jill Bolte. *My Stroke of Insight: A Brain Scientists Personal Journey*. New York: A Plume Book, 2009.

The Arbinger Institute. *Leadership and Self-Deception: Getting Out of the Box*. San Francisco: Berrett-Koehler Publishers, 2002.

*Thrive: What on Earth Will it Take?* DVD. Directed by Foster Gamble, Kimberly Carter Gamble, and Stephen Gagne. Soquel: Clear Compass Media, 2011.

Todeschi, Kevin J. *Edgar Cayce on the Akashic Records: The Book of Life*. Virginia Beach: A.R.E Press, 1998.

Tolle, Eckhart. *Living a Life of Inner Peace.* New World Library. ISBN 978-1577314868. CD. 2004.

Tolle, Eckhart. *Living the Liberated Life and Dealing with the Pain – Body.* Sounds True, Incorporated. ISBN 978-1-56455-945-6. CD. 2001.

Tolle, Eckhart. *The Power of Now: A Guide to Spiritual Enlightenment.* Novato: New World Library, 1999.

Vandekeere, Marc. *The Ultimate Lucid Dreaming Manual: From Basics to Beyond.* USA: Brainwave Mind Voyages, 2007.

Vitale, Joe and Hew Len, Ihaleakala. *Zerolimits. John Wiley & Sons, Inc.* 2007.

Wahls, Terry. "Minding Your Mitochondria." *TedxIowaCity.* YouTube Video, 17:47, posted by TedxTalks, November 30, 2011, http://www.youtube.com/watch?v=KLjgBLwH3Wc

Walker, Brian Browne. *The I Ching or Book of Changes: A Guide to Life's Turning Points.* New York: St. Martin's Press, 1992.

Walker, Ethan. *The Mystic Christ.* Norman: Devi Press, 2003. http://reincarnation.ws/reincarnation_in_early_christianity.html

Wang, Shirley S. "Psychiatric Drug Use Spreads: Pharmacy Data Show a Big Rise in Antipsychotic and Adult ADHD Treatments." *Wall Street Journal,* November 16,

2011. http://online.wsj.com/article/SB10001424052970
203503204577040431792673066.html

Weil, Andrew. *Eating Well for Optimum Health: The Essential Guide to Food, Diet, and Nutrition.* New York: HarperCollins Publishers, 2001.

Weil, Andrew. *Why Our Health Matters: A Vision of Medicine That Can Transform Our Future.* New York: Hudson Street Press, 2009.

Weissman, Darren R. *Awakening to the Secret Code of Your Mind: Your Mind's Journey to Inner Peace.* USA: Hay House, 2010.

Weizmann Institute of Science. "Quantum Theory Demonstrated: Observation Affects Reality." *ScienceDaily,* February 27, 1998. http://www.science-daily.com/releases/1998/02/980227055013.htm

Wenner, Jann S. "Paul McCartney: A Giant Among Rock Immortals." *Rolling Stone Magazine,* April, 23, 2007. http://www.rollingstone.com/music/news/paul-mccartney-a-giant-among-rock-immortals-20070423

*What the Bleep!?: Down the Rabbit Hole.* DVD. Directed by Betsy Chase, Mark Vicente, and Matthew Hoffman. Beverly Hills: Twentieth Century Fox, 2006.

Wilber, Ken. *A Brief History of Everything.* Boston: Shambhala Publications Inc., 1996.

Wilmoth, Janet. "Psychologist Offers Fire Chiefs Tips for Proactive Stress Management." *Fire Chief,* September 7, 2011. http://firechief.com/health-safety/mental-health/iverson-on-stress-management-20110907

Yogi Ramacharaka. *The Science of Breath.* USA: Empire Books, 2011.

Zoroya, Gregg. "Study Suggests Feelings of Guilt May be a Top Factor in PTSD." *USA Today,* November 25, 2011. http://usatoday30.usatoday.com/news/military/story/2011-11-23/study-of-marines-ptsd/51386488/1

# Index

## A

Acceptance  80, 129, 143, 147–149, 151,
   152, 154, 156, 159, 161–163, 167,
   177, 259, 269, 270, 277, 288, 292,
   293, 350, 365, 408–411, 415
   Accepting Reality  147, 152, 409
Additions  23
Aging  144, 145, 274
Anger  viii, 6, 97, 114, 143, 161, 164,
   175, 215, 238, 242, 281, 297, 298,
   340, 341, 344, 345, 359, 362, 363,
   421, 443
Approval  48, 49, 109, 149, 200, 208,
   381, 383, 391, 394, 395, 417, 424
Attachments  54, 98, 124, 125, 187, 203,
   268, 291, 374, 375, 378, 389, 426
Attention  xiv, 6, 12, 23, 31, 35, 37, 61,
   68–75, 78, 80, 83, 84, 90, 96, 101,
   102, 104, 105, 109, 128, 131–133,
   149, 155, 169, 182, 186, 188, 190,
   199, 240, 242, 244, 267, 268, 270,
   274, 276, 277, 283–286, 296–300,
   317–320, 326–329, 331, 334, 336,
   338–340, 345, 346, 349, 353,
   356–358, 361, 366, 384, 386, 393,
   401–403, 405, 417
Awakening  x, xvi, 1, 54, 55, 58, 71, 78,
   98, 102, 117, 121, 125, 134, 152, 166,
   222, 269, 278, 280, 319, 329, 374,
   387, 389, 390, 401, 416, 417, 426,
   433, 455

## B

Balance  6, 7, 10, 18, 24, 76, 157, 167,
   168, 180, 186, 252, 287, 331, 332–
   334, 336, 337, 391, 393, 418, 424

Beauty  xvii, 20, 79, 92, 97, 173, 189,
   205, 215, 261, 262, 293, 295, 298,
   375, 383, 386, 403
Becoming centered  109, 288, 378, 381,
   382, 388, 423, 424
Beyond death experience  3
Blame  102, 153, 181, 255–257, 268, 341,
   347, 348, 355, 371, 382, 410, 421
Bliss  23, 24, 37, 74, 77, 78, 83, 96, 97,
   99, 155, 206, 210, 292, 294, 297, 300,
   301, 303, 323, 330, 377, 378, 386,
   387, 397, 401, 405
Body  xvi, 4–10, 15, 26, 27, 29–31, 33,
   35, 36, 41–43, 51, 66, 68, 73, 74,
   76, 80, 84, 86, 91, 92, 96, 103–106,
   108–110, 112–114, 122, 123, 124,
   131–133, 135, 140, 145, 172, 173,
   191, 192, 195, 206, 239, 241, 243,
   274, 276, 277, 282, 283, 285, 289,
   290, 296, 298, 299, 308, 311, 321,
   322, 325, 326, 332, 334, 338, 339,
   350, 356, 368, 375, 391, 400, 404,
   418, 427, 438, 445, 452, 454
Buddha  vii, 11, 22, 61, 122, 149, 164,
   171, 175, 176, 199, 265, 273, 284,
   285, 303, 338, 360, 434

## C

Chakras  27, 103, 213, 432, 451
   Opening Heart Chakra  288,
      290, 291, 292, 293, 294, 295,
      297
Change  vii, viii, ix, x, xi, xii, 17, 20, 22,
   25, 39, 45, 54, 57, 61, 63, 64, 76, 77,
   79, 80, 90, 98, 101, 106, 107, 121,
   122, 124, 128, 131, 132, 137, 138,

147, 148, 150, 151, 154–156, 158,
163, 170, 180, 185, 194, 221, 223,
226, 253, 256, 267, 268, 272, 274,
277, 279, 284, 286, 291, 292, 300,
302, 340, 342–345, 348, 354, 359–
361, 363, 367, 370, 371, 374–376,
382, 384, 385, 388, 390, 399, 402,
409, 411, 414, 419–421, 423, 428,
434, 437, 443, 444, 448, 452, 454
Chi. *See* Life Force
Choice xiv, 99, 101, 102, 150, 155, 161,
162, 171, 178, 181, 209, 218, 222,
255, 257, 259, 265, 285, 332, 338,
349, 354, 355, 365, 368, 372, 389,
399, 404, 415, 421, 428, 450
Communication 40, 46, 234, 238, 239,
241, 242, 243, 246, 247, 250, 251,
309, 417, 425, 437, 452
Comparing yourself 297
Condemnation 147, 203, 216, 411
Conflicts viii, 134, 140, 141, 151, 248,
249, 276
Confronting 131, 221, 227, 336, 392
Connection 8, 24, 32, 36, 37, 39, 40, 43,
55, 62, 82, 96, 103, 112, 113, 120,
132, 141, 171, 184, 194, 200–202,
210, 220, 221, 224, 271, 277, 286,
288–290, 295, 300, 301, 306, 307,
308, 318, 326, 332, 335, 341, 352,
362, 378, 383, 384, 387, 392, 401,
402, 405–407, 411–413, 417, 419,
420, 425, 427
Conscious mind 35, 265
Consciousness, xiii, 25, 31, 33, 44, 46,
51, 52, 56, 76, 80, 91, 99, 112, 120,
125, 128, 144, 159, 178, 210, 212,
258, 269, 284, 285, 301, 302, 306,
307, 328, 341, 342, 356, 372, 383,
392, 405, 406, 410, 411, 413, 416,
423, 425, 426, 428, 449
Contentment viii, 72, 98, 99, 193, 194,
386, 393

**D**

Depression 63, 65, 345, 367, 443
Dualities 137, 140

**E**

Eckhart Tolle xvi, 27, 68, 73, 144, 298,
390, 431
Ego 12, 28–39, 42–45, 47, 51, 55, 59,
74, 78, 82, 84, 96, 108, 134, 135,
137–140, 141–146, 153, 160, 161,
174, 175, 191, 194, 200, 220, 244,
248, 249, 252–254, 267, 269, 276,
284, 288, 293, 297, 298, 306, 307,
315, 317, 327, 368, 370, 387, 391,
395, 396, 404–407, 415
    Collective Ego 44
    Ego Identification 37, 38, 44, 47,
        59, 145, 297, 406
    Separating from 36, 38, 44, 45,
        46, 134, 280, 288
Empowerment 234, 255, 257, 335, 413
Enlightenment 25, 34, 101–103, 112,
119, 125, 158, 171, 203, 212, 256,
293, 319, 335, 382, 392, 425, 426,
429, 437, 451, 454
Evolution 38, 45, 77, 90, 99, 144, 157,
185, 210, 214, 232, 253, 255, 269,
280, 291, 295, 378, 407, 417, 423,
436, 452

**F**

False Belief viii, xiv, 31, 34, 36, 53, 54,
98, 112, 143, 215, 223, 232, 265, 268,
280, 294, 339, 345, 346, 355, 358,
367, 396, 403, 406, 407, 414, 419,
421, 425, 433
    Removing False Beliefs 425
Fear 32–34, 36, 37, 52, 55, 65, 88, 97,
110, 123, 127, 132, 149, 162, 175,
187, 204, 208, 218, 219, 232, 237,
255, 258, 261, 264, 271, 289, 297,
310, 315, 339, 344, 346, 359, 363,
366, 372, 376–380, 401, 407, 414,
420–422
Forgiveness 52, 59, 60, 129, 139, 158,
164–169, 171, 174–176, 177, 181,
182, 185–187, 214, 218, 224, 259,
266, 288, 292, 293, 342, 362, 382,
408, 410, 427, 445

## G

Generalities 58, 245, 414, 415, 418

Grand Illusion iii, viii, xiv, 24, 25, 35, 54, 91, 96, 98, 102, 117, 121, 187, 219, 268, 272, 290, 296, 342, 362, 383, 384

Gratitude xvii, 13, 40, 73, 94, 112, 155, 172, 188–190, 192–197, 214, 239, 259, 262, 298, 305, 307, 309, 315, 318, 375, 379, 380, 385, 411, 413, 422, 424

Grief viii, 5, 68, 69, 74, 86, 109, 123, 150, 264, 275, 276, 281, 321, 322, 349, 354, 362, 366

Grounding 273, 286

Guides 269, 280, 305, 306, 308, 317, 424

Guilt 98, 108, 132, 160, 161, 178–180, 182, 224, 227, 229, 258, 339, 393, 408, 456

## H

Habits iii, viii, 98, 99, 117, 119, 120, 126, 128, 129, 167, 202, 239, 254, 256, 263, 276, 288, 293, 297, 298, 302, 337, 350, 397

Hamsa, So'ham technique of the Kashmir Shaivites 74

Heart 16, 55, 60, 69, 73, 74, 82–84, 86, 92, 94, 97, 105, 109, 111, 119, 131, 132, 161, 168, 170–173, 195, 202, 209, 210, 213, 220–222, 227, 255, 260, 261, 273, 276, 277, 281, 283–288, 290–293, 294–303, 307–309, 316, 320, 326, 339, 350–353, 377, 378, 381, 383, 384, 390–392, 401, 405, 406, 412, 417, 420, 423, 424, 445

Helping Others 252, 252–254

Hesychastic Meditation 273, 284, 285

Hinduism 90, 175, 256, 265

Humility 134, 141, 320

Humor 214, 323, 324, 328–330, 418

## I

Identification 31, 37–39, 43, 44, 47, 48, 53, 54, 58, 59, 98, 124, 125, 134, 135, 145, 176, 187, 203, 253, 280, 291, 292, 297, 372, 404–406, 414, 418, 426, 427

Immortality 17, 96, 436, 446

Inner Compass 111, 381, 391

Interconnectedness 301, 303, 413

Internal/ external worlds 147, 184, 358, 359, 360, 362, 363, 365, 385, 386, 419, 422

Isolation 28, 36, 55, 88, 89, 289, 297, 392, 407

## J

Jesus 73, 128, 142, 164, 171, 175, 187, 199, 211, 214, 216, 218, 220, 260, 263, 266, 284, 285, 300–303, 319, 360, 362, 365, 388, 434, 443, 445, 448

Judging 91, 152, 195, 202, 205, 206, 221, 254, 275, 278, 293, 297, 306, 349, 412

## K

Karma 157, 159, 171, 175–177, 182, 212, 252, 255, 256, 265, 267, 329, 360, 368, 391, 410, 415, 416, 419

Ki. *See* Life Force

Kindness viii, xv, 21, 50, 72, 94, 98, 198, 209, 214, 235, 300, 303, 329, 341, 391, 405, 413, 426, 427

## L

Left brain 74, 76, 205

Lessons 36, 100, 101, 115, 123, 125, 128, 136, 160, 177, 201, 217, 227, 233, 240, 257, 267, 269, 280, 345, 375, 381, 391, 392, 394, 406, 417, 426, 428, 448

Logic x, 138, 140, 147, 156, 205, 223, 225–228, 230, 258, 279, 437, 438, 443

Looking inside 17

Loss 13, 14, 33, 36, 78, 82, 87, 108, 109,
123, 124, 147, 151, 172, 185, 192,
210, 279, 289, 294, 295, 327, 338,
349, 350, 351, 355–359, 371, 377,
379, 380, 388, 406, 410, 411, 413
Louise Hay 162, 343, 433, 447
Love vii, viii, xiv, xv, xvi, xvii, 24, 31,
33, 37, 40, 45, 47, 50, 52, 55, 63, 66,
69, 72, 73, 80–82, 92, 94, 96–99, 109,
110, 119, 120, 125, 126, 133, 136,
140, 145, 147, 152, 154, 158, 159,
164–166, 169, 171, 175–177, 180,
182, 188, 189, 196–198, 200–207,
210, 211, 214, 220, 222, 228, 234–
236, 239, 251, 252, 255, 259–262,
277, 288–290, 291–298, 300–303,
307, 309, 316, 320, 323, 330, 341–
343, 345, 350–356, 360–363, 366,
368–371, 374, 376–380, 384, 386,
389, 392, 394, 396, 397, 401, 405,
407, 408, 410–413, 417, 420–422,
426–428, 431, 444
Loving kindness 300

**M**

Manifesting 256, 262, 263, 355, 383
Mind viii, x, xii, 22, 34, 35, 37, 39, 46,
47, 61, 62, 64, 65, 69–73, 75–78, 80,
81, 84, 85, 96, 98, 106, 111, 112,
119, 120, 122, 125–127, 129–134,
137, 139, 140, 144, 151, 153, 154,
166, 168, 175, 176, 182, 188–190,
192, 193, 204–206, 210, 213, 215,
220–223, 226, 230, 232, 236, 238,
242, 258–262, 265, 273–276, 278,
280–283, 285, 290, 291, 298, 300,
303, 305, 308, 326–329, 334, 335,
338, 339, 345, 348, 355, 361, 367,
376, 380, 382, 389, 396, 401–404,
407, 414, 418, 421–423, 432, 433,
435, 445, 446, 448, 454, 455

**N**

Nirvana 75, 96, 99, 206
Non tolerance 203, 298

**O**

Obstacle 267
Oh well- peace 285, 286
Oneness 141, 423
Open Heart 92, 171, 227, 277, 291, 295,
296, 299–303, 384
Other therapies 356

**P**

Painful memories 131, 161, 407
Patience xii, 134, 143, 214, 269–271
Peace vii, 10, 16, 25, 39, 50, 65, 66, 80,
96, 98, 99, 102, 119, 125, 133, 149,
154, 158–160, 162, 163, 166, 169,
174, 177, 181, 192, 194, 204, 210,
220, 224, 230, 262, 270, 271, 277,
283, 285, 286, 289, 358, 361, 363,
366, 368, 369, 371, 372, 375, 380,
386, 387, 397, 401, 403, 409, 411,
413, 419, 420, 424–428, 431, 454,
455
Perception ix, 5, 11, 14, 20, 41, 47, 52,
55, 69, 80, 82, 105, 132, 138, 154,
170, 186, 194, 221, 274, 302, 315,
348, 383, 428
Positive/ negative viii, xi, xii, xvi, xvii,
10, 12, 20, 32, 35, 36, 38, 39, 41, 47,
54, 67, 72, 84, 85, 87, 90, 97, 98, 99,
102, 107, 108, 111, 112, 113, 119,
120, 121, 123, 127, 133, 139, 141,
142, 143, 149, 151, 152, 156, 157,
159, 160, 161, 162, 166, 169, 170,
175, 176, 177, 178, 179, 180, 182,
184, 187, 189, 190, 191, 192, 194,
196, 210, 212, 215, 218, 229, 231,
234, 236, 237, 239, 241, 242, 243,
244, 248, 250, 255, 256, 257, 258,
259, 260, 261, 262, 263, 266, 267,
268, 270, 271, 272, 274, 275, 276,
278, 280, 281, 282, 283, 285, 286,
298, 306, 308, 317, 318, 320, 324,
325, 327, 329, 335, 336, 338, 339,
340, 341, 342, 343, 344, 345, 346,
347, 348, 349, 354, 356, 359, 360,
362, 364, 365, 367, 368, 372, 379,

382, 391, 392, 393, 397, 399, 400,
402, 403, 404, 405, 407, 408, 409,
410, 411, 412, 414, 415, 416, 417,
418, 419, 420, 421, 422, 425, 426
Prana. *See* Life Force
Prayer 164, 173, 196, 305–308, 314, 315,
319, 363, 380, 425
Present moment; now, 3, 4, 5, 7, 9, 12,
15, 18, 19, 20, 25, 27, 29, 30, 31, 33,
34, 36, 40, 43, 44, 45, 52, 53, 54, 55,
59, 60, 61, 62, 63, 65, 67, 68, 69, 71,
72, 73, 74, 75, 77, 78, 79, 80, 81, 83,
85, 88, 90, 92, 94, 96, 97, 101, 104,
105, 106, 114, 122, 124, 131, 132,
133, 135, 136, 137, 139, 140, 144,
145, 149, 151, 154, 161, 162, 168,
169, 170, 172, 173, 174, 175, 176,
178, 179, 180, 181, 182, 186, 187,
188, 189, 190, 192, 196, 210, 212,
228, 235, 237, 239, 241, 257, 263,
273, 276, 277, 278, 279, 280, 281,
283, 285, 288, 289, 290, 293, 297,
298, 300, 301, 307, 310, 313, 314,
316, 327, 328, 339, 343, 344, 348,
349, 350, 352, 353, 360, 361, 362,
363, 367, 370, 371, 377, 378, 379,
382, 388, 390, 392, 393, 396, 401,
402, 403, 409, 411, 415, 420, 422,
431, 433, 447, 454

## Q

Qi. *See* Life Force

## R

Reality xiii, 8, 9, 31, 38, 45, 52, 55, 56,
71–73, 75, 77, 79–81, 84, 85, 87, 96,
120, 124, 125, 143, 147–153, 156,
159, 160, 163, 172, 173, 182, 220,
221, 236, 244, 250, 253, 257, 262,
329, 343, 344, 346, 350, 354, 356,
365–370, 372, 375, 382, 400, 402,
403, 409, 411, 420, 421, 428, 436,
447, 455
Regression therapy 82, 264, 356, 357

Reiki xvi, 90, 105, 106, 113, 285, 306,
314, 315, 338, 356, 432, 443, 451,
453
Reincarnation 90, 122, 128, 157, 212,
269, 429, 436, 438, 446, 453, 454
Resentment viii, 32, 59, 65, 132, 139,
166, 167, 169, 170, 172, 174, 175,
181, 182, 183, 187, 228, 303, 339,
345, 352, 359, 363, 365, 410, 411
Resistance 87, 149, 151, 154, 156,
159–162, 274, 298, 299, 342,
407–409, 411
Responsibility iv, 20, 44, 49, 51, 52,
163, 171, 204, 213, 215, 231, 245,
251, 254, 255, 257, 258, 291, 316,
354, 355, 382, 408, 410, 416, 426
Revenge 132, 158, 159, 161, 166, 167,
169, 176, 179, 182, 184, 185, 362,
391
Right brain 75, 205
Right/ wrong 244
Rumi xv, 28, 74, 154, 388, 435

## S

Satori 152
Silence 282, 361, 388
Soul xvii, 9, 11, 30, 39, 121, 129, 186,
216, 227, 261, 268, 269, 361, 381,
436, 446
Spirit, God, Goddess, The Almighty
xiii, 17, 25, 28, 32, 34, 37, 39, 48, 49,
73, 78, 80, 99, 102, 112, 122, 125,
127, 141, 142, 160, 171, 173, 197,
203, 204, 213, 233, 253, 258, 262,
265, 269, 271, 284, 288, 295, 300,
302, 306, 319, 330, 335, 342, 360,
363, 366, 372, 376, 382, 383, 386,
387, 388, 405, 406, 411, 412, 413,
419, 420, 423, 425, 427, 428, 451
Spiritual laws vii, x, xiii, 41, 102, 113,
119, 126, 174, 202, 266, 302, 342,
349, 355, 386, 399, 416–418, 423,
428
Spiritual nature 7, 8, 54, 75, 122, 131,
389, 399, 428

Spiritual School 96, 100, 157, 320, 392,
428
Stillness 222, 431
Stress 14, 38, 47, 74, 75, 77, 97, 98, 127,
130, 155, 162, 179, 193, 273–276,
278, 285, 286, 323, 325, 350, 359,
368, 378, 401, 449, 456
Suffering viii, 8, 12, 31, 46, 54, 59,
61, 66, 71, 87, 89, 90, 98, 115, 125,
126, 138, 148, 151, 152, 157–161,
169, 176, 183–185, 194, 212, 217,
250, 253, 256, 258, 259, 265, 266,
269, 279, 318, 321, 328, 346, 347,
354–356, 359, 361–363, 370, 374,
379, 385, 386, 397, 399, 403–405,
407, 409, 411, 416, 426, 427
Suffering, its function viii, 8, 11, 12,
31, 46, 54, 59, 61, 66, 71, 87, 89, 90,
98, 115, 125, 126, 138, 148, 151, 152,
157, 158, 159, 160, 161, 169, 176,
183, 184, 185, 194, 212, 217, 250,
253, 256, 258, 259, 266, 269, 279,
318, 321, 328, 346, 347, 354, 355,
356, 359, 361, 362, 363, 370, 374,
379, 385, 386, 397, 399, 403, 404,
405, 407, 409, 411, 416, 426, 427
Synchronicity 305, 318, 437, 448

**T**

Teacher ix, xvi, 12, 26, 53, 114, 137,
139, 177, 203, 205, 208, 234, 237,
238, 267, 273, 286, 316, 361, 382,
403, 420, 435
The Physical universe ix, x, 24, 39, 54,
75–77, 91, 98, 103, 106, 108, 122,
124–127, 152, 170, 172, 176, 192,
219, 291, 353, 354, 362, 365, 374,
378, 383, 400, 404, 406, 409, 414,
419, 420, 422, 426, 427
The Power of Now - Eckhart Tolle xvi,
27, 68, 73, 144, 298, 390, 431, 454
Therapies 356
Thoughts – negative/ positive viii, 31,
35, 38, 39, 47, 55, 69, 70, 71, 78, 79,
80, 84, 85, 97, 98, 129, 132, 133, 134,
144, 148, 158, 159, 166, 175, 176,

177, 180, 181, 189, 206, 241, 242,
252, 260, 261, 262, 264, 267, 269,
271, 272, 275, 278, 280, 281, 282,
283, 286, 293, 338, 342, 343, 349,
350, 353, 354, 360, 361, 365, 367,
379, 392, 402, 405, 413, 414, 417,
420, 421, 422, 426
Time x, xvi, 3, 4, 6, 8, 12–16, 14, 19–21,
25, 29, 30, 32, 34, 35, 37, 39, 42, 45,
47, 49–51, 53, 57, 60–62, 64, 67, 72,
74, 78, 80, 82, 83, 85–89, 96, 99,
101, 103, 104, 106, 111, 112, 114,
122–124, 126, 129, 131–133, 136,
138, 139, 143, 145, 148, 151–153,
155, 156, 162–165, 169, 172, 174,
184–186, 192–194, 198, 205, 208,
215, 217, 226–228, 230, 232, 234–
236, 238, 240, 257, 259–261, 264,
265, 268, 269, 272, 276, 277, 279,
283, 285, 292, 293, 295, 297, 298,
302, 306, 308, 310–312, 314–317,
320, 321, 324, 325, 327, 328, 332,
333, 339, 340, 342, 345–347, 349,
353, 354, 356, 357, 360–363, 368,
370, 377–380, 387, 389–392, 394,
400, 401, 409, 414, 418–420, 451
Tolerance x, 53, 98, 198–201, 203, 207,
406, 411, 417, 426
Transformation iii, viii, xi, 20, 37, 38,
61, 72, 83, 98, 99, 117, 119, 122, 130,
133, 134, 147, 164, 184, 188, 198,
207, 208, 234, 252, 254, 255, 273,
303, 305, 323, 331, 337, 338, 358,
381, 389, 393, 395, 426
Traumas 161, 407
Tribalism 44, 405
Tribal Consciousness 47, 56, 58
Tribal Unconsciousness 56

**U**

Ujjayi breath 282, 296
Unconsciousness 25, 34, 35, 55, 56,
98, 126, 127, 132, 135, 142, 143,
159, 166, 170–173, 175, 181, 218,
221, 232, 249, 251, 258, 259, 268,
301–303, 346, 362, 391, 412, 426

**V**

Viktor Frankl 183, 184

**W**

Will viii, ix, xii, xiii, 10, 12, 19–24, 26,
30, 31, 33, 36–38, 41, 43–48, 51, 54,
56–59, 66, 71, 72, 74, 76, 77, 83, 84,
90, 94, 98–102, 104–107, 110–113,
119–126, 128, 130–132, 135–141,
143, 144, 147–149, 152–163, 166,
169–176, 178, 180–184, 186–189,
191–194, 196, 197, 199, 203, 204,
212, 213, 215–228, 230, 231, 233,
235, 236, 239–241, 243, 244,
246–250, 252, 255–266, 260, 269,
271, 272, 275–284, 289–291,
293–297, 299, 301–305, 308, 314,
317, 319, 320, 322, 323, 327–331,
334, 337–345, 348, 349, 352–356,
361–365, 368, 370, 371, 373–375,
378, 380–382, 385, 387–391, 393,
394, 396–399, 402–410, 412–418,
420–424, 426–429, 453

Witness Consciousness 273, 278, 389,
401

**Y**

Yoga xvi, 26, 27, 113, 273, 282, 288,
289, 296, 356, 357, 390, 434

Your story 134, 145

**Z**

Zen 103, 122, 131, 205, 206, 267, 434

Lightning Source UK Ltd.
Milton Keynes UK
UKOW06f0157130617
303198UK00004B/363/P